About the Author

CAROLINE JONES is a veteran Australian broadcaster and communicator. She has worked in radio and television since 1963, as writer, producer, director and reporter.

In 1988 she was made an Officer of the Order of Australia. In 1997, she was voted one of Australia's 100 National Living Treasures. From 1987 to 1994, she presented *The Search for Meaning* on ABC Radio.

Her previous publications include four volumes of *The Search for Meaning*, as well as *The Search for Meaning* video and audio-tapes. Judged by ABC Radio tape sales, *The Search for Meaning* was, for years, the ABC's most popular program.

About *The Search for Meaning*

An Authentic Life is a sequel to *The Search for Meaning* books and it takes their sustaining insights a step further, by inviting readers more personally into both Caroline Jones' search and their own. The book encourages the individual reader to keep a journal. It is also an ideal resource for group discussion, and it contains detailed guidance on how to succeed in these complementary ventures.

*This book shows that Caroline Jones writes as beautifully as she
listens and draws out others' stories. It offers an inspiring depth of strength,
vulnerability, humour, insight, resilience and distilled courage.*

Stephanie Dowrick

§

*Many of us have, in the past, experienced Caroline Jones' marvellous
gift in bringing forth the life stories that lie in the heart of the people she meets.
This time she gives us a magical and moving journey as she allows
us to enter her own story, and interweaves that with the stories of others.
As we read, I am sure that most of us will find that the story
which lies unrecognised within ourselves begins to unfold before us in
a powerful journey of discovery. This is a very special book.*

Reverend Dr Dorothy McRae-McMahon

§

*I am told on good authority that when the old Dutch Captains retired
from the spice trade to the Indies, they sold their 'routers' —
their charts and sailing directions — to younger skippers for high prices.
It always seemed to me to be a very fair trade: hard cash for
hard-won experience, provided always that the routers were genuine.
Caroline Jones' book is precisely that: a 'router' for the risky but
enriching voyage of self-discovery.
In the end, the voyager must make a personal choice; but all can be
assured that in this case the documents are authentic.*

Morris L. West

§

*From its ambitious title to the frankness of its discussion of family tragedy,
Caroline's book is a disarmingly intimate chronicle of the
culture-shifts taking place in our society, as many Australians switch from
the twentieth century's rationalist focus on 'seeing is believing'
to a more ancient, essentially religious position that 'believing is seeing.'*

Hugh Mackay

*This is a remarkably generous and thoughtful book. For the first time
we have been taken into the life of the person who,
more than any other in the Australian media, opened the lives of others.
Caroline has drawn heavily from the eight years she presented the
Search for Meaning on ABC Radio National. She breathed
into that program an air of respect and sometimes awe as she spoke with
politicians, prostitutes, old diggers, people who were dying, surfers,
carpenters, Aboriginal poets, gurus, healers and the rest.
It was part of her remarkable gift that each person was treated with
the same aristocratic professionalism, warmth and encouragement.
She took no position except she expected her guests to invest the same
degree of high seriousness and expectation that she did.*

*In **An Authentic Life** Caroline has come from behind the microphone
and told us something of herself. Although it is at times painfully
revealing, the book is not ultimately about Caroline Jones.
She writes to all who believe that there is more to life than our present
culture would have us believe. It is like a primer for the journey
of the spirit. She tells us some of the hard lessons she learnt, living
with the suicide of her mother, and her outrage at being unemployed.
But the focus is away from her to the grapplings of us all.
And this is what makes this an important book.*

*Caroline's own faith is in this book in a way which is gracious and
unintrusive. She writes about lofty themes that theologians and spiritual
leaders claim as their home territory. But I think she does it better.
Our Australian religious leaders might learn from what Caroline
has done here. She has found the language and the feel of Australia
where the struggle is not about issues or dogma.
It is about the desire to enjoy life, live with a clear conscience
and find a sense of spiritual home.*

Reverend Dr David Millikan

CAROLINE JONES

AN AUTHENTIC LIFE

Finding Meaning and
Spirituality in Everyday Life

ABC
BOOKS

For my mother Nancy Rae James who
gave me life and purpose.

And for my father Brian Newman James
who showed me how to live with
honesty, patience, courage, humour and a
lively interest in the world.

Published by ABC Books for the
AUSTRALIAN BROADCASTING CORPORATION
GPO Box 9994 Sydney NSW 2001

First published April 1998
Reprinted April 1998
Reprinted May 1998
Reprinted July 1998

National Library of Australia
Cataloguing-in-Publication entry
Jones, Caroline.
An authentic life: finding meaning and
spirituality in everyday life.
ISBN 0 7333 0207 6.
1. Jones, Caroline. 2. Spiritual life. 3. Interviews.
4. Life. 5. Radio journalists — Australia — Biography.
I. Title. II. Title: Search for meaning (Radio program).
128.092

Designed & typeset by Brash Design Pty Ltd
Cover design by Robert Taylor
Cover photograph by Ludwik Dabrowski
Set in 12/16pt Bembo
Printed and bound in Australia by
Australian Print Group, Maryborough, Victoria

Contents

Acknowledgements

I acknowledge my appreciation of a number of people who have helped me in the preparation of this book. I am grateful for their encouragement and their faith in me, for the contribution of their research and their insights, for appraisal of the manuscript, for technical assistance, or for their care for my health. My thanks to each one of you:

Gwen and Gerald Bohle, Margot Cairnes, Lee Carmody, the members of my CLC group, Fr Paul Coleman SJ, Peter Coleman, Stella Cornelius, Cecily Doig, Stephanie Dowrick, Len Fabre, Michele Fehlberg, Julie Fewster, Ron Flint, Stephen Godley, Bronwyn Gowing, Jenny Gribble, Brian and Mary James, Leonie McMahon, Kevin Mark, Phillip Martin, Chris Michaels, Joanne Middonte, Christian Muzard, Jocelyn Nott, Robert Owen, Lynn Parsons, Victoria Renigeris, Louisa Ring Rolfe, Annette Smith, Valerie Smith, Florence Spurling and Melvie Tait. Patti Miller has been exceptionally helpful with her appraisal and criticism of the book as it took shape.

My grateful acknowledgement goes as well to my editor, Jo Rudd, to Stuart Neal and Matthew Kelly of ABC Books, and to designer Deborah Brash.

The book has been greatly enriched by the inclusion of quotations from the sustaining stories told to me by my guests on *The Search for Meaning* programs. I am grateful to each one of them for disclosing the wisdom of their experience.

Note

Some of the the Endnotes refer to the four *Search for Meaning* books already published:

* *The Search for Meaning*, Caroline Jones, ABC/Collins Dove, 1989.
* *The Search for Meaning Book Two*, Caroline Jones, ABC/Collins Dove, 1990.

These two books are out of print, but there may be copies in local libraries. The next two books should be available at bookstores, and can also be found in many libraries:

* *The Search for Meaning: Conversations with Caroline Jones*, ABC/Collins Dove, 1992.
* *The Search for Meaning Collection*, Caroline Jones, ABC/Harper Collins, 1995.

Some notes refer to audiotapes. These are numbered and listed in a booklet called *The Search for Meaning Catalogue*, published by ABC Radio Tapes, G.P.O. Box 9994, Sydney 2001. Tel: (02) 9333 1034. A *Search for Meaning* video is available in ABC shops. ABC Video catalogue number 12574.

1 BEGINNING THE SEARCH

In the silence let us listen to our heart.
Michael Leunig[1]

Only connect.
E. M. Forster[2]

I think from the time I could open my eyes I was aware that there seemed to be something else going on amongst those around me which was not talked about ... there was another truth. It's as if I want to run up to people on the street and say, 'Look, I feel this; do you feel this, too?'[3]

THE SILENCE OF SHARED understanding shimmers in the air between us in a mid-winter ABC radio studio in Melbourne. As he leans out earnestly around his microphone, Michael Leunig's expression is transparent in its yearning to make connections.

It seems I have this search to find my people, to find my culture, to find a place where there is some common agreement; to find a common ground, my people, my society, my village, my parish, my culture, you know? I feel we live in a time when these things are shattered and cast all over the place in a great mess, and I want to keep tying it up together a bit and linking it and seeing to what extent I'm like you and to what extent you can feel as I feel. This, I think, is at the centre of what I'm trying to do.[4]

He's a bit untidy, which is endearing and helps me not to be over-awed in the presence of someone I admire very much. It's the first

1

time we've met. Why should I be surprised that he resembles one of his own homely family of cartoon characters? Mr Curly, say, with that large, perky tendril rising frondlike from his head in a suggestion of the fragile human heart and consciousness venturing forth into the world. Or the intrepid Vasco Pyjama, leaving all that is known and safe, to sail out over the horizon in a battered armchair on his own brave search. Or even one of his ubiquitous angels which Helen Garner describes as 'helpful, anxious creatures with tatty wings and daggy little nighties — airborne versions of our better selves'.[5] Yes. And some of them look like jack-knifed cats who've been picked up round the middle with two hands by small children, and can only hang, patient and pliant, until released.

Helen Garner identifies the most gruesome drawing in all Leunig's work as 'an angel submitting, shocked, to the amputation of its wings by an officious fellow wielding a pair of long-handled hedge-clippers, while another angel in flight looks down from a black seething sky, his mouth and eyes rounded with alarm, and without being shown it we know that the cause of his horror is our world'.[6] Leunig himself is alarmed by our world but he does not repudiate it. He has compassion for it and he sees that it is beautiful and he tries to work out why we are alienated in it.

I am so attuned to Leunig's sensibility that I feel naked in his presence. I am disarmed by his vulnerability, embarrassed to find such an expanse of common ground between us. I am wondering how to traverse it. We sit looking shyly at each other. We would both find it much easier to go out for a walk in the streets, pointing to things in companionable silence.

I watched a man making a pavement in Melbourne in a busy city street: the concrete was poured and he had his little trowel and there was traffic roaring around, there were cranes and machines going, and this man was on his hands and knees lovingly making a beautiful little corner on the kerb. That's a sort of love and that's important, that's very, very important. That man's job is important and he's a bit of a hero for doing it like that. So that's why love is important, because love involves that as much as it involves what happens between people. It's about relationships between oneself and the world and its people and its creatures and its plants, its ideas.[7]

Silence falls between us again, a silence of deep accord. I try to indicate my delight in his perception, but he doesn't catch what I say and I remember that it was deafness in one ear which saved him from going to the Vietnam war when he was conscripted in the first call-up. Just as well. He was finding it increasingly difficult as a political cartoonist to make incisive comments about a conflict that was causing divisions even among his close friends. He was only 24 and he was becoming disillusioned with politics. Even though political journalism was considered the most important journalism, he sensed that it was avoiding something.

One morning, with the daily deadline looming, he was trying to do another cartoon about Vietnam when he found himself drawing instead a man riding on a duck. It was the first intuitive step in Leunig's re-examination of the world, and he would take thousands of us with him, reassuring us that, although we seemed so out of step with the times, we were not necessarily mad and we were not alone. As we got to know him better, we would come to recognise this as Leunig's liberating image: the duck symbolised the man's feelings of primal freedom and playfulness. And upon his head the man was wearing a teapot, image of all that is domestic, welcoming, ordinary and unmenacing, all that brings us onto common ground — like a fool's cap worn as crown by a man in search of his own truth. As these familiars evolved off the end of his nib, they made him laugh out loud. They disturbed him and inspired him, and it was through their questions and their antics that he began to express his most personal life in public.

I'm supposed to be interviewing him for *The Search for Meaning* radio program and I'm self-conscious about it. I dread interviewing artists because, when their painting or their music-making or their dancing is so eloquent, it seems ungracious to ask them to express it again in words, which are not their chosen medium. Why should they? It seems an impertinence to ask, worthy only of rebuke. But

Leunig is prepared to do it. He's prepared to take the risk of being truthful, even if he has to grope for words in his effort to do so.

> The great secrecy that evolves as we grow older ... these hidden aspects of life — hidden sadnesses and hidden fears and hidden desires — they disturb me. They separate us. I accept that we are private people; we need our moments of reverie without intrusion, but I guess I'm trying to confess publicly by saying, 'Look, I have this really strange, rather pathetic feeling, this ignoble feeling — do you? Do you have that?' ... It's very lovely to reveal well-formed feelings and poetic feelings; it's very nice if you can do that, but I'm talking about the other feelings that are a bit clumsy ... it's about not knowing; to confess to not knowing.[8]

Time had no dominion as we yarned on about his father who used to come home exhausted at the end of the day's work as slaughterman at the meatworks; and of the strange homesickness peculiar to the human condition. We talked about who or what God might be, and about suffering, and about why men are a bit lost today. It was the sort of conversation that would sustain you for a year, something to revisit over and over again. It had taken my researcher Louisa Ring months to get the appointment for this interview, and we rejoiced together that Leunig had given us a talk that was quintessential to *The Search for Meaning* program. This broadcast would validate an expression of the inner life for many listeners. It would give us permission, as do Leunig's cartoons, to acknowledge our feelings of frailty or irrational joy; to indulge in our whimsical imaginings, to pursue our quest for an authentic life; and to take the risk of connecting with other people. He had spoken to the very heart of our endeavour.

The Search for Meaning was broadcast on ABC Radio National for eight years from 1987 to the end of 1994. It was a one-hour weekly show in which a great variety of men and women told their stories; generously revealing what, for them, was the point of life; how they'd come through the hard times; what sustained them; what they celebrated; what they believed in; what it is to be human. It made compelling listening as people took the gamble of speaking from the heart. It was real. As with Leunig, it was like hearing secret thoughts out loud, convictions about what really matters in life. And it sounded chords of recognition in listeners as it echoed their own experience, their wondering, their doubt and faith.

Over the years, we heard about the ecstasy of surfing; the passion to follow your star; the reflections of the dying; the pain of being 'different'; the insight of the blind; the terror of imprisonment; the disappointment of wealth; what it's like to go mad and recover; the fear of being ultimately alone; and the highs and lows of love. We heard profound revelations of the soul and psyche, told in plain searching language as people sifted their experience for the turning points and flashes of understanding in their quest to make sense of life.

These are matters traditionally pondered in private. *The Search for Meaning* provided a forum for them to be shared, in a public discussion new to Australia, and valuable because it identified what we have in common at the most profound level of human experience. Our mail-bag overflowed with thousands of letters of response:

When the depths of depression hit me and every grim news broad-cast confirmed my belief that the universe was crumbling, your wonderfully non-intrusive talks with brave people made life bearable. If they had come through, so could I.

The Search for Meaning has been a lifeline for me and my children as we stumbled out of a fearful relationship. Your program introduced me to people who were survivors too and rejoicing in the lessons learned through their suffering.

The program makes me feel less isolated.

It's such a relief to hear my thoughts and feelings reiterated by another woman of my age.

I feel part of the search.

It's like an oasis in a spiritual desert.

I believe this program is drawing us together as one people.

I feel calmed and encouraged as I listen to the honesty of your guests.

During the weekly hour of *Search for Meaning* I feel more truly at home and alive than at any other hour of the week.

Every such letter, and there were thousands of them, rededicated me to my purpose. Twenty years earlier my own life had been wounded by the suicide of the person in my family who was closest to me. My own sense of meaning and order were all but annihilated by this tragedy. I seemed to be suspended in space on a pendulum that swung from numbness to vertigo and back again, while somewhere inside I could hear the faint whimpering of a small, stricken animal. At first I could not think much about her death at all. My imagination would fall over the precipice of it into oblivion. Then, as the weeks and months went on, I would return to it warily, and look at some small piece of it. Gradually, as I struggled to make some sense of the unthinkable, it seemed to me that her death marked the end of an anguished search for meaning that was not fulfilled. It was unutterably, achingly sad.

She had done so much for me and I felt that I had failed her — that somehow I could have done more to sustain her, to invest her life with meaning. The fact is that, despite our closeness, I could not know the full truth of her plight. That was hidden in the recesses of her soul. It was her story and she had taken it with her, putting a stop to all further questions. Our lifelong conversation, which I had taken for granted would go on forever, had been brought to an abrupt end. I supposed that whoever I had been was broken and would stay that way. Whatever was left would have to maintain some sort of facade and pretend to normality. Yet, as it turned out, that breaking was more like the splitting open of a seed to germinate, for my grievous loss was not an end but a beginning. Although I did not know it then, she had given me my life's purpose.

At that time, grief had not yet been acknowledged as a valid rite of passage, and grief-counselling was yet to be invented. Our family got through it as best we could. I threw myself into work with an intense energy that fuelled a career in radio and television journalism. I made sure that no one got too close to me, to evade the risk of losing again. At some level I had established a sinister connection between loving and loss, as though the two were inextricable. At any rate I did not feel that, emotionally, I had very much to give.

But it was not so. It took several years but, after the numbness wore off, I emerged with an altered consciousness, like a butterfly from the chrysalis. I had developed a heightened sensitivity to people's pain. In a way never before possible to me, I could feel something of the loneliness of another *with my own loneliness*; or their bereavement *with my own loss*; or their shame or remorse or their self-disgust or their fear, *with my own*. I could feel these things in people without wanting to judge or reject them, or to stop their tears or solve their problems. I could simply be with that person in fellow feeling.

My newly awakened compassion, born of suffering, was still only embryonic but it was a gift because it enabled me to listen to people and, at times, it allowed me to be close to another person in trouble. It was astonishing to think that this empathy had come from the place of my deepest wounding. Having seen a loved one lost through lack of meaning, the quest for meaning became paramount for me. I pursued it first on my own account. Later, when an invitation came from Dr David Millikan, Head of Religious Programs for the ABC, to join his team, I was ready to take it on as a public endeavour, through broadcasting, books and tapes, all under the title of *The Search for Meaning*. I thought that if I could do anything to contribute to people's sense of peace and purpose, then that would be a worthwhile project into which I could pour my energy with conviction. I felt too that it would go some way to redeem her suffering.

As the program developed, it demonstrated a nation's ability to express its deepest values and its spirituality. It began at the end of a decade of financial buccaneering in Australia and in the year of the Australian stock market crash. In those uncertain times, in a vacuum of moral leadership, people were unnerved and looking for reliable maps by which to chart their course. In the life stories of their countrymen and women, listeners recognised the authenticity of real lived experience and were sustained by it.

Thousands of Australians own tapes of those programs which are still widely used in education, and this will be the fifth *Search for Meaning* book. In the first four, we collected the wisdom of some of the women and men who spoke on the radio programs. We all go through times when we wonder what the point of life might be but, while we puzzle over that enormous question, we still have the task of getting on with life on a daily basis. These books provide a source of deep and continuing sustenance to anybody in search of a way to live with meaning, purpose, hope, joy and some measure of peace.

This book takes the process a step further. It is an invitation to you to reflect on your own story, on your own experience, on the way you are living your life — to discover the revelation it has to offer you.

For many people, this is a curiously neglected source of insight. We can spend a lifetime looking to outward sources of knowledge as though they must be superior, while undervaluing the inner blue-print for our own integrity and direction. We have meaning in our very being. In the course of life many things happen to obscure it. This book is about uncovering what lies at the heart of your life, and nurturing it. It is about discovering what connects your life to all other life. There is no complex formula for this discovery. It is not like studying to pass an examination, or striving to reach a goal. Rather, it is a process of simplifying, of letting go your tight grip on the controls and pausing to reflect and listen. Have you not heard at times the whispered guidance of an inner voice, quickly overridden by the clamour of dogma, doubt or cynicism in the world around you? What if you were to hearken to that inner voice and accept the wisdom of its direction? That is the invitation of this book which I have envisaged as an extended search for meaning interview in which the reader is asked to reflect on the questions raised. If you accept the invitation, I believe that your response will help you to discern pattern and purpose in your life more clearly.

The book begins with a reminder that you do have a story; and an invitation to reclaim that story and search it for clues about the source from which your life flows. There are questions to help you build a clearer picture of your own identity and encourage you into a surer sense of your authenticity. Because it's easy to take life for granted, and to lose sight of the gift and the joy of it, there's a chapter on finding your most vivid experiences of being alive and giving them more space in your days. There is an invitation to examine how you deal with suffering, and to offer you some perspectives on this most difficult of life's challenges.

As well, we go in search of spirituality. What is this elusive yet crucial element of the human condition? How is it nourished in your life? What is sacred to you? Are you fully aware of the rich spiritual resources of your memory and your imagination? How well are you caring for your soul? Would you like some strategies for increasing a spiritual dimension in your everyday life?

When are you most at home in yourself? What do you need to change, in order to allow greater fullness and harmony? Are you completely time-bound or do you get occasional glimpses of eternity? What might that suggest about the meaning of life? Do you feel free? Free to choose, to change things? Is there a feeling of emptiness at the core? What could there be to fill it? What do your most treasured possessions tell you about yourself?

Have you a well-developed philosophy of life? Does it serve you well? What are your most powerful metaphors of meaning? Are they the best ones for you? Are you too busy? How does your attitude to life shape your experience? Do you feel that you must be in control of everything? Where do you experience grace and forgiveness? How well do you 'connect' with the people around you? How do you make a contribution to a just and healthy community life? Although the book discusses religious experience and belief, it does not exclude the reader for whom God has no place in the scheme of things. It is for anyone in quest of greater depth and meaning and enjoyment of life. If I use terms that you find problematic, like 'soul' and 'God', for instance, you may like to substitute other terms. It will not hinder our dialogue. Perhaps 'inner sense of being' will do for soul, and 'Higher Power' or 'Source' for God.

Just as with my guests on radio, the choice is always yours and the process is gentle. I will not ask you to do anything I am not prepared to do — first I engage with the question myself and tell you how and where I found my answers, or not, as the case may be. Next, we hear some responses from others who've made the same reflection. And then it's your turn. You may find yourself ready to contemplate the area suggested in one chapter, yet quite closed to others. My suggestion is to follow the line of least resistance. Do only what you feel ready for. This may open the way to an approach to more sensitive chapters later. Or it may not. No matter. Just go as far as seems agreeable to you. One train of thought prompts another. You will be surprised by what comes to light. Perhaps you will be stirred into action to fulfil some long-neglected heart's desire, or to free yourself from living someone else's plan.

Many guests on *The Search for Meaning* programs told me that, although the broadcast interview made them vulnerable, they were glad of the push it gave them to review their values and direction. It was like a personal stocktaking which revealed unacknowledged assets and also a few places where the cupboard was bare.

I hope that you will be reassured by the deeper discovery of your own story. I hope that, if you are feeling any uncertainty of direction, you will gain a greater sense of purpose; that if you are treading water you will find the will to swim on; that if you are lonely you will find good company; that if you fear the future you will find new heart for the journey; that if you are rejecting your age you will discover the insight it has stored up for you.

I am surprised to find that I am happier in my middle age than I have ever been before. It's not that I've forgotten the wild enthusiasms and excitement of earlier years. It's that I wouldn't exchange them for the hard-won glimmerings of wisdom I now discern, which bring peace and a quieter joy. It's not that I don't worry any more or doubt or get frightened. But I have a steadier foundation on which to deal with these disturbances, and a wider perspective in which to locate my individual experience. The getting of wisdom is a long task but, once you decide that it is *the* task of life, time and experience become your best collaborators, not your enemies.

I would like to discourage you from choosing too solitary a journey. Very few are suited to the way of the hermitage. And I imagine that few of us are aiming for sainthood, but rather for a chance to live life to the full, to delight in all its possibilities. This book sees personal reflection as having its own rich reward. It can also be regarded as a precursor to social engagement. That may be as simple as an increased capacity to contemplate other people's lives with compassion; or as active as devoting yourself to the needs of others. A vital element of fulfilled living is to feel that your society is your family, that you belong, that you are part of the whole human race, with a role to play and a responsibility for the wellbeing of the wider group. This orientates you to contribute, which is an effective route to involvement and meaning.

It can also free you from the loneliness of autonomy so prevalent in western thinking, in which the world is viewed from the exclusive standpoint of 'my rights' and 'my choice'. I am writing to remind all of us that we have the power to make a unique contribution, that everything we do and everything we are has its effect in the world, and therefore needs doing with awareness and integrity.

I have written this book because it would not leave me alone until I did. I make no claim to have all the answers but I am engrossed by the questions and I continue to search for meaning myself. I have written it for the people who have told me that they are faltering on their search; and as a hand outstretched to anyone who is finding the road too steep, in the hope that it may call even one out of the inertia of despair, perhaps simply by naming it. I have written it in profound gratitude for the experience of my own life; and to honour the story of everyman and everywoman — and of all the ancestors who have lived before me and struggled and endured to give me life.

The principal bases of my writing are my own response to life; the hundreds of personal stories told to me by my countrymen and women; my imagination; my reflection on poetry, literature, art, spiritual tradition and current affairs; the practice of my faith; the example of wise people; a habit of contemplation; and the mysterious but undeniable element of inspiration.

What this book provides, quite simply, is company — my own and that of others — as we describe our milestones and discoveries on the journey. It also points the way to books and ideas I have found to illuminate the way. It is not an end but a beginning. The only answers that will have validity for you are the ones you find for yourself, those that delight you with their rightness for you. This book is a testimony to what I have found to be true and to the questions that still await answers. I offer it to you as a companion to your own search for meaning.

You have picked up this book in order to read it, but I invite you now to consider taking an optional step. What if you were to respond to my book by creating your own? It need not be too formal an exercise. Rather than chapters of words, it might consist principally of photographs or cut-out pictures, with little writing. It might be a series of mind maps or diagrams, or symbols of your sources of spiritual nourishment and sacred places. It might be a diary, or a scrapbook. Or you may work most happily on your computer, or on video or on audiotape. You will know what suits you best.

I am suggesting this so that you will make some physical response, rather than merely stay in your head thinking about all the questions the book raises. It is more productive to be an active participant in the formation of your life than a passive consumer of other people's ideas. I am suggesting that you make a tangible record of this process in order to increase your sense of authenticity and awareness and deepen an appreciation of your own unique story. You may like to think of it as weaving your own tapestry or creating your own sacred place.

When I was at school, we had to cover our exercise books with brown paper, choose an appropriate picture for the cover of each, and print on it our name and the title of the subject, in our best script. This gave the sense of preparing a receptacle for something significant. It got us off to a good start. I am not suggesting that you do exactly the same but that you find your own equivalent way to give your journal special significance. It is going to contain the most important elements of your story, so it is sacred ground; and it is a private document, to be shared only by invitation.

The inscription of your name is important. You may like to illustrate it, in the style of medieval illuminated manuscripts, with symbols that have particular meaning for you. Are you slaying dragons at present, or on a quest for peace or beauty, or are you perhaps in no-man's land, waiting? You will be discovering more symbols for yourself as you go on, so leave space for additions.

Maybe the next page could be devoted to a simple statement of purpose. Write down what you are looking for at this time of your life. It will be interesting to check back to this page, from time to time, to see if your quest is being fulfilled, or if your purpose is changing direction and needs restating.

From there on, your journal will take its own course as you reflect on the questions at the end of each chapter of this book. If you take up my suggestion to keep a journal, you will create something of value: a fuller picture of who you are and where you are going; a testament of your priorities and desires; a mirror to your sensibility; a reinforcement of your faith in life; a record of your spiritual life, perhaps a revelation of your soul. Of course, if the journal has no appeal for you, sidestep the references to it and just enjoy reading.

What I have suggested so far may be sufficient for the introvert. For those who gain energy principally from the communication and exchange of ideas, an individual reading could well be followed by using the book as a resource for group discussion. There is a chapter on how to do this at the end of the book.

Endnotes

1 Michael Leunig, *Common Prayer Collection*, Collins Dove, 1993.
2 E. M. Forster, *Howard's End*, Hodder & Stoughton, 1973.
3 Michael Leunig in *The Search for Meaning: Conversations with Caroline Jones*, ABC/Collins Dove, 1992.
4 Michael Leunig in *The Search for Meaning: Conversations with Caroline Jones*.
5 Foreword to *Introspective*, Michael Leunig, Text Publishing, 1991.
6 Foreword to *Introspective*.
7 Michael Leunig in *The Search for Meaning: Conversations with Caroline Jones*.
8 Michael Leunig in *The Search for Meaning: Conversations with Caroline Jones*.

2 YOUR STORY: WHERE DOES IT BEGIN?

*Go into yourself and see how deep
the place is from which your life flows.*

Rainer Maria Rilke[1]

I BEGAN MANY OF *The Search for Meaning* radio interviews by exploring my guest's childhood, inviting their most vivid early memories, looking for the key that would unlock the beginning of their story. I was also seeking to identify some of their most potent images, to light the way forward.

And that is where we can begin together. I have made a sort of impressionist painting of my first few years by collecting the predominant images, the sounds, feelings, shapes and symbols of my childhood landscape. I allowed time to do this, reflecting, daydreaming, remembering. It did not come to me all at once, whole and ready-made, but gradually over a period of time. One memory unearthed another. Once I began the process, it continued to unfold in its own time. The purpose of this recollection was to reclaim the early part of my formation as a person. It gave me some surprising insights into who I am today. It showed me how I began to construct my framework of meaning and belief. It gave me some clues about the origin of my priorities and a perspective from which to evaluate my adult sense of values. Unexpectedly, it opened the way to transformation of some difficult early memories. But all that came later. At first I just remembered and this reverie on my experience was its own reward, regardless of any intent. It seems there is a benefit in reflection that we have all but lost in busy, modern life.

See if you can read my recollection like a net through which you are fishing to retrieve your own story, so that my images become hooks to catch your own. Your experience will differ from mine, but the very contrast may help you to bring something long forgotten to the surface. This is not intended as an exercise in psychoanalysis but rather the assembly of the pieces of a jigsaw puzzle — something you may do for pleasure on a rainy afternoon. There are still parts missing from this memory of my early life. What I have recalled is not the truth, the whole truth and nothing but the truth, but a version of my story, for that's how memory works. As time goes by, I expect I will recover more of my childhood story.

Something else happened as I was making my recollection of childhood. Fragments of other people's memories came tiptoeing forward to make themselves heard. I felt them peering over my shoulder and I had to heed them, for at some level of my memory I carry the stories of hundreds of others, like a sacred library. I have no choice in this. They are part of me because they have been told to me. They do not belong to me but they will be with me always. When I am bewildered, they keep me company; they ask the questions that I ask; and they give me hope and sometimes answers. I leaf through them, turning the pages slowly, looking for clues, searching out courage or clarity; or, to borrow Thea Astley's perfect term, 'a moment of consequence'. Once someone has told me their story I cannot do other than keep it and treasure it. So you will hear them joining in, as I explore the vivid memories of my early years.

§

I AM VERY SMALL, at the centre of a series of concentric circles, widening ripples. I am sitting hugging my knees and smiling with my mouth closed. I am an only child. I am reassured by small enclosed structures: our rooms at home, little lidded containers, bowls and basins, the inside of flowers, everything rounded is pleasing.

In the innermost circle, we are all female: Granny, Aunt Beryl, my mother and me. We live in a small weatherboard cottage with a corrugated iron roof on which we can hear the rain drumming. It's my grandmother's home. We have come to live with her because my father has gone away to the war. The houses are strung like beads along the main northern highway. Where it passes through the town, it's called Mayne Street, Murrurundi. The abbreviation is 'Mdi'. At the edge of town it becomes again the New England Highway, as it was all the way up the Hunter Valley. People still travel in horse and cart, and sulkies, up Mayne Street. Granny's cane chairs are comfortable on the bullnosed front verandah, shaded by a yellow flowering vine. There are tall, scarlet hollyhocks leaning at rakish angles against the front wall of the house. There's a white picket fence and a gate with a musical 'clack' to the latch.

Within my small enclosed world, I feel the painted smoothness of the cream weatherboard walls; I see the yellow cut-glass front doorknob, the pattern on the hall runner, the fireplace in the living room, the poker and tray to gather morning ashes; and, on the bookshelf, a verse from Rabindranath Tagore written in white ink on a black card: 'I shall pass this way but once, therefore any good that I can do . . . .' There's a stiff ribbon threaded through one corner of it.

The dining table is round. I turn the little filigree key of the sideboard door to get things out to set the table. Heavy silver-plated spoons and forks with rounded handles that fit comfortably into the palm of your hand. Serviette rings are engraved silver, each one numbered. Beside the dining table a large, freestanding wireless has a woven cover over the speaker. I sit on the floor in front of it, gazing at it, absorbed as I listen to Miss Ruth Fenner on *Kindergarten of the Air*, following her instructions to sing, imagine, play, answering her questions out loud.

One day we receive a standing telephone, which never becomes commonplace. Mum and Gran hold it warily and speak into it loudly, slowly and distinctly, as though they are addressing a foreigner. We have an ice chest. The ice man carries big, heavy blocks of ice in hessian with a grappling hook. He comes up the side path to the back door. The milkman comes, in his horse and cart, to fill our white enamel billycan. We know him well. Once he took me on the milk round with him. It was so cold early in the morning that I could see my breath, like puffs of steam, and I had to wear my blue knitted pixie hood.

I have my own bedroom but often I sleep in the double bed with my mother. I am lying in bed while she works at the marble wash-stand, decorating lidded bowls with barbola flowers for dressing tables. Barbola is a work in clay, delicate, attractive. She uses improvised tools like a butter knife to curl rose petals. The bowls are sold to the chemist to supplement my father's army pay. I am warm and comfortable, slowly pulling feathers, one by one, out of the eiderdown. In the other hand I am feeling a small empty, flat, round Max Factor tin which used to contain rouge. I am sleepy but my eyes travel round and round the familiar landscape of the room, in a habitual pattern. From the bedstead of carved varnished wood to the big wardrobe, to the flowers on the white jug and basin. Everything is in place. I am quite content. Outside, only feet from our window, a long army convoy drones heavily northward. The bed is trembling from the passing of the trucks and occasionally the china jug rattles in the basin. Yet it seems to me that we are safe in here.

§

IT'S THE WARDROBE that brings Mark Spigelman's story out of the shadows of my memory. He's only tiny and he has curls. They are killing Jewish children in the streets so his father has hidden him in the cellar for safety disguised as a little girl. Mark reminds me about his experience of wardrobes:

> I spent five years of my life sitting in dark rooms underground and in wardrobes, thinking about what would happen to me, and I'm not going to think about it any more ... I can't cry. I've never cried in my life. I probably never will. I knew in my youth that if I cried I could die. I admit that it took a little bit of doing for a three-year-old child to spend days on end in a hollowed-out sort of hole in the ground. And I apparently stayed there for something like three months without seeing the sun and played with rats. And somehow or other I knew that if I heard a voice I had to be quiet, and I knew

that if I heard a German voice I'd be dead — and I still wake once every couple of weeks with this terrible dream, of hearing a voice, and saying 'I'm dead', and then lying perfectly still and not moving.[2]

Mark tells me that he's still discovering his childhood. He had put a heavy gate in front of it and, every time he opened the gate a crack, a little more of the horror escaped. It didn't please him so he closed it again. But now he's beginning to open the gate slightly wider because he realises that closing it does not make the memory go away. Mark is only two years younger than I am. While he is in Poland, hiding in wardrobes or in the hole dug by his father in their cellar in the ghetto, I am in Australia, in my mother's bed with the army convoy rumbling north. We are small children on opposite sides of the world, yet we have a common enemy. Mark knows what an enemy looks like and sounds like and smells like, but I am not so clear about it. All I have to go on are the hideous caricatures of Hitler and Tojo, designed to stiffen public resolve for the war effort, but they do not seem very real. As for hiding, I can only conjure games of hide-and-seek with other children where you want to be found so that you can squeal and laugh and watch the discovery of all the others.

As Mark tells me his terrible memory, I try to imagine myself into the wardrobe and the hole in the ground with him, into the claustrophobia of his confinement, into the dryness of his mouth as he stifles the instinct to cough or to cry out, into the taste of his fear. The main thing I can sense is how little he is, like me; how much smaller than everyone around him, how defenceless, but my imagination keeps sliding away from his images and I return to my familiar circuit of the bedroom, my glance roving from the carved wooden bedstead, to the flowers on the jug and basin, to the wardrobe. The wardrobe looks different now with the possibility of Mark hiding inside it, but my consciousness scuttles sideways from the thought like a soldier crab making for the safety of its hole in the sand. I pull the covers further up so that only my eyes are free. My warm breath smells faintly of feathers under the eiderdown. And where was I, yes, the jug is rattling in the basin and now it seems a little less certain that we are safe in our weatherboard cottage in a small country town in Australia. For Mark's story has become part of my knowing and I will have to carry it with me.

§

OUTSIDE, UNDER THE GRAPEVINE at the back, Granny teaches me to read and write on the slate. Capital 'C', small 'a', small 't'. The slate pencil shrieks on the slate. She is laying the foundation for a life-time of stimulation, company, meaning and spiritual nourishment and I am thirsty for what she has to teach me. Granny is gentle. She squeezes grapes through a wire strainer to extract their juice. Black Isabellas and mauve Muscatels. The skins and seeds are discarded. The juice is elixir. Its sweetness floods my mouth and while I am drinking it I can think of nothing else. Granny was born a MacDonald of the Isles, descended from the renowned Flora. She was one of three sisters, beauties who married three English brothers travelling on the same boat to Australia last century.

Sometimes, in Murrurundi, great hailstorms sweep in from the north-west, shredding violets and breaking windows. We set saucepans under the drips and hide under the dining room table, to shelter from splintering glass, until it's over. Afterwards Mr Rixon gradually works his way along the street, mending windows. After one storm, when the Pages River was in flood, we found a half-drowned kitten at the bottom of the back paddock. Sheltered in a shoebox beside the kitchen stove and fed milk with an eyedropper, she grew up to be Mrs Tiggy Winkle. Once, impulsively, she sank her teeth into my knee. My mother made me chase her and hit her with an umbrella. I cried and resisted. I couldn't bear to hurt her. Unlike Mark, I cried easily.

Aunt Beryl explores her way tentatively into the morning, engrossed in the labour of drawing enough air into tubercular lungs. She is quiet and affectionate, known as Brownie. All these women have time for me, time to teach me crochet and stocking stitch and manners; and how to cut the biscuit dough into shapes. But there are secrets in the crevices of their conversation to which I am not admitted. Something terrible has happened but I am not told about it. It lives here with us, hanging in the silence, creating an air of melancholy and suppressed anxiety which I breathe in without knowing it. Nothing is ever quite certain. However, they all ask me about school, and listen to my answers. I am well aware of being loved. My mother is the most preoccupied because she is responsible for all of us and she is only young, in her mid-thirties. We talk to each other calmly.

§

IT'S THIS COMPANIONABLE TALK, murmuring back and forth among our family, that beckons the story of Anka Makovec forward into my memory. She is listening, wistfully, under the kitchen window, to the way we speak with each other. She's the same age as me and she's limping. She's two years older than Mark and they share a common enemy. Her childhood in Slovenia was a nightmare. Her father wanted a son but she was born the fourth girl and she was not welcome. Her English is strongly accented:

Soon after, the war broke out. And we survived through the war. I remember as a child of two, three and four, I remember vividly the villages burning, the people being murdered — hanged. I remember my neighbour's four daughters being shot by the Nazis because their father was a partisan in the Resistance. And my father . . . he used to drink before, but then he really went earnestly into that, and he treated my mother extremely badly and us children with her. I remember — I must have been only four years old — I remember my mother was thrown out of the house by my father, beaten up and . . . it was snow outside and she took us littlies into our neighbour's barn, where the cows were, and she talked to the old cow to stay down there. 'Keep my children warm', she said, 'keep my children warm'. And she tucked us close to the cow and hugged us to the cow so we could get the warmth from Mother and the cow.

Years went by of this terrible situation with my mother; eventually I think the sheer atrocities upon her dignity made her fall into alcoholism herself. So by the time I was five or six, they were both alcoholics. We were hungry during the war but still we used to trap animals in the forest and we used to go and see the traps before we went to do anything else. I remember going practically every day across the road to our neighbours where I felt that tremendous hunger for love that I always yearned for. I was kind of stealing it from that family. I recall even sneaking in the night to under their kitchen window, just to listen to the way they talked to each other, because it was love in there, it was love in that house and there was no love in our house.[3]

Her voice has dropped to a rasping whisper as though these memories cannot yet be spoken out loud. She stops. I wait to see if she wants to go on, but that seems to be all for the moment. She's content to listen.

§

SO IT'S TRUE. There really are starving children in Europe to make Australian children like me feel guilty when they won't eat their vegetables, and this wistful little girl is one of them. Everything she and Mark have told me casts light and shadows on my own memory and shifts its perspective. Their fearful memories help me to know how secure I am in the enclosing circle of this house of women in which I live, by the chance of geography and the whim of circumstance. It provides everything I need: love, approval, encouragement, learning, the magic of wireless bringing in news, plays and the *Amateur Hour*, and food that I will take less for granted from now on. Outside is peopled by strange unpredictable elements like big boys, one mentally handicapped boy ('retarded' was the term used at that time), black children who can run fast, dogs, army trucks and the annual Bush Carnival over the road at the showground. But there's no terror. The biggest event in my childhood was when Wirth's Circus came and I saw lions and clowns for the first time. The smell of strange animals made me nervous and excited, in a secret way. One boy laughed so much at the clowns that he fell down between the tiered wooden seats and hung suspended by his fingers, the laughter knocked out of him.

Our bathroom is separate, out the back. When Mum lights the chip heater, set with kindling and newspaper, it gets up a pulsating roar and coughs scalding water into the bath, freestanding on its own squat legs. The lavatory is a long walk up the back yard, over a lawn full of bindi-eyes, past the rope swing Dad hung from the apricot tree when he was home on leave, past the tank, past the well, past the clothesline held up with a forked wooden prop; behind the shed where grandfather Ashley Needham Pountney used to publish *The Murrurundi Times*. It's under a fig tree, furnished with a box of ashes and paper torn into squares threaded on a loop of string. There is no need to close the door. You can sit on the smooth wooden seat in privacy, looking out into the tree, searching for ripening purple fruit among the convoluted fingers of its leaves. 'Nightsoil' men come once a week to replace the pan.

The whole territory of our place is marked out by trees. I know each one and climb them all. Different trees for different moods: apricot, apple, nectarine, poplar. An apple broken in half crossways reveals seeds in a star pattern. Take a bite and its bitterness puckers your mouth. Trees provide me with adventure and refuge. The apple tree is welcoming, with smooth bark and widespread, gently inclined limbs. The poplar is dense and difficult, especially on the way down, but in the top of it I am triumphant and I spit to the ground far below, to prove something. The bark of the apricot tree corruscates the inside of my thigh as I grapple for a way up the trunk to the lowest branch.

§

ANOTHER CONTEMPORARY, Phillip Adams, has music in his childhood. Although he's in Melbourne, he's living in his own war zone, wishing to be somewhere else:

I used to create environments for myself with music and when I think back, when I was a kid I used to get very esoteric music. I remember getting some of the first Indian records you could get in Australia. I'd seek out very bizarre, strange musics. At the same time of course I was filling my little room, my little beleaguered room, with images of places that were as far away in time and space as they could possibly be. It was one of my defences from my lunatic stepfather. So just as the walls were covered with images of the pyramids, with images of ancient civilisations, the music in that room was also esoteric and strange. Later on in life I started replacing the photographs on the walls with the real things. That was the trigger mechanism, I think, for collecting antiquities.[4]

§

I HAVE A CUBBY HOUSE in a shed up the back, behind our cottage, and I gather coloured glass and pieces of broken crockery, from the garbage tip, to keep there. Treasures. I am looking not for escape but for evidence of beauty. I love coloured glass and the patterns on china. And, like Phillip, I carry the compulsion into adulthood, until my walls are crammed with paintings and my shelves with ornaments.

Mostly we know women. We know the people in each house on the street. We know the people in all the shops. A succession of women visit us from around the town and from country properties. They come with eggs and a billycan of milk or even cream. They are not related but might as well be, through friendship and shared need in uncertain times. I call them 'aunt'. After years of association they all call Granny 'Mrs Pountney', except for the closest who might on occasion use the intimate 'Mrs Pount'. The formality is no barrier to their fondness for each other. Visitors are made welcome. The first sign of them is the clack of the gate latch in the picket fence, facing Mayne Street. There is always a cup of tea in willow-pattern cups and something homemade to eat.

Occasionally, a man comes with one of the honorary aunts, her husband or son. The backs of their hands are like tanned hide. They smell of leather. Their riding boots creak. Plaited kangaroo hide belts hold up their cream moleskins. Coming in the front door, they take off their broad-brimmed felt hats to reveal an area of shocking pink across the forehead above weathered faces. They are a bit too big for our chairs, and their voices are louder and deeper than I am used to. I find them secretly attractive but intimidating; another race, powerful, potentially dangerous. I have heard them laughing together when they stand talking beside their utes in the main street. In the laughter of men, I hear an unfamiliar note. It contains its own hidden messages which I feel may not be to the advantage of women. Visiting their places, I have seen them wrestling huge merinos in the shearing shed and breaking in horses, so I know their strength. They all like my mother, and I find this disturbing. I retreat into shyness but I am watching and listening to everything.

At Christmas time we could have been lonely but instead we are invited out to Blandford, where the Haydons, Aunt Maud and Aunt Bubby, embrace us into their extended family. The old homestead sprawls in the heat under its corrugated iron roof. At our arrival, after church, a dozen wildly excited sheepdogs strain barking and break-neck at their kennel chains under pepper trees. The smell of turkeys roasting in the great Aga stove drives me wild with anticipation. Conveniently, I suppress the memory of seeing chooks' heads cut off with the axe, appalled that they run round the yard for a minute, headless and spurting blood from the neck, before they realise they are dead. Long trestle tables are set up on hospitable verandahs under grapevines. The skin of the turkey is crisp and delicious around slices of white meat aromatic with sage and thyme. Rich gravy is poured over browned wedges of roast potatoes and pumpkin.

Later, I bite on the metal of a sixpence hidden in the Christmas pudding, skilfully served by Aunt Maud to ensure that no child misses out on a prize. A profusion of honorary aunts and uncles bellow conversation at each other across the table. A number of them are deaf and inclined to scorn their hearing aids, and it is easier to shout at everyone than to distinguish the deaf from the others.

After Christmas dinner there is dressing-up and charades in the long cicada-shrilling afternoon, while aunts snore gently on cotton-quilted sleepout beds under the dense and kindly shade of a giant mulberry, their gnarled hands at rest at last. And finally the delicious, electrifying chill of a plunge into the deep green swimming hole, off the end of a long, slow-swinging frond of weeping willow on the river bank. The day at Blandford is one of ecstasy. I never recaptured the flavour of it until I read *The Darling Buds of May*, H. E. Bates' evocation of the idyllic life of the Larkin family, in post-war southern England. There was always room for a stranger at Ma and Pop Larkin's generous table.

It's Mark again:

> Christmas 1944 and we were with a lady called Mrs Matoniowa. She actually hid us for the last three or four months of the war. Her husband was a German collaborator and he was due for the chop (by Christmas '44 everybody knew that the Germans' days were numbered). And apparently she decided to hide a Jewish family in her farmhouse, so that we would be witnesses to how good she was. In fact, it worked bloody well, because my father stood up and said, 'Yes, she hid us'. And until the day she died, from Australia every month we'd send a parcel to her. So it helped her and it helped us a little, too. But I'm diverting . . .
>
> Christmas Eve 1944 . . . Mrs Matoniowa walked into the room and she had two big slices of black bread with cream cheese and sugar, and two lollies, one in a grey wrapper, one in a blue wrapper. And I'm quite certain this is the first time in my life I remember eating anything sweet. I don't know about you, but, as life goes on, you have a sort of thing you say, 'Is it better than this or worse than this?' Well, since that day any meal I have is a percentage of how good those two bits of bread and those lollies felt. I've been to some great restaurants in my life. Some of them have even come up to 75 per cent of that — that was the greatest meal I've ever had in my life. I'll never forget it. You know, I was four; there were several things I hadn't done in life. One of them, obviously, was to eat sugar. That meal is just a total instant recall: my mouth salivates, I know exactly what it was.[5]

$$\S$$

How dramatically different our lives are and yet our memories set each other off. Perhaps it is because we are the same age, and born into wartime, that we feel bound together in sympathy and mutual curiosity. While Mark is tasting sugar for the first time in Poland and Phillip is running from his stepfather's madness in Melbourne and Anka is trapping animals in the Slovenian forest for food, I am shopping safely with Granny Pountney in Mayne Street, Murrurundi. It is reassuring to feel the respect and acceptance of being part of Gran's modest entourage. By material standards in Australia we are poor, but so is everyone else. The prevailing currency is a sense of values subscribed to by the community at large. It is based in Christianity and although, as Protestants, we are suspicious of Catholics, and they of us, we hold many similar values.

At this time, Aborigines are virtually invisible to whites, except as domestic servants, stockmen, unacknowledged mistresses to country men, or bush people corralled on reserves. They look uncomfortable in the town, awkward and out of place. Murrurundi, 'nest in the hills', is an Aboriginal name, a suppressed reminder that this is the country of the Kamilaroi people, but I did not know that until much later.

§

NOW, IN MY IMAGINATION, Kevin Gilbert is tapping me on the shoulder to let me know that he and his mother were nervous about coming to town. They found town alien. It was like walking into an enemy city, he says. It wasn't this town, but it's a shock to hear my people classified as enemy. He was born in a tent on the banks of the Lachlan River, but for him its name was Kalara, which means the ever-flowing river. Thinking of the river, his memories flow:

> I remember the early years; I was the youngest of eight children in the family, and I remember the children and the animal life, fishing, fish jumping in the river, Aboriginal relatives coming and visiting, and then the big occasion of going across to town. We had to cross the Goobang Creek over the Chinaman's Bridge and we had some friends in the Chinese market gardens and the little Chinese shop; they were always warm, flowing people. The rest of my people were over on the Aboriginal mission, which was like a refugee camp. My other main family, which is my grandmother and aunties and uncles, refused to live on the mission so they lived on the lagoon, called the Murie. These were very early and precious memories. All the other children were at school and I used to play on my own on the river banks, and there was only my mother and I most of the time so there was a very close bond. My mother used to take in washing at the local butcher's and I'd accompany her when she was doing that.[6]

Kevin's mother was Wiradhuri, his father Irish/English, but that provided no passport into the white world.

Mark and Anka break in to tell Kevin he was lucky to be playing on the river bank. (Now I am beginning to wonder if it is legitimate for me to bring them all together like this. They have each told their stories to me at different times but they do not know each other. Their meeting place is only in my imagination, yet they seem to have things to tell each other and to hear from each other.) Mark reminds us that he never played with another child until he was nine and the war over. It was going to be the most exciting day of his life, he thought. He was going to school for the first time to play with other children. He had dreamed about it, but when he got there no one played with him. The children's parents had told them that the Jews were to blame for the war and, since he was the only Jewish child left alive in that district, they called him insulting names and beat him. He says it was one of the great disappointments of his life but he didn't cry because he had not learned how to. (Was this the start of his training to become a children's doctor?)

Kevin keeps silent, probably because Mark's story reminds him of times when he too was called insulting names and beaten, and he doesn't like to think about it too much. He's saving it up to write in his poems later, when he's grown up, after he's been brutally bashed, over and over again, in Grafton Gaol.

When the white man took his bloodied boot
From the neck of the buggered black . . .
Did you expect some gratitude,
His smile, 'Good on you Jack?'
When your psalmist sang
Of a suffering Christ
While you practised genocide
Did you expect his hate would fade
Out of sight with the ebbing tide?[7]

§

THE DOOLEYS in Murrurundi are Catholic. Nonetheless we shop at their Emporium. Inside it is pleasantly cool and you can't see anything for a few seconds until your eyes adjust to the gloom. Customers are served at a long wooden counter. I climb onto a high chair painted pale green to sit beside the hinged Arnotts biscuit tin with a rosella on the label. Mark watches with his eyes popping while Gran pays for half a pound of sugar and half a pound of tea with shillings and pence and ration coupons. Miss Dooley puts the money and coupons into a brass cylinder and they are catapulted up, singing on the high wire, to the office. The change comes back the same way.

'Always the right change at Dooley's,' Gran says. 'You can count on that.' She thinks the best of everyone, even Catholics.

After a call at Mr Sutton the chemist, who walks leaning backwards, and another courtly interlude with the butcher, we walk home along Mayne Street, past Dr Middleton's, past the Commercial Bank where my best friend Sue lives, past Peter the Greek's which gets flooded when the river comes up, across the Pages River bridge, past the Post Office. We call in to the Eleys. Their front gate makes almost the same clacking sound as ours. Sitting on their cool front verandah, shaded by vines, Gran and Mrs Eley talk. Miss Gypsy Eley, who has lived with her mother and cared for her as long as anyone can recall, helps me to practise making a posy for the church flower show. She picks a few small flowers from the profusion of her cottage garden. She watches me patiently while I arrange a tiny bunch of columbines, violets, pansies, Sweet Alice, love-in-a-mist and maiden-hair fern. When I cannot hold them all together and drop some, she is calm in suggesting another way. When we're happy with the posy, she ties the stems with a scrap of wool, and shows me how to fold paper around the stems for decoration. I am enchanted by it. She has enabled me to make it my creation. I carry it home to Mum as a prize. Neither she nor Miss Eley ever goes visiting without making up a dainty, fragrant posy of whatever they can find in the garden.

We walk to the Church of England across the swing bridge. Granny is a member of the Women's Guild. She is on a roster for doing the flowers, and polishing altar brass, collection plates and candelabra. Harvest Festival is celebrated literally, in unconscious perpetuation of its pagan origins. The church is decorated with great sheaves of wheat, giant pumpkins and fleeces of wool. My mother plays the organ but she finds church melancholy, a depressing duty. I win a prize for 'best buttonhole' at the church flower show. My mother and grandmother and Aunt Beryl know everyone. People like them. At home we say prayers every night:

> *Now I lay me down to sleep*
> *I pray the Lord my soul to keep.*
> *If I should die before I wake,*
> *I pray the Lord my soul to take.*

This is a pleasant, comfortable ritual and, although I have very little idea what it might mean, later it will become my nightly mantra.

Occasionally, we take a picnic to Paradise Park, at the edge of town, a barely tamed expanse of land ascending into a rock escarpment. It is a brooding, unfamiliar place, humming, mysterious, potent and completely indifferent to us. We are not at home here, yet something attracts us to come and endure the strange atmosphere for as long as we can. Eventually, conversation dies out into an uncertain silence and, although no one mentions it, we all seem relieved when it's time to go home. One day, for an outing, my mother and I walk up a slope on the other edge of town. We try to lie down and relax on the hill-side. It is impossible. We are both nervous, too exposed. Something else is here already but we do not know what it is. We come home rather shaken, in silence.

§

IN MY STORE of memories, Patti Miller is dancing from foot to foot. She knows something important about this. Patti grew up on her family's farm near Wellington, New South Wales. That area began to be settled by Europeans within 40 years of the white settlement of Australia. Her family, the Müllers, as they were originally named, were among those early settlers. Patti was the fifth generation of the family to know these few square miles of country. She did not know, as a child, that this is also Wiradhuri land. Yet she felt a potent communication from it. She explains:

I know this country as an animal knows it ... I know the gradient of the slope across to the orchard, and the flat land where the creek spreads out behind the wheat-shed, and the gentle rise from the house to the sheep yards and the empty space behind the sheep-killing tree and the sheds.

I know the shifts in the spirit of each of these places: the faint danger of the slope beyond the creek, the loneliness of the land behind the sheds, the mystery and loss in the flat salty land where the gums have died, the light-heartedness near the windmill and horse paddock and, less than a hundred yards away, the solemnity and strangeness around the top dam. I walk about the farm and my heart shifts, responding to the changing spirit, to the distinct dreaming of each ... I can only suppose I was responding to stories I hadn't heard ... Can stories hover in the silence for years, soaking through the skins of children, even European children already filling up with English stories?

I had nothing to explain the ground beneath my feet or my connection to it. If I knew the stories of my own place, I might have walked across the land, reading its history. The land might have sung and I might have followed the songlines. But my ancestors came with stories of English seasons and gods and obliterated the sacred text of the red soil and silver rivers. Like many before, I waited in vain for the awful silence to speak ...

The Aborigines of the Wellington area had stories which named everything. As a child I didn't even know the name of the people who lived on this land before I did. Before my father's family took the land from under their feet ... My ignorance has been absolute. And my loss.

My story is that I was born on Wiradhuri land, surrounded by family, and we thought we owned the land. But it owned us. Now it is owned by others and we grieve, all of us, but most of all my father fades without his land. Sold 15 years ago and still Dad cannot bear to drive past the beloved land. We grew and explored and knew the ground beneath our feet, it was our mother, but for Dad it was like a lover. He cannot think of anyone else ploughing the land ... The land owns us and we cannot escape it. It must have sung its story to us in our sleep.[8]

§

WAS IT THIS same spirit of place, as yet indecipherable to us skinny little white kids, which called so clearly to Anka Makovec in faraway Slovenia, and set up a longing in her to come to meet it in Australia? This is how she remembers it, in a dramatic chapter of her life which began when she was struck down by osteomyelitis at the age of ten:

The closest hospital was a day away on the train. But one of our neighbours, they thought I was a pretty good little kid and they saw that I was getting really bad so they said, 'We've got to find a truck and take this kid to the hospital.' We started at five o'clock in the morning and reached the hospital about eleven at night. I was unconscious by then. My leg was huge and blue in colour; the skin was just like glass. And the doctor, I think he was a military doctor, came and looked at me and he said, 'I don't want this child to die. Go into the village and wake me two assistants. If I don't cut this open or cut the leg off, she will not reach the morning.' So he sawed the bone out and during that procedure I came to, to my senses. And I could see my leg open, and I could see on the ceiling what burst out of it when he cut it. And I just remember his beautiful loving face and I thought, 'I can see love on this man' and something just surged into me — a tremendous will to survive.

A year later, pus was still coming out of her wound. She was on crutches and in plaster but her father, who complained that he had too many mouths to feed, carried her across the mountain and gave her to a farmer as an indentured labourer. After six months she escaped and, still on crutches, made her way home across the mountains. It took her two days.

On my return I met a person who introduced me to the village library. And in that library I found an article on the Aboriginal culture and I saw a bark painting and I was totally moved. I thought, 'This is another world. This is such a refined . . . this is such a wonderful art.' And I thought, 'My God, one day I'm going to meet these people — I am. Not a penny on me and on crutches but one day I'm going to go to Australia.'

Notwithstanding her crippled leg, Anka trained as a nurse. She came to Australia and worked as a nurse and later became a postmistress and a wilderness guide in Tasmania. She formed deep friendships with Aboriginal people. It was she who importuned Roger Climpson to portray some Aboriginal people on *This is your Life*, starting with poet Kath Walker, Oodjeroo Noonuccal. She nursed the great artist of the Lardil people, Dick Roughsey, Goobalathaldin, at his place Jowalbinna on Cape York. So her childhood dream came true as her own long quest for the sacred was profoundly enlightened by Aboriginal spirituality.

Well, one doesn't use the word 'sacred' lightly. I don't use it lightly, because I've searched for it for so many years. In the wilderness, when you are totally away from the artificial things, when you are there for days, probably weeks, you feel the presence of the Great Spirit. And I'm saying 'Great Spirit' because in Aboriginal culture I have found it. The whole of humanity is under the umbrella of its great love. And it's not only humanity. It's the whole of the world: living things, flowers, trees, rocks, everything. It's in touch, it's in tune with the Great Spirit. And those who, for instance, are rock-climbers, like I am . . . before I learnt about this, when I was out there alone with the rock, I knew there is a spirit in the rock . . . I knew it before I heard it. And then, years after, I heard Helen Keller saying, 'The rock — she doesn't hear, she doesn't speak, but she has the life embodied in it, the life of the world. She has a spirit.' And that came totally in tune to what my Aboriginal tribal friends were saying. Then it all came together and I thought, 'Well, Jesus is a part of that Spirit. All people are a part of the Spirit. It's just a matter of that great tuning-in.'[9]

Jesus had been left behind long ago in Anka's grim childhood in Catholic Slovenia. Now she met up with him again in the Australian wilderness.

§

RELIEVED BY the spiritual homecoming of Anka's story after such a desolate beginning, I am more grateful than ever that my childhood home is familiar and predictable. As the circles of my environment widen, I feel less secure. When we go on the train to spend a few days with my father, near his army camp, I sleep under a soldier's khaki greatcoat in the luggage rack. My father is away for four years at the war that is also Anka's war, and Mark's, and the war of Patti's father and Kevin's older brothers who enlisted in the army. One of Kevin's brothers was only 16 — he was the youngest Australian commando.

We pray for my father, at night. We miss him. He comes home very occasionally, for a short leave. It's exciting to see him, yet his true place in the scheme of things is a puzzle to me. He brings us luxuries — once, a bottle of lemonade; another time a magical fold-out cardboard storybook. He replaces me in my mother's bed. He is embarrassed and scolds me when he catches me looking at him through a hole in the bathroom door while he is showering. One year, he makes a little table and two chairs for my Christmas present. I love them so much that I am reduced to shyness and retreat into silence. He is big, with a powerful presence, rough-textured, very clean. I know I loved him because we said so and it was implicit, but mostly he was absent and my daily experience of practical, tangible love all came from women.

I'm looking at a black and white photograph of me and my mother taken on a box brownie camera. I'm in my stroller on the back lawn, about 18 months old. There are sweetpeas growing against a paling fence. I look blissful with a bow in my hair and Mum kneeling beside me on the grass. Her hair is fastened back from her forehead with a bobby pin, gleaming in sunlight. She looks pleased, relaxed, all her attention focused on me. We are enough for each other.

Anka and Kevin, Patti, Phillip and Mark have gone back into my memory for the time being. I am grateful for their company there.

For your Journal

* Revisit your childhood home, literally or in memory. Wander through it, looking into rooms.

* Reflect, daydream, remember. What did you like, dislike in your house?

* Talk to parents and grandparents or others who knew you as a child.

* Who else was there? Look at old family photographs.

* What is your earliest memory?

* What sounds, images, feelings, touch, tastes, aromas do you remember? Where did you experience them? What time of day?

* What did you love to do?

* Did you have a favourite toy or book? What did you like about them?

* What was your first secret?

* What were you afraid of?

Write down the remembered images or record them as a drawing, diagram, map or painting; or perhaps an album of photographs with captions. Reflect on your remembered images and let one image unearth another. They will come to you bit by bit and gradually form into a whole.

For invaluable guidance in recovering your story, I commend to you a book called *Writing your Life* by Patti Miller (Allen & Unwin 1994).

Endnotes

1 Rainer Maria Rilke, *Letters to a Young Poet*, trans by M. D. Herter, Norton, 1993.
2 Mark Spigelman in *The Search for Meaning: Conversations with Caroline Jones*, ABC/Collins Dove, 1992.
3 Anka Makovec in *The Search for Meaning Book Two*, Caroline Jones, ABC/Collins Dove, 1990. Also Tape 25 in *The Search for Meaning Catalogue*, ABC Radio Tapes.
4 Phillip Adams in *The Search for Meaning*, Caroline Jones, ABC/Collins Dove, 1989.
5 Mark Spigelman in *The Search for Meaning: Conversations with Caroline Jones*.
6 Kevin Gilbert in *The Search for Meaning Collection*, Caroline Jones, ABC/Harper Collins, 1995.
7 From 'The Flowering' by Kevin Gilbert in *People Are Legends*, University of Queensland Press, 1978.
8 Patti Miller, *The Last One Who Remembers*, Allen & Unwin, 1997. Also Tape 235 in *The Search for Meaning Catalogue*, ABC Radio Tapes.
9 Anka Makovec in *The Search for Meaning Book Two*.

3 YOUR STORY:
HOW DOES IT UNFOLD?

*It is the recognition of one's actual truth,
the truth of one's actual life, that is so lifegiving.*

Harold Brodkey[1]

YOU WILL NEED to spend time with your memories and contemplate how you feel about the process of recalling childhood. You don't have to judge your recollection and the people in it, nor impale it like a butterfly on a cork for interrogation or blame. This recollection can be a gentle process, an end in itself, conducted in a mood of reverie. It is likely to arouse a range of feelings. For me, the process produced a sense of expansion. It helped me to feel more authentic, reminding me that my story does have a beginning and continuity, and that it involves a lot of other people. It also brought me to tears more than once. It made me homesick for a time when I was secure and innocent, a time when I seemed to be mostly happy. I felt a poignant and helpless love for the child I remembered.

There were moments of vertigo in which that little girl in the photographs seemed a separate identity, gone forever; and I longed to reconnect with her, in whatever way that might be possible. As well, there was a sense of fear that I might be the only person who could truly know her, and that there are probably limits even to that knowing.

What to do with this turmoil of responses? One way to take in that early part of my story was to identify its elements and to see where, and in what form, they are present in my life today. It began to seem important to identify my own symbols and images and their meaning for me, rather than be seduced by those of others. It is easy to become engrossed in a fast-food diet of fictions from popular culture which suppress attention to the integrity of your own story unfolding, and leave a feeling of emptiness in their wake. In this chapter, I'll identify some of my own prevailing symbols and explain how I've reflected on them. The reflection requires time and contemplation. It is more a work of the imagination than of logic. It is savouring rather than analysis.

You need to turn a symbol over and over in your mind or, better still, let it turn while you observe it. See it capture and then refract the light, like a prism. See it like the patterns in a kaleidoscope, assembling and reassembling with each turn of the cylinder. A symbol is never a static diagram. It is saturated with meanings that will expand and shift in emphasis and nuance over time.

I can identify one significant symbolic resonance between childhood and maturity in my image of family. In wartime, the concept of family was redefined by the absence of men and the survival needs of women and children. A wider image of family opened up, in which people who were not related offered care and interest where they saw it was required. And that is the pattern of my life today. As a person who married and divorced in my twenties, I have, in mid-life, no primary commitment to a partnership. As many other single people know, this can be categorised socially as a condition of inadequacy. Yet the reality is that, like many other single people, of all ages, I maintain ties of friendship, love and responsibility with a number of other people, only a few of whom are related by blood. The valuable role in society of a married couple with a conventional family is easy to see, while a single person's contribution may be less evident, but still considerable in its effect.

Like many other single people, I have created my own family and it is extended beyond blood relationship and personal acquaintanceship out into the wider community. I think of listeners and correspondents to *The Search for Meaning* programs as part of my widely extended family, for they have provided support and direction for my vocation. My single status has been determined by a variety of circumstances, but at this stage I can see that it is also my personal preference. It is a situation in which I can be effective in terms of what I perceive to be my life purpose, both as an individual and a member of the community.

While my primary family responsibility is to my elderly father and stepmother, I am in touch with quite an extraordinary number of people, in varying degrees of intimacy. I would not be able to maintain these friendships to the same extent if I had exclusive obligations in a partnership and to my own children. For one thing, my capacity to be available to a large number of people is nourished by my solitude which diminishes if I am enclosed in one exclusive relationship. In my life there is a blurred line between the personal and the vocational because my main interest lies in being part of awakening people to the possibilities of living life to the full, with meaning and purpose. This interest brings me into contact with a great network of people of like mind, and invites me into various situations where people are in pursuit of meaning.

It is reassuring for me to see that this image of a large extended family has its roots in my childhood where the unusual circumstances of wartime brought people into new relationships through mutual need. It is an attractive and satisfying image for me because I have seen how well it sustained people in difficult times. It is an idea of family linked not only by blood but by the needs of the common good. I have seen misery and loneliness result from a determination to live in an overly independent way that results in the isolation of an individual or a nuclear family. I place great value on knowing the people in the local shops, at the local library and the local church. I may not know everybody well but we share a common interest in our district and its people, and it is easy to smile and pause for a short conversation in order to maintain these community contacts.

Another predominant and related symbol of my early story is 'the sustaining community of women'. One day I was pressing the avocados in a local shop, unobserved, I hoped, to select a ripe one. I became aware that one of the local woman doctors was standing near me doing the same thing to the nectarines, right beside a handmade sign saying 'Please don't squeeze me till I'm yours'. We are acquaintances only, but sufficiently interested in each other's lives to have a short conversation about our family situations. We have met like this a number of times over the years.

Reflecting on this meeting later, I noticed with a little surprise how deep was my pleasure in the encounter. Some of the feelings aroused were reassurance at being recognised (a reminder that I exist); a sense of belonging in the community; a sense of pride in her achievement as a woman who had graduated in medicine at a time when that was unusual for women; a sense of honour that she thought it worth spending a few minutes in my company; a feeling of comfort that we both had family concerns and an acknowledgement that these were legitimate concerns.

This experience is significant for me today because it harks back to the rich symbol of a 'sustaining community of women' in childhood. Of course, as a child, I took it for granted that several women cared about us, called at our house, telephoned us, invited us out to their farms. It is only today, many miles along the road of experience, that I see it for the treasure it was; for the emotional, physical, spiritual and psychological support that it provided our household in wartime. And I see how, albeit unconsciously, I have sought to reproduce it in my life today. It has resurfaced as an important plank in my sense of values, one to which I am prepared to contribute attention and energy.

My women friends are not all single. Many happily married or partnered women still seek the company of women. Quite often it is the differences and contrasts that make the sexual relationship between men and women stimulating and complementary, while the conversation and concerns of women are based in that particular shared understanding of what it is to be female. Women (and men in whom the feminine qualities are developed) will often express their feelings and identify the location of their vulnerability. It is common for women to relish the discussion of the challenge and nuance of relationships. They are likely to be interested in the psychological, physical, emotional and spiritual wellbeing of women and children and perplexed sometimes by the contrasting priorities and behaviour of the husbands, brothers and sons with whom they live. Few of these subjects would be the first choice for men, unless they were attending a discussion group specifically for the purpose, but they are frequently grist to the mill of women's talk which is often concerned as much with the process of life as with the completion of tasks.

There is another aspect to this symbol of the sustaining community of women. At some stage in my adolescence there was an element of claustrophobia in the circle of women which urged me to escape it, to flee from its safety into the unknown world of adventure, work, individuality, men, challenge and risk. This presents me with a contradiction, and contradiction often gives rise to anxiety. The western system of thought trains us to think in opposites and to try to resolve contradiction when we encounter it, by choosing one side and rejecting the other. This often results in addled thinking and needless suffering, and I want to explore it here and now because, frequently, it poses an obstacle to the search for meaning.

We *are* complex and contradictory. That is the nature of the human condition. It is not to be resolved but relished and explored for its nuance and possibility. Where you find contradiction in your own life, you may like to hold the apparent opposites gently in tension with each other. Let them conduct a dialogue with each other, without one having to win and the other lose. You can mediate between them, see what it is they have to say to each other, for there is much insight to be gained in paradox. It is because I took that outward journey into the masculine-dominated public world that the 'sustaining company of women' is something chosen afresh and with deeper pleasure today, in the light of contrasting experience, *which also had its value*. It is the very contradictions which enrich this symbol and make it rewarding to contemplate. The writer Barbara Blackman told me that the principle of many insights she gained in the East was *not either/or, but both*. It is a profoundly useful concept to incorporate into your habits of reasoning, in order to think more freely, to gain a more imaginative view of the world and to avoid the limiting pitfall of fundamentalism — taking everything literally. But what is the authority, or the origin of this concept?

It is found first in the *Tao Te Ching*, thought to have been written by Lao Tzu, a contemporary of Confucius, some five centuries before Christ. Other scholarly theories place it in the third or fourth century BC and suggest more than one author. Bede Griffiths, in his book *Universal Wisdom,*[2] says that, whatever its authorship, the *Tao Te Ching* belongs to that breakthrough in human consciousness which occurred in the first millennium before Christ, and is a supreme example of the great mystical tradition that underlies all religion. The *Tao Te Ching* affirms, as the Hindu Upanishads and Buddha had done, that the ultimate reality has no name. While Hinduism speaks of ultimate reality as Brahman, and Buddhism speaks of it as Nirvana, the Chinese preferred to refer to it as Tao, or the Way.

> Tao is the 'rhythm' of the universe, the 'flow' of reality, like the 'ever living fire' of Heraclitus or the field of energies of modern physics. Its character is the union of opposites, the Yin and the Yang, the passive and the active, the female and the male. This leads in Chinese philosophy to a profound sense of the complementarity of all existence. The western way of thinking, based on Greek philosophy, thinks in terms of opposites, of good and evil, truth and error, black and white. Its way of thinking is logical, based on the principle of contradiction. But the Chinese mind, and with it the eastern mind as a whole, thinks more in terms of complementarity. It is aware of the Unity which transcends and yet includes all dualities, of the whole which transcends and yet unites all its parts.[3]

The west was offered this insight later by the Christian philosopher, Nicholas of Cusa, a cardinal of the Roman church, who spoke of the coincidence of opposites. Yet, as Bede Griffiths goes on to point out, 'for centuries now the western world has been following the path of Yang — of the masculine, active, aggressive, rational, scientific mind — and has brought the world near to destruction. It is time now to recover the path of Yin, of the feminine, passive, patient, intuitive and poetic mind'.[4]

The *Tao Te Ching* speaks of 'something formlessly fashioned, which existed before heaven and earth. Without sound, without substance, dependent on nothing, unchanging, all pervading, unfailing. One may think of it as the Mother of all things under heaven. Its true name we do not know. Tao is the by-name which we give it'.

> The Hebrew people, from whom the western world received its religion, belonged to a patriarchal culture and saw their God in masculine terms, consciously reacting against the cult of feminine deities among the surrounding peoples. But the Tao is essentially feminine. The most typical concept in the *Tao Te Ching* is that of *wu wei*, that is 'actionless activity'. This is the essence of the feminine. The woman is made to be passive in relation to the man, to receive the seed which makes her fertile. But this passivity is an active passivity, a receptivity which is dynamic and creative, from which all life and fruitfulness, all love and communion grow. The world today needs to recover this sense of feminine power, which is complementary to the masculine and without which man becomes dominating, sterile and destructive. But this means that western religion must come to rec-ognize the feminine aspect of God.'[5]

Bede Griffiths put this opinion into practice in his own life. An English Benedictine monk, he went to India to discover 'the other half of his soul'. He became a sannyasi, integrating Indian tradition into his monastic life. He told me that, after a stroke, late in his life, he felt himself to be flooded with a new experience of feminine sensibility and spirituality which was indeed a revelation of 'the other half of his soul'. Highly educated in several disciplines, including science and religion, he wore his learning with grace and generosity, speaking in straightforward language that anyone could follow. I recorded an interview with him for *The Search for Meaning* when he was on a winter visit to Australia from his ashram in southern India.[6] He had made a concession to the cold by donning a pair of socks with his sandals and his saffron robe was covered with a borrowed woollen overcoat. His skin was translucent; he was very thin, very thoughtful. He listened with full, calm attention, yet I felt he also had a line of communication open to some universal dimension and that he might dematerialise into it at any moment. Bede Griffiths was a leading international figure in crosscultural spiritual dialogue. His openness to exploring the deep connections between the spiritual traditions of the world won him many followers.

Because of our conditioning in the argumentative, adversarial pattern of western thought, the concepts of the *Tao Te Ching* are foreign to us, but they reward deeper reflection and I have found they help me to make clearer sense of my own experience. For instance, I have worked happily for many years principally in the company of men. The conversation there is different *and* I enjoy it *and it* is not enough for me. I need the company of my own sex as well, for the sustenance of its unguarded candour, the earthiness of its humour, the particular way in which it interrogates the world in search of meaning.

Today I have a number of women friends whom I value deeply. Invited into the company of women, I go with confidence and trust. I do not anticipate competition from women as I do sometimes from men. I anticipate mutual interest, common ground, readiness to listen, to share experience, to support, and to enjoy the relationship with no defined end in mind. I anticipate kindness and an intuitive challenge devoid of the killer instinct. Of course, I find these qualities in some men as well. This is to do with attitude of mind, not with biological gender. The need for women's company does not cancel out the need for men's company. Each is important to me. Each complements the other. So Barbara Blackman's observation, '*not either/or, but both*', and the traditional wisdom on which it is based, gave me a richer way to think about my own experience, my own journey and its symbols.

Several other powerful symbols surfaced in my childhood recollection. One is my enjoyment of safe enclosure as a vantage point from which to view the world. Murrurundi is nestled among hills. It was at Murrurundi that an extra engine, billowing steam, was coupled to north-bound trains to pull them up the steep climb of the Liverpool Range, which stood as a rampart behind the little town. At the other end of town, the enclosure opened out into the valley of the Hunter River which ran through rich seams of coal and fertile grazing and vineyard country to join the sea at Newcastle. The golden paddocks and misty blue hills of that landscape are imprinted on my consciousness. Our cottage was an enclosure, and my room and my mother's bedroom where she worked, and especially her bed, and the little powder tin I took to bed. Hiding in the trees I climbed is another image that belongs to this symbol, as is the sound of army convoys and rain pelting on the corrugated iron roof, reinforcing my innocent sense of safety within the flimsy weatherboard walls.

The image of enclosure is a classic feminine symbol found in myths and literature down the centuries, and it is open to varying interpretations. For me the most clarifying approach is to identify where and how that symbol surfaces in my life now. Today I live in a small home unit, from which I look out over a world of river and trees, sailing boats and ferries. I have no hankering for a larger living space. At night, music drifts across the water from lit-up party boats. I enjoy seeing them and knowing that people are having fun but I have no desire to join them.

I appreciate handling ceramic lidded bowls and small enamelled boxes. I prefer a domestic garden to a bush walk. I like to shop locally rather than in big supermarkets. I enjoy a meal with a few, more than a gathering of many. I have found my professional vocation in listening — the providing of a safe enclosure in which something may be told. The potency of these images of enclosure is enriched by my reproductive biology as a woman, which is interior, hidden and capable of nurturing. I am grateful for this insight to Robert Lawlor, who wrote of it in his book, *Earth Honouring: The New Male Sexuality*.[7]

And my temperament is introvert, relishing the inner life of the imagination — thinking, reading, reflection, music, cinema — above participation in big crowd events, idle chatter or the hurly-burly of parties. Perhaps because the extrovert, the 'outgoing' personality, is prized in our society, I used to think that my tendency toward enclosure was a sign of inadequacy. Today, with an understanding of the variation in psychological types, I accept that it is legitimate to have a preference for introversion, and that sometimes I can also manage to take part in a big occasion, without accusing myself of contradiction.

Sometimes we allow ourselves to be limited by an image carried from childhood. For instance, like me, you may have felt shy as a child. Because we never learned a strategy to overcome this, we expect that, each time we go to a gathering, we will feel shy and have a terrible time. Yet, lo and behold, we find ourselves in a job that requires attendance at big gatherings. What are we to do? Do we admit defeat and give up the job? Surely not. What we need is an effective way to deal with this problem. Can shyness be cured? Do we go into psychoanalysis, or assertiveness training? Well, both may be helpful, but a more direct strategy might be simply to go to the next gathering. We may still feel shy at the gathering; we may still feel terrible, but we have chosen to go along anyway. The experience has not killed us and it is likely that we will gain in confidence from the sheer bravado of doing it. At any rate, we are no longer limited by our shyness.

This useful strategy is suggested by US psychotherapist Dr David Reynolds.[8] He has brought two Zen-based therapies to the West and he calls his approach 'constructive living'. To bring about change, he advocates side-stepping thoughts and feelings and just taking action. He points out that a lot of people fear flying but they still use aeroplanes because they need to get somewhere. They do not stop being frightened of flying, but they fly anyway, and it does not kill them, and they get to their destinations. Therefore, in the most practical possible way, they have 'overcome' the problem of the fear of flying.

Sometimes a childhood memory provides a useful symbol of warning. I remember my mother chopping wood for the kitchen stove, the bath chip heater and the open fire in the lounge room. Watching her, I was uneasy. I knew that it was wrong somehow, without understanding why. For me, this symbolises an image of women making too many sacrifices for the welfare of others, at their own expense. This was especially evident in wartime when men were not there to share the burdens of maintaining a family. Of course, the men were making sacrifices elsewhere. I also remember the unmarried women who had been tacitly elected by their families to stay at home indefinitely to care for ageing parents. While many dutiful daughters fulfilled this destiny with admirable grace and patience, no doubt it caused a measure of sadness and frustration.

There is a good deal of learned argument about the way in which childhood formation affects adult life, for better or for worse. I can only say that the recollection of childhood helps me to make meaning in my life today. For instance, the echo of the symbol of 'enclosure' between childhood and maturity gives coherence to my story, a pleasing sense of pattern and continuity. Yet I do not see one as just a replication of the other, any more than a butterfly is a copy of a caterpillar. One is an evolution of the other, achieved through experience and changing circumstance and sometimes grace, of which I will write more later.

At this point, it's wise to be on guard against sentimentality or a naive nostalgia. If I had stayed living in a weatherboard cottage in a tiny country town, I may have experienced it as imprisonment, frustrating, even stifling. It is because I have broken out of enclosure at times, or been expelled from it, and known its opposite, that I can relish it now by choice and with more insight. However, I also need to beware that the symbol of enclosure does not become an idol. My solitude today is precious but I need to be alert to when it needs interrupting with the stimulation and chance of the outside world, beyond my safe enclosure.

Something similar is true of flowers. They have been a lifelong symbol in my story, changing in their meaning over the years to enrich my evolving experience of life. In childhood they illuminated the magic of a garden I explored minutely. I took sensual pleasure in distinguishing the velvet texture and chocolate smell of a hidden violet from the astringent pungence of a hollyhock, its leathery magenta throat powdered with saffron yellow pollen. These were private discoveries. Flowers also drew me into the circle of women who prized the arrangement of cut flowers as evidence of the domestic arts. Later again, they became tributes from a suitor, waxy pale-green orchid heads tortured into a corsage to pin stiffly on the bodice of an evening dress, socially essential evidence that one was partnered. At another time, they were the reward of my labour in the garden. And sometimes, coiled in melancholy wreaths, they have said good-bye to friends.

How does this symbol emerge in my life today? A bunch of flowers from a cottage garden still gives me greater delight than a florist's arrangement, however elegant. I rejoice in flowers and find it hard to imagine life without their beauty. One morning I went to the flower market to place an order for a friend's wedding. I was soon intoxicated with colour and perfume, wandering in ecstasy among the banks of freesias, hyacinths, lilies and daisies. Great fronds of creamy pink orchid hung suspended in cellophane. Ranunculus and Iceberg roses swelled out of buckets, row upon row, ravishing and extravagant under the great vault of the market roof. A woman grower rubbing her eyes with fatigue told me she'd been out of bed at three o'clock that morning to pack dozens of purple iris into her truck. I wondered at the hazard of her venture — to gamble a family's livelihood on such ephemeral produce. And I thought that, for her, flowers may carry quite a different constellation of emotions from my own.

As a symbol, flowers are dangerous as well as beautiful. Their fragility and brief blooming are reminders of the transitory nature of my life. I find them alluring yet some instinct draws me back from drowning in them. See how the symbols both reveal and conceal. If you take them literally, and if you try to resolve their contradictions, you are robbed of their poetry. You will miss the secrets they offer you about your life.

Perhaps the most pervasive emotional quality threading its way through my life is a sense of melancholy. I inhaled it as a child from my family when, concealed from me, they were grieving the shocking and inexplicable death of my mother's sister. By melancholy I do not mean depression, but rather a wistful sense of the limitations of life, the richness and brevity of it, the vulnerability and tragedy of it, for which we are never adequately prepared. It is a sense that is evoked by the minor keys of music, by much Australian painting and poetry, by the night cry of the plover, and by the smell of violets. It is not an individual loneliness but rather a recognition of the struggle of the human condition, of our yearning to be at home in ourselves and in our lives; of our longing for communication, and of the many barriers to its success. It is a feeling that, if I began to cry, there would be no staunching the flow of tears from the well at my centre.

I do not regret the presence of this element in my perception of life, although it catches me unawares when I see sadness on the face of a stranger in repose, or the silvering of a poplar leaf in the wind. Now that I have befriended it, I would not be without it simply because it opens me to the pain of the world, and to the sweetness of the experience of life which is the more exquisite and intense because it can vanish at any moment.

As a guide to unearthing your own potent patterns and symbols, and the information they contain for you, it's fascinating to explore the experience of others. I have always wondered how different my view of the world may be from everyone else's. I wonder if my idea of the taste of grapes is anything like yours, for instance, and how we would establish that. Not easily through words, which are so ambiguous.

The writer Barbara Blackman was the subject of the painting that won the Archibald Prize for portraiture in 1997. Painter Nigel Thomson chose her because he wanted to symbolise the isolation of a blind person. No doubt it is a fine painting, yet his image of Barbara did not accord with my own. When I talked with her on *The Search for Meaning* program in the late eighties, she did not tell me the story of an isolated person. She explained that she had been 'an only child, but not a lonely child'. She accepted solitude as a natural state and found the world wonderful and people friendly. She was her own companion, and talked things over with herself. She says, 'At four years of age, I discovered the nature of my being. I said to myself, "I am I. There is no other I than me. There will never be another me. I will never be anything else but me. But this me that I am is not just my body. My body is kind of acting it out. And I am outside of that."'9

As an only child, I had never enjoyed such confidence in my own identity and I was astonished by her precocious understanding. She continued, 'Well, that discovery then governed my life. It allowed me to be brave, or to be reckless, which is the same thing, because from that viewpoint the experiences that I have are circumstantial and the self beyond that is the "real". There had to be a meaning to it, a connection between the two, and I went through my growing up desperately trying to find out what it was.'

Barbara Blackman has lived an adventurous and creative life without eyesight but with much insight. In her maturity she resonates with the Sufi philosophy of living 'a life guided from within by that which is infinite'. She is part of a wide network of friends and fellow scholars of the esoteric and the search for meaning. Certainly, in her book of autobiographical reflections, *Glass after Glass*, she reveals her desolation at losing sight:

> Books were my craving. Charles read to me incessantly. Sometimes others: John Brack, when I was laid up with a burned foot, called in on me on the way home from school, and read me Beerbohm, Chesterton and Belloc. In mid-decade (1950s), I found my way to talking books and the unlocking of doors to an inner life of my own. I was exploring my blindness, that isolation, that life sentence for a crime I had not committed . . . [10]

Yet it seemed to me that she took with her, into blindness, a deeply rooted resourcefulness. The rest of the book, and my knowledge of her, leaves me with the impression of a life lived to the full, with a multitude of connections on which she lavishes unusual attention. After we had met for the radio interview she stayed in touch. With a confident intuition for kindred spirits, she introduced me to the writing of May Sarton[11] who would articulate for me, above all other writers, my own experience of solitude. Barbara wrote me marvellous letters on her talking typewriter, full of generously elaborated ideas for the program. It was reassuring to be taken seriously by someone of her artistic and intellectual stature, especially since *The Search for Meaning* had provoked a couple of media pundits into glad criticism of my departure from the orthodox adversarial style of interview. These chaps liked a bit of blood on the floor at the end of a program, and I was not providing it.

Although I deplore the fact, I take far too much notice of criticism. I can quote verbatim the words of an adverse mention in the press years ago. It stays with me, neon-lit, to undermine my confidence in weak moments. Yet I had encouragement as a child, at home and at school, and I have thousands of letters from people who say they have been helped or stimulated by my work. Somehow a sense of authenticity eluded me and I could not take these good experiences in, to become part of me, to build up my sense of being at home in myself. I recall a school report which claimed that 'Caroline is too easily influenced by less intelligent students'. I was offended by it at the time, for its accuracy.

For most of my life, I had none of Barbara Blackman's enviable sense of self and I have sought membership of any milieu where I might catch it, like measles perhaps; or where, as a chameleon does, I could borrow someone else's colouring. This led me into risk-taking that grew, unlike Barbara's, not out of self-confidence but out of a desperate desire to belong — somewhere, among my peers. I am sure that is the reason I married, and why I did not succeed in marriage. If you do not take an authentic self into partnership, there is no substantial entity for your partner to encounter, to get to know and to grow with. Instead I became an expert at adaptability. It was a social asset. It absolved me of the need to search out my own identity for many years; and since journalism in my training days rewarded objectivity it was the ideal job for me — it gave me dispensation from forming any opinions of my own.

Other people are constantly writing scripts for us to fulfil according to their own needs. Someone needs us to be a dutiful child; someone else wants us to be a lover or an artist's muse; yet another needs the undivided attention of a doting mother. Because we need love, attention, approval and belonging, and we want to do what is noble, we strive to be what others want of us, but the demand of these various roles can be confusing, and reinforces the need for each person to find a sense of identity, integrity and direction. For some, like me, that is to embark on a long search.

I have heard it suggested that, for each person, life sets an individual riddle and the adventure is to solve that riddle. Certainly, some people identify early incidents that have produced a recurring pattern. Writer Clare Dunne told me that she sees her delayed birth, held back by the lateness of the doctor, repeated as a motif throughout her creative life. Just when a piece of work is about to come to fruition, some obstacle or setback intervenes, as if her delayed physical birth must be played out again and again psychologically. Then, after numerous delays, she achieves her objective in a rush, one piece falling into place after another in quick succession. Eventually, through the study of Jungian psychology, she recognised the connection. Now, her awareness of it lessens its potential to frustrate. She is able to laugh about its manifestations. She can distinguish the past event from present reality, assess the options of her situation more readily and take some action, rather than remaining enmeshed in the pattern of the past.

And I was intrigued to hear a similar experience from the English biologist, Rupert Sheldrake. In his childhood he was surprised to see lengths of rusty wire hanging from willow trees on his grandmother's farm. When he asked, he was told that willow stakes, cut for fence posts years ago, had come to life and sprouted into trees, taking the fencing wire up into the air with them. Much of Dr Sheldrake's scientific work has been devoted to replacing the utilitarian perception of nature with a vision of nature alive. He spent years at Cambridge, studying plant physiology, particularly the development of cuttings and isolated pieces of stem and their ability to regenerate roots and shoots. Later, he was in India for a long period, working on cropping systems that involved cutting back plants and studying their regeneration. His book, *The Rebirth of Nature: The Greening of Science and God*,[12] is about how our idea of Nature as inanimate and mechanical is giving way to a vision of Nature as being, once more, organic and alive.

He told me that remembering the childhood image of the willow trees was for him a tremendous revelation.[13] Being a scientist, it set him questioning. He said that when he badgered his colleagues to identify the earliest source of *their* scientific specialty, he unearthed some parallel stories. One rather serious German academic was forced to contemplate the possibility that his own distinguished research had received its first impetus at his grandmother's kitchen table as he watched her making dumplings. Apparently he was not amused by the idea.

These reverberations of the patterns of childhood into adult life are interesting enough to warrant exploration in our own experience.

Some images may be carried like stigmata from childhood well into maturity, consciously or otherwise. Les Murray told me that, as a child, he suffered schoolyard bullying. This was a powerful element in the formation of the great poet's philosophy, evident both in his writing and his political position. While that wretched childhood experience caused personal pain, it also gave birth to a deep resonance with the wounded, the disadvantaged, the one who is different from the herd, and a passionate desire to give them a voice. This sensitivity is one of the finest qualities of Les Murray's poetry. [14]

Les Murray was always conscious of this aspect of his motivation but some adult behaviour is driven by buried memories. I was told the story of a married couple who were in constant conflict over money. The husband was the paid worker in the family. His wife felt that he was mean with housekeeping money, giving her only a small amount each time, denoting a lack of confidence in her. Not until the husband reflected deeply on his childhood story, in marriage counselling, did a reason for this emerge. He remembered that his mother had done the same thing to his father. Parsimoniously, she had doled out little bits of money. As a child, he had been offended by it and had vowed that, when *he* married, *he* would take control of family finances. *He* would not allow a woman to do that to him. Consequently, as an adult, he was engaged in unconscious retribution. When he had brought the experience from the past to the surface, he could start to think differently about present reality. He could choose to behave differently. The change became possible only through his remembering.

Recollection is not always a comfortable experience. Recalling childhood may bring painful memories, yet even the difficult memories can produce revelation. An image from childhood may seem too sensitive to contemplate. Then further reflection can break it open to reveal the unexpected kernel of a deeply held and positive value in adult life. Natural therapist Dorothy Hall told me the story of a painful memory from her austere childhood in Scotland and how she had won some meaning from it:

I remember one thing that shaped the rest of my life perhaps. My father walked round and round me in the kitchen one morning and he looked me up and he looked me down (I was 13 years of age, I remember it vividly) and he said, 'Well, we didn't make you beautiful, so you'd better get some sense!'[15]

I was apprehensive about what Dorothy might have done with this incident that had made such an indelible imprint in her memory. I thought she might say it had crushed her spirit or demoralised her. She explained that the first effect had been to give her a very poor concept of her own attractiveness. She came to the conclusion that no one would want her as she was, so she decided to develop something else that people would want. As a child she hated her stern Scots father and not until she was adult did she realise that he had provoked in her a quality of toughness and resourcefulness that was useful — the energy of her hatred became transformed into zeal to toughen up other people and help them to face life. And that was one of the bases for her vocation as a popular therapist and author in the area of natural health. It is always an inspiration to discover how a person has turned adversity into some positive value in their life.

And so it was with Nick Carroll. No one has done more to bring the ecstasy of surfing to life on the printed page. Yet his love affair with the ocean began after a childhood tragedy at the age of nine:

Tom and I and my sister stopped trusting human relationships when my mother died and so I turned to the ocean and I thought, 'Well this never changes, this isn't going to betray me, this isn't going to disappear. This can absorb all my fears and concerns and worries and insecurities as a person.'[16]

Nick's loss in childhood has not left him with a distrust of family life but rather a devotion to it. When I spoke to him in 1989, he said,

Success for me would be to have children and to bring them up well. Having children and bringing them up well, I think, makes running BHP look silly. It requires immense ability to give, rather than to keep thinking of your own goals. You've got to just give all the time and I haven't tried that yet. It's probably going to be a very challenging experience. Very much one to look forward to.[17]

The great Aldo Gennaro della Francesca devoted his life to healing through art. His genius was to help people to find their creativity. Around Australia he worked with people on the fringe of society, the intellectually disabled, relocated Aboriginal families, prisoners. You may remember a wonderful documentary on television called *Stepping Out*. It showed Aldo working for weeks with a group of Down syndrome residents of the Lorna Hodgkinson Sunshine Home in Sydney. With Aldo's encouragement, they created a glorious performance of music, mime, dance, colour, light and energy to be staged at Sydney Opera House. The documentary followed the whole process so that we saw shy, awkward amateurs blossom into an eagerly artistic performing company. *Stepping Out* was a magical, moving film directed by Chris Noonan of *Babe* fame; it was shot for Film Australia by Dean Semler who later won the Oscar for *Dancing with Wolves*.

Aldo enriched the lives of many Australians. His genius was to show people that they were beautiful, creative and acceptable, and that they were not alone. He pushed back petty limitations and stereotypes to clear a space in which people who had been ignored and relegated to the margins of society could venture out to be who they are, in safety and in the radiance of the patient love he had in abundance — a love which encouraged, and which held the wounded spirit of a person, like a shivering dove in gentle hands, until it regained the body warmth to fly once more.

When he was dying of AIDS-related illness, Aldo reflected with me on the events that had shaped his life. On the appointed day, he was well enough to come into the radio studio, on the train. It was a cold winter and he was swathed in a theatrical black wool cloak, with a black hat and his tiny dog Dolores peeping from the top of his backpack. It was an emotional occasion that ended in tears, but somehow we got through the recording, with many stops and starts. He had had a very difficult childhood in Chile, yet it would provide the discipline for his mature vocation. He discovered that his mother, while carrying him in her womb, was still grieving for a lost baby. He was born into her mourning. His life was punctuated by several dramatic periods of silence. At age four, he lost the power of speech for 18 months and his father nicknamed him 'giraffo' (head in the clouds). He felt like an observer of life, while wanting to be part of it. At 14, he wrote a poem which read, in part: 'We are angels of broken wing in a dream of a god who went to sleep and forgot us.'[18]

Looking for spiritual understanding, he entered the austere Augustinian religious order where much time was spent in silence. His loneliness deepened in the academic competitiveness of the monastery. But in the long silences he also became aware of a collective consciousness which informed all his later creative work. It allowed him to communicate, in situations where words were ineffectual, with the soul and spirit of a person diminished in speech or hearing or intellectual capacity. And he was rewarded for this capacity.

If you recall the documentary *Stepping Out*, you will remember the touching scenes in which the performing artists clustered around Aldo until he resembled a decorated Christmas tree — how they wanted to be near him. He told me that working with the Down syndrome residents was the first time in his life that he had experienced love, and it made him weep to recall his happy time with them. The Lorna Hodgkinson Sunshine Home is not far from my place and I often see the residents venturing out to walk to the shops or catch a bus. Sometimes, people stare at them because they are different. And they are different indeed for they have a wonderful secret. They have danced on the stage of Sydney Opera House and they have brought the natural spontaneity of their being and the sweetness of their love to many people, including Aldo Gennaro.

There is a common thread in several of these stories. These people were not cured of their particular frailty or suffering, nor psychoanalysed out of it. They acknowledged it, and did not let it paralyse them. Instead they used it to do something. Our society encourages the repression of pain. We seek to minimise it through drugs, alcohol, sensation, busyness, the amassing of possessions, hunger for more and more information, and a readiness to be submerged in other people's stories — television fantasy and careless gossip about celebrities. In this way we are diverted from the unique insight embedded in our own life experience, our own story — it is there if only we will search it out and engage with it, to see what it has to teach us.

As I collected all these stories from other people, a train of thought began to thread its way back through my own story. It was then that I glimpsed, in the photographs of myself as a shy only child smiling with mouth closed, the genesis of the adult who learned that the habit of listening could be put to good use. And that opened the door to another possibility. Perhaps life was not just a random series of unrelated events. Maybe almost everything in my life, including the excruciating elements like shyness, were stitches in a garment that I had been knitting unconsciously for many years, to some purpose visible only in retrospect. If that were so, then it redeemed a lot of suffering, and recovered pattern from what had seemed to be chaos. Of course, it also begged the question of who might be the author of the garment. Was it I alone? Was I programmed solely by my genetic inheritance? Could there be, as well, a creative source or prime mover in my destiny who could see the whole garment while I was still shortsightedly dropping stitches. I did not know the answer but I found the questions intriguing.

These questions sent me sorting through my habits and accomplishments and preferences of today in search of their genesis. Suddenly, the symbols and images of a lifetime sparkled out at me like a seam of opal in rockface. I could see that they were many-faceted. Yes, moving around in my youth had been unsettling, yet it taught adaptability to life outside my comfort zone and exposed me to a variety of people and situations — exactly what I would need to pursue my purpose when that became clear. Yes, adaptability was a minus in that it delayed the formation of individual identity. It was also a plus because it laid the foundations for a capacity to listen. I had done something useful with it.

Yes, my father's absence on military service in my childhood was a loss for me, yet it sowed the seed of an understanding that would

come much later, a concept of love in the spirit, which is not diminished by physical absence. At some level, I had taken into myself the
knowledge of his love. He was not there in person but we kept on
loving him and he kept on loving us.

When this understanding of love in the spirit came to my conscious understanding, only recently, it was very important to me
because I could project it onto other situations in my life. For instance,
it lessened the devastation of physical separation from loved ones, and
even of death. If we can love and know each other in spirit, which
belongs to the realm of the eternal, then in a sense we can never be
parted. To know that I can love and be loved in this spiritual way also
increases my sense of inner legitimacy. If this is possible, then I am
some one, not no one.

My father's absence also alerted me to the concept of responsibility
to the world beyond home. My father had been very happy in his
domestic situation with a young wife and a new baby, yet he had
sacrificed that personal contentment to do something in a wider
cause, that of his country's need. At that time, to answer your country's
call to arms was a matter of duty and honour.

And so it went on. One insight drew out another and another, just
like the feathers I used to pull out of the eiderdown on my mother's
bed. You may find that your own prevailing symbols are delightfully
odd. Search them out gently and contemplate them with compassion.
They may come as quite a surprise to you. Whatever you discover, the
exercise of making your recollection of childhood is likely to bring
new understanding to light and help you to know yourself more
deeply. You may also like to ask some questions of your recollection.

$\mathcal{F}or$ $your$ $\mathcal{J}ournal$

* What are your predominant symbols and images? What have you always liked or disliked? Let your answer be concrete (stones, autumn, little boxes) rather than abstract (truth, love, anger). Record them in some way in your journal — as a sketch, a photograph or cutout picture, or a story.

* What do they say to you today?

* About which of them are you most curious?

* Is there a motif from childhood that has recurred through your life? Is it a creative motif for you? Is it limiting your ability to act freely? Do you need to let it go?

* How have any of the dark events produced light over the years?

* Is there still some healing needed?

* What is the overall emotional feel of the recollection?

* What are the most vivid details of sight, sound, smell, touch?

* How has this remembering given you a clearer sense of who you are and where you are going and how you relate to the rest of the world?

$\mathcal{E}ndnotes$

1   Harold Brodkey, *This Wild Darkness: The Story of my Death*, Metropolitan Books, 1996.
2   Bede Griffiths, *Universal Wisdom*, Fount, 1994.
3   *Universal Wisdom*.
4   *Universal Wisdom*.
5   *Universal Wisdom*.
6   Bede Griffiths, Tape 184, *The Search for Meaning Catalogue*, ABC Radio Tapes.
7   Robert Lawlor, *Earth Honouring: The New Male Sexuality*, Millenium.
8   David Reynolds talks with Stephanie Dowrick on an audiotape called *Living with Change*, ABC Radio Tapes.
9   Barbara Blackman in *The Search for Meaning Collection*, Caroline Jones, ABC/Harper Collins, 1995.

10 Barbara Blackman, *Glass after Glass*, Viking, 1997.

11 May Sarton's books include *Journal of a Solitude* (The Women's Press, 1973) and *At Seventy: A Journal* (W. W. Norton & Co. 1987).

12 Dr Rupert Sheldrake in *The Rebirth of Nature: The Greening of Science and God*, Random Century, 1990.

13 Dr Rupert Sheldrake in *The Search for Meaning: Conversations with Caroline Jones*, ABC/Collins Dove, 1992.

14 Les Murray, Tape 55, *The Search for Meaning Catalogue*, ABC Radio Tapes.

15 Dorothy Hall in *The Search for Meaning Book Two*, Caroline Jones, ABC/Collins Dove, 1990. Also Tape 6, *The Search for Meaning Catalogue,* ABC Radio Tapes, and *The Search for Meaning* video.

16 Nick Carroll in *The Search for Meaning Collection*, Caroline Jones, ABC/Harper Collins, 1995.

17 Nick Carroll in *The Search for Meaning Collection*.

18 Aldo Gennaro in *The Search for Meaning Collection*, Caroline Jones, ABC/Harper Collins, 1995. Also Tapes 65 and 148, *The Search for Meaning Catalogue*, ABC Radio Tapes.

4 DESIRE OF THE HEART

I think that what we're seeking is an
experience of being alive so that our life
experience on the purely physical plane
will have resonances within our
innermost being and reality, so that we
actually feel the rapture of being alive.

Joseph Campbell[1]

WHAT DO YOU LOVE TO DO? What engrosses you? What are life-giving experiences for you? Under what circumstances do you feel most alive, most joyful? What is your heart's desire? These are potent questions on which to reflect. Identifying your own most vital occasions of being alive may help you to live more happily, with increased energy and a surer sense of purpose. Finding what you love to do may also lead to the relief of loneliness and to feeling more at home in yourself and in your life, more sure of who you are.

One of my most life-enhancing experiences is dancing. As so often happens for me, I was led to it, not through my strength but through my vulnerability. At a wedding reception where the guests were enjoying themselves on the dance floor, I didn't know the dances and couldn't join in. I watched in dismay from the sidelines, regretting that I had not given myself more time for fun when I was young. I smiled a lot and pretended that I was happy watching but inside I had succumbed to a sense of inadequacy and isolation. Next day, common sense returned and I telephoned the nearest Arthur Murray school.

In the dusty recesses of my memory there was an old radio commercial that promised 'Arthur Murray teach you dancing in a hurry'. My first appointment was appalling. The music was painfully loud and the ballroom artificially lit in a pretence of permanent glamorous evening. I felt awkward, embarrassed and inappropriately middle-aged as a patient young teacher gave me the first lesson. Experienced students lilted and swooped around us, emphasising my stilted, perspiring incompetence.

It was difficult to go back for the second time but I forced myself to do it, so strong was my desire to learn. On my third visit, another student spoke to me, for which I was grateful. She was Caroline, too, but school custom favoured a gracious formality in address and behaviour, especially between student and teacher. It's six years now since I began dancing. I was 'Miss Jones' on the first day, and so I have remained. It is another world, existing in a time warp, as displayed so hilariously in the film *Strictly Ballroom*. The film was a caricature of the dancing scene I know but it was also a splendid exploration of the theme that what we are seeking, above all, is our own unique expression of being alive. And dance provides an excellent metaphor for life. We do not want to dance someone else's steps, dictated by authority, represented in the movie by the tyrannical governing body of dance. We want to dance in the way that is true to ourselves, and ideally we will not be diverted from our desire. At my dancing school, one student told me that she had not danced for 22 years because her husband did not care to. At length, her longing to dance prevailed. With tears in her eyes, she pressed one hand to her chest as she explained to me, 'I have to do it. It satisfies something in here.' This is truly an experience of being alive, and it is not to be disregarded.

We were an odd mixture of ages and personalities, but we connected through our passion for dancing; and belonging to that collective passion helped me to validate an element of my personal authenticity. As I became part of the culture, I learned the language of dance and the subtleties of appraisal. I discovered where to buy shoes and which bootmaker charged least for resoling pumps with suede. I bought quantities of cheap tulle to make dancing skirts and learned from the others where to get diamante and sequins at wholesale prices. It was sheer fun, frivolous and wonderfully entertaining.

We all had our heroes among the teachers and the advanced students and dreamed of the day when we too would develop a distinctive style and make complexity seem fluid and graceful. We were encouraged endlessly and assessed on our achievements and our individual expression of the dance, not on our mistakes. One by one, we realised our dreams. It was exhilarating to see a confident performance from a fellow student who had started off with two left feet, just like me, only a year or so ago.

I am deeply grateful to the teachers, both male and female, who have shared their dancing experience with me and helped me to get so much out of it. Dancing is one of my best experiences of being fully alive. When I am dancing I feel beautiful and free. My body, mind and spirit are integrated into a focused, harmonious whole. I feel at home in myself. I am happy. The concentration of it leaves no room for other concerns. The physical effort extends me. I love the art and the exertion and the sweat of it. I feel that I could dance my way into eternity. The lesson always ends too soon. But then I can sit and watch the others with vicarious pleasure and the aching feet borne gladly as the mark of the initiate. It's a fine form of self-expression, liberating bodies which have forgotten how to stretch, releasing joy too long subdued, enabling grace through discipline, creating beauty in partnership.

Best of all, I have taken the experience of dancing into myself, into my soul. It has become part of me and it sustains me, so that, one day when I cannot dance any more, I hope the change will not break my heart. I will still belong to dancing. I will be able to think about it, appreciate it, and to know that I am more 'me' because of it.

§

THERE ARE MANY different ways in which people find life-enhancing experience. The writing of journalist Martin Flanagan is distinguished by his unerring eye for hopeful moments of life in the minutiae of every day, his capacity to take them in, and his skill in communicating them to his readers.

The other day I was in a train station, and I saw this little fellow who'd be about forty, a little plump bloke, and he had this look of great joy on his face and he had this little pup in his arms and I went over and started talking to him and he'd just bought the pup at the market, and he had a look of great love on his face, and to me that was a wonderful thing, that was a great moment. And that was . . . you know, that was a little item of evidence.[2]

It is the sort of scene that I, too, relish and take in, and I appreciate Martin Flanagan's decision to conserve this vivid glimpse of the evidence of love. In recording the incident, and many others like it from everyday life, he expands the definition of love to more generous boundaries than we might normally consider.

Too often, it is locked into a crudely determined category with sex predominant and all the other types of love diminished — filial love, parental love, extended family love, the love of friends, the compassionate love of charity, love of country, love of community leaders, love of art, love of domestic pets, love of nature, love of life, love of God, and so on. If we pay no attention to these varied and important loves, they wither in meaning, like plants unwatered, and life is the poorer as a result. The English language is curiously impoverished in its provision of words for love, in comparison with other languages which have many words to express the nuances of this central characteristic of being human. Martin Flanagan makes us a gift when he draws attention to such matters in the popular media of communication, which are the primary source of most people's information. He is enhancing the reader's experience of being alive. He is expanding an understanding of what constitutes the experience of love and fulfilment.

Being loved and affirmed, in a way that accepts you as you are, may be the most profound of all the experiences of being alive. When you are loved in such a way, and if you are able to trust that love and consider that you are worthy of it, you can feel as though you are a flower unfolding in the warmth of the sun, able to display the full potential of your being. Then it becomes easier to give love, to be generous, to rejoice in life and to imagine that anything is possible. I was fortunate enough to be loved as a child, and since then I have known many other experiences of being loved in an accepting way. Eventually, as my sense of inner authenticity grew, I was more able to trust these experiences, to feel worthy of them and be nourished by them. And it is empowering to consider that, by loving in a similarly accepting way, you can bestow such benison on others, helping them to realise the fulfilment of their being.

Sometimes the experience of being alive is heightened in risky situations. New South Wales Greens party politician and activist Ian Cohen told me about his experience of being fully alive at such a time. A powerful new image was imprinted on Australian history the day he rode the prow of a gargantuan British aircraft carrier into the Brisbane River on his surfboard. Pictures of his dramatic antinuclear protest went round the world. Here's how he recalls that moment:

> At those times I become possessed by an energy that's so positive and so strong that my nerves leave me the moment I hit the water. I feel so secure, with the warmth of the water and the feeling that I'm flying, because of that medium. It's like a meditation. At that moment in my life there's no question. There's absolute conviction. With the intensity of the police and a warship bearing down on me, I get to the point of being absolutely centred. And there's no anger. It's more a feeling of rejoicing in being able to make that statement so strongly and so clearly. It's my statement of non-violence. My deliberate vulnerability shows that the hulk of a massive nuclear warship can also be vulnerable. Militarism can be seen as absurd.[3]

Most of us will never emulate the daring of this action, and we do not need to. The thing to pay attention to is the quality of the experience. In which situations do you find a quality similar to that described by Ian Cohen? He includes the elements of positive energy, absolute conviction, being centred, rejoicing, and an impression of both meditation and flying. Perhaps the most unexpected element was his deliberate exposure to vulnerability.

I can think of several activities in which I have known some of those elements. Skiing was one in which the risk was all-engrossing and I could do no other than centre my gravity, acknowledge my vulnerability and my terror, convince myself that I would survive the madness of the downhill speed, and rejoice in the exhilaration of flying. A swim in the ocean has some similar qualities, without the danger of speed. It is the sheer childlike play of surfing that I delight in, the freedom, the lightness, the emotional and spiritual cleansing of it, the good sleep you have that night.

It is not difficult to understand why many people have such a passion for sports. It is inspiring to play a game to the best of your ability, as it is to watch the highest achievements in sport. I see it as a metaphor of what is possible in human endeavour. Reverend Peter Nelson, chaplain to the Australian Institute of Sport, suggests something even more interesting about sport as a lifegiving experience. He says that one of its chief attractions is the occasional peak experience in which an athlete transcends pain and extreme physical effort in a moment of ecstasy when everything is just right. You'll find more about this in the chapter on Australian mystics.

Peter Nelson mixes with elite athletes, but such occasions are not reserved only for champions. He recalls his own moments of elation when the cricket ball hit the bat right in the centre, solid and satisfying. He suggests this is an integrating experience in which players know a sense of connection, identity and fulfilment. If they can take that in to become part of them, the knowledge of it acts as sustenance during the next arduous day's training, and the next.

Martin Flanagan has been interpreting the human passion for sport for years in the press, especially in *The Age* newspaper. His skill in writing about it is enriched by the fact that sport has been a lifegiving experience for him. He told me that sport was the first theatre he ever went to:

It was in sport that I first saw deep self-expression; where I first saw passion; where I first saw imagination; where I first sensed the potential of drama and for a long time, possibly up to the age of 16, maybe 17 or 18, it was the only place I perceived those things and that interest has lingered. The other attraction for me to sport is its folklore, because I believe I come from a folk culture, and one of the lines I wrote was: 'My grandfather could write no more than his name but he read the *Sporting Globe*', and that's a connection I have with him. I never met him but I understand what sport was to him.

In the realm of pre-affluence Australia, sport was one of the few male decorations. And I understand that I come from that place, and I've enjoyed the people I met through it. I've always been in a peculiar position in that I'm sort of halfway between the athletes and the aesthetes, but on the whole I found the athletes more accepting of me.[4]

Many people say that what they most love to do is fish. Fishing is the leisure activity with the highest participation in Australia. Why do we go fishing in such extraordinary numbers and with such intense devotion? It's not because we're hungry. And sometimes no fish at all are caught, but does that stop the fishing? What can be the allure of those tedious hours spent waiting in discomfort for an uncertain reward? You see people out fishing in all weathers, dodging waves breaking on dangerous rocks; standing all late afternoon and evening on the beach; bobbing up and down in small boats; perched on the wharves around the harbour, patiently pulling in the line each time a ferry comes. Fishing enthusiasts travel with great inconvenience to remote areas in search of the perfect trout stream. People who fish are quite devoted to it, in a quiet way, preoccupied, detached. But why?

Benedictine nun Kym Harris has a theory about fishing. She had a sister who fished undeterred for seven years before catching anything. Kym puzzled it out. Writing in the Australian Christian Meditation Community Newsletter of Autumn 1995, she said that there are few activities more conducive to contemplation than fishing. She suggests that people do not go fishing to get anything. They love to fish in order just to be. She invites us to consider the circumstances: unless it's the thrill of the hunt in big-game fishing, or an excuse for a grog-up, people fishing are mostly quiet, gentle in movement and speech, the stillness broken only by regular rhythmic baiting and casting. They are gazing at the water and the sky, attentive to the tide; they are taking these things in. Even in company, there is a degree of solitude and silence. And of course fishing crosses boundaries of language, race and age.

Kym Harris's proposition is that we live in a culture that expects us to do things and produce tangible results, and that fishing provides a deeply desired excuse to be still, to wait beside the water and feel the transformation take place as, slowly, another level of consciousness rises. Beyond words and ideas there is a sense of communion with nature, a calming of the spirit. The inner depths are acknowledged and they expand in a way that is difficult to describe but of immense importance to those who fish. And of course people fish in water, a powerful icon of this nation and a symbol of the unconscious, that deep realm in which universal connection may reside, according to the insights of Jungian psychology. So fishing can be seen as a symbolic dive into the mystery, a ritual of being, a connection with the infinite, similar to the practice of meditation, an opportunity for some care of the soul.

You may find that it is lifegiving to sing in a choir, resolve a conflict, see a wonderful film, read a good book, cook a special dish, have a conversation in which you are really heard, make love, exalt in a service of worship, be trusted to care for a friend's baby, put all your concentration into learning something new, extend yourself in the practice of your craft, get your point across at a meeting, mend something you did not think you could fix, or achieve a goal at work.

It is not the sheer amassing of these experiences that is important, but the capacity to take them in so that they become part of your inner self and continue to sustain you when they are no longer happening. From listening to others, I recognise in myself a tendency to skim over a lifegiving incident, to waste it, as though there were plenty more where that came from. This probably has its origin in the sanction taught in childhood against self-indulgence. But now I believe that I need to integrate these things that I love to do into my life. It is easy to be spendthrift of such experiences and to hasten on to the next of many activities on my list. In this way my days are reduced to a blur of activity in which little is absorbed in the way of spiritual nourishment; and life becomes a self-defeating series of tasks that is never completed.

It is important to identify what gives you life, to reserve space for

life
✳

it and pause long enough to honour it. At some level you know about this need when you refer to something as 'good for the soul' without registering that you might mean this quite literally. It is as vital to your wellbeing as food and rest, for it is building up those inner reserves that give you a healthy sense of your authenticity as a person and enhance your capacity to encounter others well. Without this inner resource, we are susceptible to misfiring in communication and relationships; and we are prone to loneliness, which is one of the worst afflictions of western society today.

In her book, *Intimacy and Solitude*,[5] Stephanie Dowrick makes an interesting analysis of loneliness. She suggests that you are likely to feel lonely when you are experiencing yourself as fragmented, incomplete or invisible to those around you — when what you *don't have* dominates your thinking and feeling. This emphasis on lack can give rise to a longing to bring some element into your life from the outside to fill the void and, as it were, bring you back to life. The longing may be for a partner, a baby, a new home, a better job, a different appearance; and, while these are all real needs, they will not fulfil your lonely yearning if you are not able to take them in.

authenticity

Stephanie Dowrick identifies a sense of 'inner legitimacy' which allows you to take in and be nourished by what comes into your life. This 'inner legitimacy' allows you to accept love, to integrate, own and trust good experiences, to feel you are worthy of having them and, crucially, to be sustained by them later when they are no longer happening. Without this sense, all your wishes may be met but you may still feel unsatisfied.

When I read this, it explained something important to me about my own life. For many years I lived with acute personal loneliness. During that period, I was devastated that, even when I had public success, I still felt lonely. Indeed, the loneliness was at its worst when I won some award for my work, and that was inexplicable to me. Without understanding how, I felt that somehow I was cheating. In fact, my problem was that I could not take in the achievement, and experience happiness and fulfilment from it. My wildest dreams of professional success were being met and yet I could not own them or trust them or feel worthy of them, so my loneliness continued and worsened until I reached a crisis (discussed later in the book, in the chapter called 'But who am I?').

Stephanie Dowrick goes on:

> At the core of loneliness often lies a fear of abandonment, usually experienced as a fear that the loneliness — the feeling of *not being wanted by someone,* of not being recognised, or understood, or sought after, or appreciated — will go on forever. No rescuer will come …
>
> And behind the fear of abandonment is something else: a lack of trust in your own self. (Do I exist in any meaningful way? Does my existence matter?)
>
> And if you are already locked in with someone and still feel lonely, that can be experienced as most terrible of all because then the illusion is gone that further ahead you might be rescued or saved.
>
> For I may leave you, perhaps everyone may leave you, yet if you could trust your own self you would know that, even then, you are with someone, *you are with your own self.* Not only that, you have all your experiences of connection — and these cannot be taken from you. They are part of who you are.
>
> I am aware this is a mighty hard lesson to take up, especially when you are struggling with feelings of emptiness or even despair. On the other hand, it is also hard to live without self-knowledge and without self-love.[6]

But how are we to obtain this crucial self-knowledge and self-love? Stephanie Dowrick reminds us that, as babies, our very survival depends on the attention of our carer, most likely our mother. However, an adult needs to learn that wellbeing does not depend on anyone else, that we need to accept the limitations of what others can supply, and build up our own rich inner world. The aim of this is not to become absolutely self-contained, but rather to 'develop your self so that when you communicate with others there is someone there, inside you, whom you are in good contact with and who is free enough from self-doubt and self-absorption … For men just as much as for women, self-nourishment and the capacity to nourish others are the best possible — the only possible — bulwarks against loneliness.'[7]

It took me a long time to appreciate all this. In our culture, we are seldom offered these valuable insights. On the contrary, those who hold power in a consumer society have a vested interest in persuading us that we are incomplete, that we have many needs, and that we can only be satisfied by getting (preferably buying) things from outside ourselves. This message invades our consciousness from an early age and is constantly reinforced by the media. It requires some effort to reject the bombardment of this propaganda and to seek out sources of true nourishment in everyday life.

For instance, we may love the garden or feel restored by working in the paddocks. We hear music with deep pleasure; we enjoy making a cup of tea and are refreshed by pausing in a busy day to drink it; a conversation may reach a warmer depth than usual; we are moved by smoothing a baby's downy head or hearing the wisdom of an old person; we are captivated by a new moon; we look forward to the next chapter of a good book, and relish the look and smell of a beer even before we taste it. In these ways and many more, the mind, body and senses become thresholds for nourishment of the sense of inner legitimacy, building rich defences against loneliness. When I asked Stephanie if there was such a thing as instant, self-help relief from the pain of loneliness, she had a positive suggestion:

> It is possible, when you are feeling lonely, and uncomfortable about that, to bring your attention right into the present, becoming con- sciously aware of the body you are inhabiting, the earth you stand on, the breath that is coming in and out of your body, and that you are someone, not 'no one'. Bringing your awareness of 'self' back home in that way can be surprisingly calming, centring and restorative, and can often shift you into a state of solitude where you are, once again, at the centre of your own life and therefore comfortably able to reach out beyond your own life to others.[8]

Stephanie Dowrick suggests that solitude is a component of her own peace of mind when she writes:

> Solitude can be an emotional lifesaver. I know that is the case for me and, given a choice between an eternity in which no solitude was

possible and an eternity in which solitude only was available, I would be very hard put not to choose solitude: the chance to go back into myself to renew myself; the chance to check out what I am feeling and thinking; the chance to drift and dream and think at my own pace; the chance to cease to be attentive to the needs, demands or simply the presence of other people. It is in times of solitude that I feel restored to myself. I really could not do without it.[9]

Of course, you are most likely to appreciate solitude when you have attained a reasonable steadiness in your sense of self, a measure of self-acceptance and a feeling of standing on solid ground within. The cultivation of your best moments of being alive is valuable precisely because they concentrate your attention in the present, and contribute to that sense of inner legitimacy which allows you to take in and be sustained by good experiences.

I am sure that experiences like dancing, swimming and skiing, among other things, have played that role in my life. It is years since I ski'd but I still carry the knowledge of it with me. It became part of me. I integrated the experience of braving the risk of it and the thrill of pointing my skis straight downhill with cold air rushing against my face. I can remember that falling and being winded was nasty but it did not kill me; it was part of a wonderful adventure that lodged in my imagination as evidence of personal competence and courage, and made its permanent home in my inner self. Dancing and swimming are current realities. They have each contributed to filling inner emptiness. They have built up a feeling of self-confidence and self-trust, and nurtured me — and that is why I have enjoyed them so much. And then there are the many instances, associated with those experiences, of being taught and affirmed and cared for. If only we can take these feelings into ourselves, they will provide nourishment for the future. Much of this book encourages you to identify, develop and nourish your inner resources.

It is worth asking other people for their most lifegiving experiences. Although they may be different from your own, it can be enlightening and provocative to hear about them.

I was curious to know what Aboriginal adventurer and writer Burnum Burnum would nominate as his lifegiving experiences. It is easy to assume that, because of their strong spirituality, Aboriginal friends have refined living to a fine art, in spite of all the pressures of contemporary life. What he told me came as a surprise:

> When I go to Uluru and Katatjuta in the desert, I always take the slow movements of Mozart with me because the ocean and the music of Mozart are the two major energy-giving factors in my life, and they're very, very important. Mozart's music relaxes me. It makes me incredibly happy. And in the same way, being near the sea, breathing the air of the salt water and being in the sea and then coming out and allowing the sun to dry the salt to my body is very important. Mozart's music and the ocean have made an impact on my life which I find quite extraordinary and it's something I don't even care to explain away. It's just what's happened to me as an individual and it fits in perfectly with my true spirit and nature.[10]

In this description, Burnum Burnum conveys a sense that he was able to take in the music of Mozart and the refreshment of being by the sea; that these things became part of him and sustained him even when he was no longer experiencing them. That is what was so valuable about them. Burnum Burnum had every reason to lack a sense of inner legitimacy and to feel very lonely indeed. He was born on a piece of bark under a gum tree at Wallaga Lake on the south coast of New South Wales, the centre of his father's traditional land. He was taken from his people, raised by Baptist missionaries, made a ward of the state, and became one of the first Aboriginal people to matriculate, in 1954, from Kempsey High School on the New South Wales north coast. In Australia's bicentennial year, he planted the Aboriginal flag on the white cliffs of Dover, to take possession of England, in a gesture of ironic genius. Burnum Burnum loved Mozart. He liked to point out that, in 1770, when Aboriginal people discovered Captain Cook sneaking up the east coast of Australia, Mozart was 14. In the 18 years between Cook's departure and the arrival of Captain Arthur Phillip, Mozart created 500 masterpieces.

It helped me to hear Burnum Burnum nominate music and the sea as lifegiving experiences because I realised that I could say the same, yet I had taken both for granted. He alerted me to their significance and to my need to give them an acknowledged place in my life. Burnum Burnum found it easy to identify his lifegiving experiences and he treasured them because, as he put it, they fitted in with his true spirit and nature.

The same is true of Barbara Blackman. After a cancer operation, the loss of her marriage and a move across country, she knew feelings of abandonment and was in need of a fundamental experience of being alive. This is what happened:

The little inner voice said, 'Lie upon the landscape of your country'. Probably this had come up from the depths, from something very early in my life. My father died when I was three. He was a surveyor and, when he knew he hadn't long to live, he took my mother and me to camp with Aboriginal people, whose ways he loved, out on Pumicestone Creek, Caloundra. We went fishing and cooked round camp fires, and I think we were deeply happy. So that must have been what spoke to me now at this time of bereavement which the end of a marriage is. So that's what I had to do.

People had said to me, 'You'll get bruised from lying on the ground. You'll get the trots from bush tucker, you'll get sores.' But I knew. I knew from the very first night when I lay down under the stars upon the sands of a dry river bed under the sky, I felt happy — happy in a way I had never felt happy before. Then, the more I got to feel myself one with the old slow time of rock and the near fast time of birds flitting by, the deeper that happiness became. We stayed out for six months. Oh, the remote places we went to, the silences — the way we were able to pull fish out of the sea and eat them — and the crabs, the wallabies, goannas . . . I had never been part of nature like that before. And I was healed. Healed of the sorts of fears I might have had as a middle-aged blind person living by myself for the first time.' [11]

Years later, Barbara Blackman still lives in bushland. At the age of three, she had been able to take in the sustaining experience of living in the bush so that it remained within her, to be called upon years later, in her loneliness. At a time of severe disorientation, she remembered a way to come home to herself.

Natural therapist Dorothy Hall likes to get her hands into the soil, to be in tune with the energy of the earth, to lie with her back and her palms on the ground, or against the trunk of one of her great pine trees, and 'quietly remove whatever is the intruding energy, and plug into the larger energies again'. As well, she needs to contemplate beauty as 'an antidote to pain'. She told me she was surprised how many of her patients over the years had felt guilty about pleasure or had simply neglected the need for it. Although full of news about what was wrong and what they lacked, when asked what they really enjoyed, they looked at her blankly and required prompting. Dorothy urged them to identify what, for them, was pleasure, beauty, what was a positive experience of life.

'Find it and do it! Whether it's driving a racing car at 150 km an hour; or ocean-sailing; or a bowl of fruit and a closed door and Beethoven. Do that thing!'[12]

Australian film producer George Miller enjoys an international success for his films, including the *Mad Max* series, *The Year my Voice Broke*, *The Witches of Eastwick*, *Lorenzo's Oil* and *Babe*. When I talked with him about his creative process, he identified daydreaming as a vital component. Never bored, he has loved to daydream since childhood days in the intense heat haze of Chinchilla on the edge of the Darling Downs. Daydreaming was not punished by George's parents, and he says that his career has grown out of it. It was not the only component. He has medical training and is devoted to research and painstaking preparation. His intellectual effort provides a solid base from which his instinct and imagination take flight.

This is a strong endorsement of Shakespeare's admonition: 'To thine own self be true ... thou canst not then be false to any man.' Many children are corrected for daydreaming. I doubt that it's taught in any curriculum, yet here's one of the most successful men of a generation telling us the crucial value of daydreaming in his life.

Listening to George Miller, Burnum Burnum, Barbara Blackman and

Dorothy Hall reminded me that I am inclined to ration my lifegiving experiences and the contemplation of beauty for fear of self-indulgence, of wasting time. I see this now as a lost opportunity. If there is vitality, consolation or the promise of wholeness in an experience, I need to include it in my life and take it in to become part of me, to nourish that sense of inner legitimacy and being at home in myself which is an important protection against loneliness. Such personal enrichment may also come in more sombre moments, such as spending time with a friend who is dying (see later chapter on suffering).

Stephanie Dowrick writes of self-nourishment and the capacity to nourish others as being the best possible bulwarks against loneliness, and this turned my thinking to friendship. Friendship is all too easily taken for granted, yet friends enhance the enjoyment and stability of most of our lives. This is not true for everyone. Some people find their company principally in the mind, in their own world of ideas, but for many of us our friends are a crucial ingredient in the richness and variety of being alive. Insight can be deepened in a challenging conversation between friends. Experience may be more vivid in a friend's company. Suffering may be comforted or even illuminated in the empathetic presence of a friend. Even hard work can be turned into fun, in good company. An invitation from a friend can raise the spirits and give reassurance that you are pleasing company. In many ways, friends increase your understanding of who you are by remembering things about you, telling you new things about yourself, and reflecting your image back to you, in affection or even in irritation.

Sometimes the real sustenance of friendship is not realised until you have a falling-out. Then suddenly you find yourself humbly prepared to seek reconciliation in a heartfelt desire to reinstate the shared understanding that has been a source of strength and pleasure for both of you.

Some of my friends are people I have never met, but with whom I have enjoyed a correspondence. They wrote to criticise or encourage or put another point of view. And we entered into communication for a time. They have touched my life and enriched it.

I have often been astonished to be offered friendship and wondered how I have deserved it. I could not see why someone would put themselves out for me, or want to spend time with me. Gradually I understood that friendship is not rational; that it is quite undeserved, a gift bestowed on me for which I need simply to be grateful. I have learned slowly how to be a friend through the people who have befriended me. I try to emulate their gracious acts of thoughtfulness. I think that I am not a very good friend and would like to be a better one. For me, this is mainly a question of devoting more time to friendships. As an introvert, I can be deeply nourished by just holding the knowledge of my friendships in my consciousness. I have integrated them and they are part of me even when we are separated. But I cannot expect my extrovert friends to be satisfied by that. Very understandably, they like to do things together. However much I fall short in being a constant friend myself, I do honour friendship and accord it a status akin to marriage, partnership or parenting.

Sometimes hurt is caused when the strong friendships of single people are relegated to an inferior status by the marriage of one of them. Suddenly, the bond of marriage assumes supreme importance and takes precedence over existing friendships, even though they are of long standing and significance. After all, some friendships can last much longer than marriage. It is desirable to seek a creative way to carry friendships along faithfully in tandem with marriage, for marriage partners cannot be everything to each other throughout life. Such an expectation places undue pressure on a marriage. Friendships will still be needed and still be precious, for each partner. Friendship has its own integrity which should not be diminished by other, more formalised relationships, but rather enjoy a respected status in its own right.

Friendships vary in their degree of intimacy. Sometimes they are based in a common interest. Sometimes they attain the depth of kindred spirituality. But it does not follow that they are then bathed in a rosy glow, immune to conflict. Sometimes they will let you down. Friendships can be as testing as any other relationship, but that is part of their rich resource. Even by challenging us, they help us to grow. Whatever the depth of their significance, friendships are in need of acknowledgement and conservation.

I suggest that a new page of your journal be dedicated to writing a list of your friends. (If you would not find this helpful, what about a list of the ideas, principles, concepts, theories and systems that are most significant to you?) You may also like to identify what you value most about each one, and the way in which each, whether friend or idea, contributes to your sense of meaning. A list will help you to reflect on who your friends are, as you enter their names in this special place where you are recording the story of what matters most in your life, and what gives you life. You might like to include some of the people who support your health and wellbeing — dentist, doctor, chiropractor, yoga teacher, football coach, even a favourite singer who expresses emotions for you. And what about the people in your local shops or on the other end of the line at the Flying Doctor Service? Leave space for the list to be expanded. Instead of a list, you may prefer to put photographs. Come back to the page from time to time, to be replenished by these important people and reminded that your life is not an island but is intertwined with many other lives from which you gain and to which you contribute meaning.

The Lebanese poet, Kahlil Gibran, in *The Prophet*,[13] has written one of the most beautiful appreciations of friendship. It reads in part:

And let there be no purpose in friendship save the deepening of the spirit.
For love that seeks aught but the disclosure of its own mystery is not love
but a net cast forth: only the unprofitable is caught.
And let your best be for your friend.
If he must know the ebb of your tide, let him know its flood also.
For what is your friend that you should seek him with hours to kill?
Seek him always with hours to live.
For it is his to fill your need, but not your emptiness.
And in the sweetness of friendship let there be laughter, and sharing of pleasures.
For in the dew of little things the heart finds its morning and is refreshed.

Gibran's reflection expresses the need to encounter your friend from a position of self-knowledge and self-acceptance, and with the gift of your own inner resources, rather than inflicting him with your emptiness.

Finding and taking in what you love to do does not necessarily require comfortable or peaceful circumstances. Indeed, it is in hard times that you may find most need of its sustenance. Jana Renée Friesová, in her wonderful book, *Fortress of my Youth*[14], describes her adolescent years as a prisoner of the Nazis in the Czech ghetto town of Terezín. Here, living in terrible hardship, she witnessed the deportation of thousands of her Jewish compatriots to Auschwitz. People were selected at random to be herded onto cattle trains heading for the gas ovens and extermination. Yet Renée Friesová records extraordinary facts about how people chose to live in this environment of sustained mass cruelty.

The Jews who were herded into Terezín were allowed to bring from their homes a scant 50 kilograms of belongings. Yet some chose to take up precious weight with dismantled musical instruments, sheet music, opera scores and books, paints and brushes. Renée Friesová says that, in doing this, they were carrying

> … an awareness of their own capacity, an awareness of their past and their responsibility to it. It became evident that intrinsic human creativity can endure under any circumstances. For those few who were to survive, it became apparent that even the most horrifying situations can sometimes strengthen people and liberate qualities of which they themselves were not aware.[15]

Choirs and chamber music concerts were arranged on a regular basis. Daily in the courtyards, artists sang, acted, performed magic tricks and read or recited poetry. The illusion of prewar cafés gave unhappy people moments of forgetfulness and joy. Operas were performed. The inmates of Terezín included distinguished musicians, composers and singers, dancers, actors and producers. Even as each concert was in rehearsal, cast numbers were depleted by the constant selection for transport to Auschwitz. As people disappeared, their spaces were filled and the music went on. Even as a teenager, Renée Friesová was captivated by the artistic passion of her people doing what they loved to do; and what gave them proof of life in the shadow of death. After 12 hours of forced manual labour in the fields, she would hurry in the evening to wherever the music was happening. She writes:

> Those who did not believe that an emotionally and physically abused group of people could sing 'Let's rejoice, let's be merry', the opening chorus of *The Bartered Bride*, listened with tears in their eyes. They listened with joy to a miracle. More than ever before, they realised what it meant to be a human being.

And here is her revelation:

> The hours and hours which I spent, incredibly happily, in the cellar of the Madchenheim (a performance space under the girls' dormitory) and in the back row of the choir during performances of *The Bartered Bride*, *The Kiss* and most especially Verdi's *Requiem*, were the most profound experiences of my life and cannot be compared with anything that happened later.[16]

What an extraordinary statement that is, yet she wrote it from the vantage point of age 70 and its authenticity is unmistakable. It is worth reflecting on these passages from Renée Friesová's book to see what effect they have on you. For me they provide a deeply registered consolation. Her book feels like a treasure that I could hold in both hands in a time of trouble, for courage and comfort . . . as though her story could seep into my bones, or into my knowing, and nourish my capacity to endure. Yet what is it? It is the record of people in a desperate plight insisting on doing what they loved to do; expressing, even in captivity, the freedom of their spirit; doing what maintained their humanity. And such is the power of their story that it becomes sacred ground for others to walk on. It's a recollection of lifegiving experiences in terrifying times. It shows what is possible and teaches something of value about what matters in life. And it stirs my desire to discover more of the sustaining story of the Jewish people, in their books of tradition, for surely that is the sacred ground upon which they were walking in Terezín.

The talk given by Tasmanian poet and writer Margaret Scott when she launched the English translation of Renée Friesová's book in

Australia illustrates how one person's story may nurture another. It happened to be the week after the Port Arthur massacre in which 35 people were killed in April 1996. Dr Margaret Scott lives on the Tasman Peninsula just a few miles from Port Arthur and is part of the community there. This is an excerpt from her speech:

> To have been thinking, just before that event, about the experience of a young girl who lost many friends and relatives to human viciousness . . . to have been contemplating the way in which she came through to lead a fruitful, meaningful life — this, as it fell out, provided me with the best possible means of coping with what occurred on Sunday April 28 . . . without Renée's book the horrors of last Sunday would have proved harder to bear. Renée has much to say about the importance of the arts for herself and the other prisoners at Terezín. She shows us that the arts are not what so many in these days would have us believe — effete self-indulgence or, at best, something to be valued as potential exports. They are the food of the spirit. They exist to keep us alive as human beings. For showing us this and for showing us how evil can be defeated, we owe Renée and her translators a great debt.

So teenage Renée Friesová's story from wartime Czechoslovakia speaks across the years to Tasmanian poet Margaret Scott in 1996 . . . and provides lifegiving solace at another time of evil tragedy. Margaret Scott went on to write her own account of the events at Port Arthur in April 1996.[17] Her book, in turn, will become a sustaining experience for its readers to conserve in their imagination, to expand their own sense of inner strength.

It is most important to identify those experiences that give life and to seek them out. Someone who has analysed this need in a simple and effective way is career counsellor Barbara Sher. In a book called *Live the Life you Love*,[18] she urges readers to list everything they have ever loved to do, from childhood to the present. Even the apparently trivial loves should be included, for they are all clues.

Next she tells you to identify what you enjoyed most about each activity and invites you to watch out for the themes emerging as you work through your list. Then you imagine 'the fabulous career' you could have built on each of your loved activities, had you devoted yourself to developing it. Having reached the pinnacle of success in your imaginary brilliant career, you project yourself forward five years to see how you might modify or enhance your career. It is a spendid exercise in creative imagination. I found it very worthwhile in uncovering some neglected heart's desires, for which I'm now making space in my life. My list of things I've loved to do ran to 26. Here it is:

* playing with my cat
* reading books
* daydreaming
* making posies
* listening to conversation
* having nice clothes
* organised games and sport
* teaching
* driving the car
* meeting a kindred spirit
* going to plays and films
* ferry rides
* playing the piano

* collecting things for my cubby house
* being at home
* climbing trees in the backyard
* going to school and learning
* listening to *Kindergarten of the Air*
* gazing at things
* swimming in river holes and the sea
* being in bed, with rain on the roof
* having friends
* storms
* working as a broadcaster
* dancing
* painting

From this list, some predominant themes emerged:

* Love to work with beauty, colour, pattern
* Need for artistic expression
* Need time for daydreaming, imagining
* Finding out about people, relationships, life
* Enabling people to realise their creativity
* Need for kindred spirits
* Life needs to be interesting
* Love of learning
* Need for rest, and for being as well as doing

* Need for outdoor physical activity within safe boundaries
* Enjoying myself
* Feeling fit

It was revealing to note which things I was actually doing. While finding out about people and encouraging people have been well satisfied in my professional work, the enjoyment of beauty, colour and pattern has been neglected, as have friends and the need for physical activity. To remedy this, I've started classes in swimming, yoga, cooking and Italian language, and I've done some long-overdue redecoration of my home. The renewal of painting and piano lessons is the next objective. And I still want to spend more time with my friends.

The swimming classes reminded me of the vital importance of including more regular physical activity in my life. This is something I've drifted in and out of, treating it as an extra that I would fit in occasionally when there was time. As a result, it was frequently left out, and I was the poorer for it. It is easy to fall into the way of living almost constantly in your head, thinking, planning and sometimes becoming stressed with an excess of mental concentration. Physical exercise such as dancing or a long walk or a swim is such a necessary relief from this that, as soon as you do it again, you realise what you have been missing. Perhaps the benefit of it can be explained very simply by the fact that exercise brings more oxygen into your brain, gets the blood coursing more vigorously and tones the muscles and organs so that you enjoy a new sense of wellbeing and awareness of your body.

I find that it also lifts my spirits. Through physical exercise, a feeling of oppression can be dissolved; a mood of optimism returns and everything seems more possible than it did an hour before. It is worth remembering that one can turn to exercise for a lift in a time of low spirits. I go to an aquatic centre regularly and find it a place where I can stop doing the mental shopping list and just be alive, in my body, in the present. It is good to look forward to this as a carefree interlude in my week. It's a pleasure to go to a place where everyone is enjoying themselves and remembering how to play. I love to watch the children, in groups of about 20, taking their swimming lessons with exuberant energy and excitement. Shivering and hugging themselves, they look up eagerly into their teacher's face drinking in the instructions and bursting to try their new strokes in the water. Brilliant in their iridescent costumes of many colours, they are absolutely engrossed in what they are attempting and it is a joy to see them delight in their growing prowess.

I find it very relaxing to be wet all over and to move weightlessly through the bright blue water. When the class is finished, I am rejuvenated. I am walking more easily; tension has been dissolved and pains have disappeared; I feel as though all the fragments of me have been integrated into a whole person once more. I have made a resolution that to neglect this is to cheat myself of fullness of life. I hope I will keep the resolution.

Closely allied to this is the necessity to maintain and enhance the experience of being alive by eating health-giving food. You will have your own ideas about what constitutes a good diet but it defies common sense to think that we can eat carelessly and expect good health and good spirits. While not true of some outback regions, in most of Australia we luxuriate in an abundance of fresh and varied foods. I also believe in drinking plenty of water and getting enough rest. Some people give more attention to the tuning of their car than to their own body. It is easy to neglect these practical matters and then wonder why we feel depressed or exhausted or unsure of the meaning of life.

Barbara Sher makes an interesting analysis of the way people get side-tracked from doing what they really love to do, and the disappointment and frustration that result. She contends that what you love to do is likely to be an expression of your unique gift to the world. We get diverted from it by duty, by thinking we're not good enough or by living out the expectations of others. She points the way out of this dilemma by suggesting that you start doing some of the things you say you love, to see if they are genuinely lifegiving enthusiasms when put into action. She observes, from her personal and professional experience, that creating space in life for the things you love can make a significant difference to your wellbeing and peace of mind. It may take a shift in thinking. Many of us have been taught that what we love to do should take second place to what we ought to do, for fear of self-indulgence.

You may like to try Barbara Sher's plan — to identify the things you love to do, the activities for which you have plenty of energy, the experiences that give you life. It's almost too simple, isn't it? But I would take the argument even further: I suspect that doing the things you love to do, following your heart's desire, will nurture your sense of being at home with yourself and in your life. I believe too that your heart's desire may represent a call to vocation, a signpost to your particular pathway, the one for which you have a special gift, the one that will fulfil you. It may not become your whole life's work but it could provide a deep satisfaction, even as a hobby or voluntary work, to nourish you and free you to meet other less captivating responsibilities more readily.

For your Journal

* What do you love to do?

* What are the underlying themes?

* What gives you energy and creative fulfilment?

* What space are you allowing these things in your life?

* What have you always wanted to do and haven't yet done? Write down some ways of making these things possible.

* Is some change needed to enlarge your experience of being alive?

* How will you make that change? When?

* What plan do you have to do some regular, enjoyable physical exercise?

* Make diagrams, sketches, take photographs or find pictures to visualise your experiences of being alive.

* What are the various ways in which you experience love in your life?

* Open a page on which to celebrate your friends.

Endnotes

1 Joseph Campbell with Bill Moyers, *The Power of Myth*, Doubleday, 1988.
2 Martin Flanagan in *The Search for Meaning: Conversations with Caroline Jones*, ABC/Collins Dove, 1992.
3 Ian Cohen in *The Search for Meaning*, Caroline Jones, ABC/Collins Dove, 1989.
4 Martin Flanagan in *The Search for Meaning: Conversations with Caroline Jones*.
5 Stephanie Dowrick, *Intimacy and Solitude*, William Heinemann Australia, 1991.
6 *Intimacy and Solitude*.
7 *Intimacy and Solitude*.
8 Personal correspondence.
9 *Intimacy and Solitude*.
10 Burnum Burnum in *The Search for Meaning*, Caroline Jones, ABC/Collins Dove, 1989. Also Tape 13 in *The Search for Meaning Catalogue*, ABC Radio Tapes.
11 Barbara Blackman in *The Search for Meaning Collection*, Caroline Jones, ABC/Harper Collins, 1995. Also Tape 35 in *The Search for Meaning Catalogue*, ABC Radio Tapes.
12 Dorothy Hall in *The Search for Meaning* video. Also *The Search for Meaning Book Two*, Caroline Jones, ABC/Collins Dove, 1990.
13 Kahlil Gibran, *The Prophet*, Heinemann, 1926.
14 Jana Renée Friesová, *Fortress of My Youth*, 1996, Telador Publishing, P.O. Box 130, Sandy Bay, Tasmania 7006.
15 *Fortress of My Youth*.
16 *Fortress of My Youth*.
17 Margaret Scott, *Port Arthur: A Story of Strength and Courage*, Random House, 1997.
18 Barbara Sher, *Live the Life You Love*, Hodder & Stoughton, 1996.

5 CARE FOR THE SOUL

*I have come so that they may have
life and have it to the full.*

John 10:10

*It is when you are really living in the present,
working, thinking, lost, absorbed in something you care
about very much, that you are living spiritually.*

Brenda Ueland, American writer/editor/educator

ONE OF the best contemporary writers on the need to restore soul
to life is Thomas Moore. He treats the soul as a reality and discusses
it in language that is readily understood. In his book *Care of the Soul*,[1]
he claims that loss of soul is the great sickness of the 20th century,
both a personal loss and a bereavement for society. He argues that
when soul is neglected it does not go away; it appears in obsessions,
addiction, violence and loss of meaning. This neglect of the soul is
evident, he claims, in the many people who complain of emptiness,
vague depression, disillusionment, a yearning for fulfilment and a hunger
for spirituality. It is common to try to fill the void with entertainment,
power, sex, drugs, possessions or a glut of information, in the belief
that more and more of these commodities will fill the emptiness. But
this is to mistake quantity for quality, the quality of soul.

I write of 'soul' meaning the essence of a person, or the source of
a person's connection with God — the universal, infinite, eternal or

divine dimension from which soul comes and to which it belongs. Some readers will relate to the inclusion of 'God' and 'divine' and some will not. Some may prefer to substitute other terms — 'personal integrity' or 'inner self', for soul and 'higher power' for God. If you will read your own interpretations into the terms I use, these differences need not hinder our dialogue. I am interested in communication rather than fine points of theology. I also refer to the soul, meaning the essence, of a society.

No conversation about such a mysterious entity as 'soul' will be clear-cut, but I am trying to articulate my own understanding of the idea. I think of soul as the animating spirit of a person — their 'me-ness', their unifying principle, their personhood.

In the increasingly secular western world of today, the term 'spirit' is in more common use than 'soul'. We speak of the spirit of a person or a team as having a discernible quality. We say someone has a courageous spirit and we speak of a strong team spirit. Many people interchange 'soul' and 'spirit' and retain quite a satisfying idea of what they mean. Unlike the body and the material world, the human spirit or soul is intangible, yet few would deny its existence. For instance, there would probably be general agreement about the meaning of 'selling your soul' to obtain something. Most people would take that to mean sacrificing one's integrity to obtain a benefit.

While soul may not be easy to define with absolute accuracy, we are familiar with its characteristics. The soul is concerned with the deepening of everyday experience, so that it may nourish itself and be in touch with its source. I imagine my soul to be aware of two worlds at once: the cosmic dimension, and me as a unique individual. It is the location where I might encounter the divine, or the infinite, in some moment of grace; the region where I can hear the great singing silence of the spheres, as one does when gazing in awe at the night sky. It is with my soul that I am capable of a total response to a total reality.

I imagine my soul as traveller on an eternal journey, enduring in a way my individual mind and body are not. My soul harbours the intuition that, in some mysterious way, I am made, deeply known and claimed by an infinite creator, that I am acceptable for myself, and uniquely gifted; cared for and safe at some deep level beyond the turbulence of circumstance. Thomas Moore's consideration of soul is expressed in images of fullness, and this rings true to me because I think of soul as being the place of my fullest life. My soul is that part where I am not fragmented; where all elements of me can find focus and harmony; where I sense that I am part of some coherent pattern, although I cannot see that whole pattern; where I feel connected with other lives and so have compassion or fellow feeling for other lives.

Similarly, I can relate to Thomas Moore's assertion that, for its satisfaction, the soul needs to have a considered view of the world, a set of values, a sense of relationship to the whole, an attitude to death and a myth of immortality. Here, he is using the term 'myth' to mean guiding story, such as Judaism, Buddhism or Aboriginal spirituality.

Thomas Moore suggests that living with attention to soul is not to do with striving for perfection nor with attaining salvation, although it may well have the effect of bringing more wholeness and integrity to life. The soul needs to 'breathe', that is to say, it needs a spiritual life for nourishment and suffers when deprived of it. This spiritual life, or spirituality (one's relationship with God/the absolute/the source), may be nourished in many ways: in abandonment to the present moment; in beauty and in all the arts; in love; when you are holding a baby in your arms; in suffering; in ecstasy; in compassion; in silent contemplation, meditation or prayer; in religious ritual; in rewarding work or the enjoyment of food and drink; in reflective conversation; and in those encounters which touch your sensibility and which you take into yourself as sustaining memories.

A spiritual life may require going to synagogue, mosque, church, temple or a sacred part of the land in order to move your consciousness out of the material world into the spiritual. In these designated places, there is symbolism, ritual and liturgy devoted to spirituality and to honouring that which is divine, infinite or eternal. You feel the change of atmosphere as you arrive. There is a different energy or spirit there. Even people for whom formal religion is no longer valid will go at times to sit in a sacred place, almost against their better judgment, because there is something there for them. That something is the ambience of prayer, reverie and communion with the infinite, with which such places are saturated. They are places that greet the soul directly and speak its language.

The soul also finds sustenance in more domestic settings, like the family home, where customs and values have created a spirit handed down over generations. According to Thomas Moore, the soul finds sacredness in the ordinary, and may benefit most when its spiritual life is performed in the context of mundane daily life. This is a most helpful idea and makes the task of caring for the soul seem attainable, for many spiritual experiences come to us through our thoughts and through the senses in everyday activities; they need not be placed in a compartment for the profane, cut off from spirituality. Spirituality may reside in your response to beauty, or in a modest act of kindness. Those occasions when you feel most truly to be yourself are likely to be times when your soul is being cared for.

My soul is the home of my spark of life. It is the sanctuary for my story. It is the place of deepest meaning, sometimes only dimly discerned; and a place to wait, in trust, for meaning to come. Yet I do not imagine it as a passive place. It seems to me that I have responsibility for the care of my soul, in cooperation with its originator. In this, the holy spirit is a concept that has powerful meaning for me. I think of it as my partner in care for the soul; as the messenger, the energy, the breath, the emotional communication, the imagination or the animating principle of the divine or the infinite. I could as well describe holy spirit as being wholesome energy, since the words 'holy' and 'whole' share the same origin. Maybe science cannot measure it yet, but I experience holy spirit as a potent, all-embracing energy which frees me from individuality and connects me into the infinite. For me, that is also a connection into the divine, because I relate to the idea of an author of creation, but not everyone would want to make that connection, preferring to keep the concept of 'infinite' as impersonal.

We may have individual experiences of the presence of holy spirit or holy energy in which it seems that we are being played as an instrument. These can occur as coincidences, or as experiences of unaccountable help or guidance — moments of inspiration when we know just the right thing to say, or when we can't hit a ball wrong, or when a solution springs to mind. At other times, holy spirit is a communal experience. An example would be a symphony concert, where there are many people involved — the composer, the conductor and all the musicians, and certainly the audience whose presence receives the music and responds to it. Their listening provides an essential part of the equation — it enlivens the spirit or the energy of the occasion. All these individuals participate in an act of creation which is larger than the sum of its individual components, and which connects them in a powerful way, beyond words.

I have also felt this experience of holy spirit at a multicultural celebration, where people of many backgrounds danced and sang and shared their foods and mingled with each other for a long, rich Sunday. It was profoundly moving to be part of such easy, natural communication. It conjured a vision of what is possible, of how different we all appear to be, and yet so intimately related to each other, in a spiritual sense. There was a rightness about it, a wholesomeness for which we long, at some level, and which we recognise readily, and with relief, when we experience it. Such a day gives tangible reality to a concept like 'multicultural society', taking it out of the realm of theory or ideology and giving it faces, voices, tastes and relationship. I have seen this occur, too, where black and white Australians meet for the first time on a social occasion. Stereotypes and political theorising give way to mutual curiosity and communication. To me these are holy encounters, in that they create the conditions for wholeness; the holy spirit is at work.

The holy spirit was also abroad at the funerals of Mother Teresa of Calcutta and Diana, Princess of Wales; and at the memorial service for our own Professor Fred Hollows. These occasions united people in their loyalty to a sense of values that emphasises care for each other. People wanted to show this, to express it communally. To do so, they came out of the privacy of their homes and gathered, in public, to support what they consider to be desirable in human life and wholesome for our society. Sometimes we can see these qualities most clearly when we have just lost an exemplar of them. We may not choose to think of these as religious occasions, yet it is on such days that we see the soul or spirit of a society, the essence of it, what is most wholesome and lifegiving about it, most enduring, the expression of its deepest aspirations. At such times, we are reinforcing the integrity of a group identity. We are honouring the qualities for which we want to be known in the world, and by which we want to be remembered.

§

ON MY EIGHTH birthday my father gave me a book by Dorothy Ann Lovell, called *In the Land of the Thinsies*.[2] It gives me a sense of identity and confidence to see that he inscribed the book with my name and the date on the title page. His gift acknowledges that I was already an avid reader, a passion of his own which he passed on to me.

The book intrigued me then and I read it again now with new insight. It tells the story of schoolgirl Jill who slips through the crack at the bottom of the escalator and finds herself flattened into a cardboard cut-out, like everyone else in the Land of the Thinsies. Soon she meets the Flower Woman from Piccadilly Circus, flattened out and aching for something round and comfortable — 'balls and balloons and babies, you know'. Jill engages the Flower Woman in conversation.

'Why is everyone so thin?' she asked. 'Don't they eat anything?'

'Oh, yes, they eat right enough,' the Flower Woman replied, 'things like wafers, and pancakes, and very thin slices of bread and butter . . . But it wouldn't make no difference if they stuffed all day, they'd be no fatter than wot they are.'

She paused suddenly and, putting her hand on Jill's arm, looked anxiously into her face.

'Have you ever seen anyone in London like me?' she asked. 'Anyone with my face and clothes, only thin?' Jill thought for a moment.

'Well, yes,' she said, 'I have.'

'Where?' asked the Flower Woman breathlessly.

'In Piccadilly Circus,' said Jill. 'On the fountain steps in the middle, you know. There were quite a lot of pretend Flower Women there when the war began and the real ones went — cardboard women, and cardboard baskets of flowers, and a few cardboard policemen, just to make it look as if there wasn't a war at all … They were put there to cheer people up.'

'Cheer people up!' echoed her companion bitterly. 'You can't cheer people up with dummies.'

Jill didn't know what to say. Could it be true that the Thinsies would remain thin always, including herself? Would she never be able to roll down grassy slopes in the parks again … or eat doughnuts, or curl up in a cushiony chair?

As she wandered on through the Land of the Thinsies, Jill met more demoralised people preoccupied with eating their thin food and resting. They had given up trying to find a way out, and this strengthened her own resolve to find the way home to a world of fullness.

Given the date of its publication, this book may be an allegory of the way in which life was diminished by war, and an exhortation to rediscover a greater abundance of life in the new peacetime. Or it may be simply an imaginative adventure story for children about losing the way and finding it again. But 50 years later, its theme and symbolism seem peculiarly relevant to contemporary life in western society. It's as though we have slipped through a crack in reality into a one-dimensional place with the fullness ironed out of it by a materialistic post-postmodern secular system of thought which claims that there are no absolute values; and an administrative system which bases most of its decisions on the mean criteria of economics.

Much public discussion today is as unsatisfying as the watery soup in the Land of the Thinsies. It's not that we don't talk enough but that something important is constantly left out. We are thirsting for spirituality but we are offered shopping. We are bombarded with information for which we have no use. We are primed for disillusionment by media commentators whose subtle cynicism saps our confidence and undermines our institutions. We are presented with confrontations which we have no means to resolve. We are assaulted with public scandal, corruption and immorality for which we are offered no remedy. We are taught to argue in terms of our rights rather than our responsibilities; to assert ourselves as competitive individuals rather than cooperative members of a group. We are exhorted to indulge ourselves and keep our options open, rather than make commitments. The technocrats produce more labour-saving electronic wizardry but offer no creative alternative to the desperate workers made redundant by their inventions. We have constructed for ourselves a soulless landscape inducing psychological inertia in which it is easier to eat and sleep than to search for fullness of life and solutions to huge social problems.

In the Land of the Thinsies, Jill eventually found a slot machine which sold her a return ticket to the rounded world. But she had to stay awake and searching to find it.

§

PARADOXICALLY, EVEN IN this spiritually lean time, it is the media that present us with the occasional wise voice. Tiptoeing in wispy images through the pages of two of Australia's major newspapers, *The Age* and *The Sydney Morning Herald*, cartoonist Michael Leunig finds countless poignant ways to signal that we're on the wrong track, and to indicate a better direction. Like a butterfly hovering in front of a speeding express train, he flutters delicate wings of warning. The missing ingredients, he indicates over and over again, are heart and soul. When we leave them out of our calculations, we are in peril, things don't work, we are unhappy, we are not kind to each other, we do damage to our surroundings, we lose our children, we are confused. But when we recall that we have heart and soul and live accordingly, we can smell the daffodils, glimpse angels, wish on the moon, be good to each other, get things working quite well and even enjoy some peace of mind.

Leunig is a crucial prophet of our time, and the editors who publish his countercultural philosophy are to be congratulated. No doubt their decision is pragmatic as well as enlightened. Even if they distrust what he portrays, or cannot understand it, they know that Leunig has a following. Leunig identifies our plight. His solitary human, an

Everyperson travelling on foot, peers forward into the landscape, his possessions tied in a knotted handkerchief on a stick over his shoulder, his uncertain way lighted by the lamp in his right hand. With the crescent moon above him, he presses on, dogged and hopeful. Sometimes his predicament is more urgent; wide-eyed with alarm, he is perched atop a fast-unravelling flotsam of outer space junk, labelled 'postmodern secular thinking'.

Leunig's genius is to leapfrog over the carping protests of the narrow rational mind by using images that speak directly to the soul, the spirit, the psyche and the heart — all those wider capacities of knowing that we have been taught to distrust, and are missing like homesick children. He has coopted the symbolic language of dreams, using cartoon images and puns that sidestep our scientific scepticism to spring straight into the unconscious. No, of course we don't believe in angels and devils and sin and evil and broken hearts and souls, that superstitious detritus of the past. Yet all our modern scientific certainty is defenceless against the childlike musing of Leunig's characters. With unerring instinct, they sabotage every speck of intellectual intolerance and fashionable immorality in the public arena. Indeed, it is fascinating to see them doing so in the very newspapers whose content they see through with such round-eyed innocence. These cartoon creatures are foolish and frail and searching and they are instantly recognisable. They are us. And we want to see where we are heading.

In what must rate as the most original departure in popular modern media, and certainly the most important, Leunig has written prayers in the newspapers, poetic prayers about the mystery and darkness of life, the joy and the pain of love. He has prayed in that most public place about death and loneliness and the comic absurdity of the human condition. In his *Common Prayer Collection*,[3] Leunig has drawn a person kneeling before a duck. The duck symbolises 'nature, instinct, feeling, beauty, innocence, the primal, the non-rational, the mysterious unsayable, qualities which . . . can be attributed to the inner life of the person, to the spirit or the soul'. The act of kneeling suggests humility, an attempt to come closer to the soul, to try to communicate with it. The man senses the enormous influence of his soul on his life. Although invisible, its inner presence is often 'wild and rebellious or elusive and difficult to grasp: but the person knows that from this inner dimension, with all its turmoil, comes his love and his fear, his creative spark, his music, his art and his very will to live'.

Perhaps he has never mentioned this to anyone, but he believes in it; he is curious about it, he wants to explore it. He knows that being in touch with it leads to a better relationship with the world around him. He feels that great misery and loneliness result when he loses touch with his soul. Leunig reckons that whether a person calls this inner life by the name of spirit, soul or God, he wants its vitality, depth and guidance. He wants to nourish and strengthen it, and as he does so his life takes on an increased sense of meaning.

Leunig dares to hurl such outmoded concepts as these into the cynical climate of late 20th century Australia and he goes on to claim that the personal act of communicating with the soul — or neglecting to do so — is also a social and political act because it affects so many people who may be connected to the searcher. I suppose we've all met the boss given to making big decisions for others while his own house is in disorder; and the person living modestly with integrity and kindness who gives hope to those around her.

If you can travel this far with Leunig's vision, the next logical question is how to subscribe to it, how to find and nurture this hidden treasure of healing and transformation. He suggests that the first step is to acknowledge its existence and honour it in ritual of some kind. Even shaking the hand of a friend is such a ritual, he says, in that it reaffirms recognition and connection. Each time it happens, something important is strengthened. As Leunig puts it, 'the garden is watered'.

Leunig's prayers, now collected in book form,[4] offer words for 'the small ceremony which calls on the soul to come forth'. Accessible, whimsical and profound, they are written in praise of tomatoes, birdsong and domestic animals. They ask for help in times of weariness, contradiction or a broken heart. There are prayers for private intentions and prayers for the world. Leunig acknowledges that the search for the soul or god or inner voice or higher power takes many forms, that it involves struggle and that each person must find his or her own way. He sees the search and the relationship as being a lifetime's work. He gives the undertaking legitimacy. He leaves it open to personal choice but, like Thomas Moore, he suggests that the consequences of ignoring the quest include loneliness and alienation in an experience of life that sounds akin to the Land of the Thinsies.

This is significant information for a society that offers its youth little or no spiritual education and wonders why they become self-absorbed or demoralised to the point of self-destruction. It is valuable information for a society based on adversarial thinking, in which too many decisions result in winners and losers. If Leunig is right, then perhaps the next essential trip for humankind is not to Mars or into virtual reality but the more challenging and rewarding inner journey to an encounter with the heart and soul.

Unless you belong to a spiritual community of some sort, this can be a lonely journey. In our society, the language of soul is given little currency, so we discuss it rather shyly and often privately, aware that many of the opinion-makers who set the agenda for public debate do not allow its legitimacy. In such a climate we need reassurance that the spiritual life exists and that exploration of it is a valid project, rather than a superstitious flight from the real world.

While the soul may well be nourished by experiences of the body and the mind, its principal instrument is the imagination. To live more spiritually may be achieved by bringing imagination to parts of your life where it is lacking. One of the most eloquent illustrations of this can be found in the brilliant 1987 film, *Babette's Feast*, directed by Gabriel Axe, and featuring Stephane Audran. This film, which is available for hire on video, portrays a curious incident in an isolated, austere Lutheran community in the 1870s, somewhere in Scandinavia, where life is governed by simplicity, thrift and plainness in all things. The people are striving for goodness and yet their piety and self-denial have produced a meagre existence that seems to contain little joy.

Into this Spartan atmosphere comes a foreigner. She is a penniless refugee, a Frenchwoman named Babette, who is prepared to work as a housekeeper for her board and lodging. Suddenly Babette comes into money and, in a grand gesture of generosity, instead of taking the opportunity to leave, she spends all her windfall on expensive provisions for a banquet such as this village has never imagined. Mysterious boxes of goods start to arrive, containing wine and fine cutlery and glassware. A live turtle is delivered from which she will make soup — and then there are quail and fruits and many other exotic delicacies. A rumour begins to circulate that, in former times, she was chef in a fine Paris restaurant.

Anticipation mounts as days of preparation follow. Babette is in her element, utterly concentrated. For the rumour of her profession is true and she is pouring her talent into a masterpiece with which she will say thank you to her benefactors.

Eventually, the evening of the feast comes. Tentatively, the restrained villagers take their places at the table, whose setting is a dazzling sight, and they are served with unaccustomed subtleties of flavour in one remarkable dish after another. Their expressions are a revelation as they show astonishment, then denial, in a reflex action repudiating such richness of pleasure. But gradually they unbend into a natural sheer enjoyment of this exceptional meal. They eat as though they had never tasted food before and indeed they had not tasted anything prepared with such exquisite imagination. As the wine flows, inhibitions are loosened, old secrets revealed, and reconciliations made.

The film is powerful on several levels. On the surface, it is an entertaining story of the enjoyment of food. And then it is a celebration of ritual, in which Babette may be seen as 'priest', for food is a potent metaphor in many religions for absorbing the divine into the body, in order to achieve communion. Combining her knowledge of food with her gratitude, Babette has given the people a spiritual experience to nourish their souls and expand their view of where God's providence may reside. Her vision is very different from that of the villagers. But she has delivered it to them with a grace more likely to convince than a hundred sermons.

As well, it is a gloriously reckless undertaking on her part. At the end of this one night's banquet, she will again be a penniless housekeeper working for her board in an insular village in a foreign land.

And the village will return, no doubt, to its previous simple customs. Yet, as the departing dinner guests dance in a circle under the cold starry northern sky, we suspect that nothing will ever be quite the same again. And for Babette? Well, honour has been served. She has paid a debt of kindness. And she has paid it with complete integrity, giving it absolutely all she had to give — physical energy, heart, soul and worldly wealth. Her soul is nourished and expanded. For the time being, it is satisfied.

In the people's relishing of Babette's beautifully prepared food, there is a reiteration of Stephanie Dowrick's theme in her analysis of loneliness — that we need to be able to take in the good things that come to us in life, to make them part of us, in order to build up a sustaining inner world. *Babette's Feast* shows that this nurture of the soul takes some effort and attention, and a great deal of imagination.

The spiritual life might be described as a combination of these elements. While it is catered for in formal religious practice, many people today find organised religion unsatisfying and are searching in other places. Thomas Moore claims that, without some formal religious practice, spiritual life is weakened and the soul deprived of valuable symbolic and reflective experience. Yet he understands the contemporary influences that may estrange people from the religion of their child-hood. This is demonstrated by the evolution of his own spiritual life.

Brought up in a fervent Irish-Catholic family, he gravitated into training for the priesthood. He enjoyed his years in the seminary, singing Gregorian chant, meditating and studying theology. In the late sixties, just before he was to be ordained priest, he heard the call of the outside world in which peace and love were being preached in a secular way, and he answered it. He left the seminary and, while searching for a new direction, went into casual work in a chemical laboratory where a colleague irritated him constantly by telling him that, although he may have left the seminary, he would always do the work of a priest. Moore denied it, saying that he was finished with the study of formal religion.

Subsequently, he discarded the aspects of formal religion that did not nurture him, and pursued study of the subjects that did, including art, music, psychology and theology. Today he is a practising therapist who writes popular books. His subject is the transformation of psychotherapy, through recovery of a religious tradition called 'care of the soul' which, in the middle ages, was indeed the work of a curate or priest. His work has nothing to do with the established church but he did not throw away the teachings in which he was raised. They are the ultimate source of his spirituality although he thinks of himself now as someone in whom Catholicism is being shaped and lived in a radically reformed way. Thomas Moore returns frequently to his theme that spirituality is expressed not only in the eloquent language of the world's great religions, but in the smallest of daily activities.

Throughout *this* book, there are ideas about how the everyday may be made sacred for each of us, how we can create our own spiritual havens, our own tabernacles of holy things, our own rituals of devotion or attention to the divine. If you are keeping a journal, you are already doing this. Your journal is a sacred book in which you are caring for your soul. For some, spirituality is nurtured in a special place in the landscape to which they feel close relationship. Or your shed may be the place in which you are doing some spiritual work as you use your imagination to turn wood on the lathe, or fashion clay into pots. For another, the spiritual life might be sustained sitting on the verandah, gazing over the paddocks at sunset; or listening in awe to the presence of your baby in the womb, feeling your attention turning inward, your priorities changing and your reflection deepening to encompass the mystery of this new life.

To consider soul and the spiritual life only in ethereal or rarefied terms is to follow a false trail. A delicate birch tree with slim white trunk and leaves silvered by the breeze could suggest a touching image of the soul. But it is only half the story. That tree is able to enchant you with its slender beauty only because its roots are anchored in the earth, invisible in darkness, searching out water and nutrient in the richness of decaying matter, fertilised by manure and mulch, aerated by earthworms. The tree may grow and bloom and make a home for nesting birds and expire lifegiving oxygen into the air, but only for as long as it is supported by its roots.

Similarly, to live with care for the soul is not to live carefree and unencumbered in a sort of spiritual haze, with your eyes cast heavenwards. More likely it means to live with heightened sensibility and a readiness to roll up your sleeves and commit the very essence of yourself to making a difference in the awkward messiness of everyday life. This will open you to encounter darkness as well as light in yourself and in the world; and to empathise with suffering, as you travel the road to that self-knowledge and self-acceptance which are the foundation of soul. Thomas Moore warns that to care for the soul is not to solve the puzzle of life. On the contrary, it is to deepen your appreciation of the paradoxical mystery of life and to find a way to live in the paradox, rather than be destroyed by its contradictions.

The powerful conditioning of the contemporary western world makes this difficult for it seeks to persuade us that the only goal of life is the pursuit of happiness. We are taught to love the light, the surface of things, daytime, summer, fun and talk, but they are only half of our human condition. They are incomplete without the twinning of darkness, roots, the inner, night, winter, suffering and silence. If we are to know the essence of ourselves, the contrasts must be allowed to encounter each other, to enrich each other, to have their rightful time and place, to serve their purpose. It may be that we love our gardens and our bushwalks because, without a word, they remind us of the natural cycle of life and death and our place in it. Nature shows us the ravages of fire in the forest and also the new green sprig shooting from a blackened stump. She shows us mushrooms springing from cowpats, ferns that sprout from fissures in sheer rock. In great trees, she shows us the success of endurance, through all seasons, which comes of transforming everything, patiently, into growth, of drawing deeply for life on the subterranean darkness.

The attempt to describe the spiritual aspect of human experience is risky because it draws you into the use of unscientific language, too imprecise to be convincing in a world suspicious or contemptuous of religion. It becomes easier to discuss the spiritual life obliquely, by describing those circumstances in which it is nourished.

Someone who interviewed me asked me what form spiritual experience takes in my life. We were in my home. I had made some blueberry muffins and we were enjoying morning tea. And I said to her, 'Well, this is it.' She looked nonplussed but it was the truth, for me anyway. We were sitting at the table, sharing food, enjoying each other's company, and reflecting on matters of ultimate meaning, with a bit of sun shining in the window to warm our backs. For me, that is a spiritual experience, in that it is a wholesome experience, a unifying experience, something to take in for nourishment so that it becomes part of me; so that it builds up the rich resource of my inner self or my soul.

My spiritual life is experienced in countless ways. They are very real to me and many of them are ordinary enough. I am conscious of the spiritual life when I feel guided to a decision; when I am awed by a storm, or see parents' adoration of their new baby. When I am very thirsty and drink a glass of water, that is a spiritual experience; as it is when I meditate, ponder, pray or listen; when I am dancing; when I am absorbed with my journal; when I remember, imagine or daydream; when I know the love of a friend; when, out of the blue, someone helps me or listens to me or gives me an insight; when difficult things are made easier for me; when I hear a person's story; when I am forgiven; when I am given the grace to be gentle or forgiving; when I feel trusting and optimistic in a difficult circumstance; when I hear an orchestra, 100-strong, in full flight; when the grey herons wheel home to roost in the old pine trees outside my window at dusk; when I cry over precious faded photographs of my family in early days; when I win a laugh from my 91-year-old father; when a shy topknot pigeon comes to sip water from the bowl on my balcony; when I am moved by a person's sorrow; when I am cared for through the skilful touch of my doctor, dentist, chiropractor or masseur.

Similarly, my spirituality is aroused by actions that offend against the soul of life: when I see on television people being hunted from their homes or children who have been maimed by war; or when I see the natural world laid waste, or cruelty to animals; or when morality and compassionate values are undermined by the powerful in society. These things are an affront to the wholeness of life, to goodness, and, if we are to care for the soul of human society, we need to take a stand against them.

My experience is that I alternate between times of spiritual renewal and periods of spiritual barrenness. The latter include moments when I feel rejected or alienated from people; when I can feel nothing; when I cannot find meaning; when I am rude or impatient; when I feel used rather than treated as a person; and in those moments when I become aware that I could act with violence. This is the human condition. We are constantly aware of a conflict between good and evil, not only in the world, but within ourselves. The spiritual life is no exception. It can lead to excess and directly into darkness. History is disfigured by hideous conflicts fought in the name of religions. It has been so, down the centuries, and we need to acknowledge the fact and nourish our souls to deal with it, for that is our best defence.

It is worth spending some time to identify the circumstances in which your own spiritual life may be enlivened, so that you can seek them out and revisit them. Worth noting, too, the occasions of spiritual desolation for, painful as they are, they may be fertilising your compassion for some future insight or creative action. I first found the complementary images of spiritual consolation and desolation described in the spiritual exercises of St Ignatius of Loyola.

In some societies, spirituality seems to be in the atmosphere, taken for granted like the air we breathe, a natural element of life not set apart from the everyday world in a church, mosque, synagogue or temple. The Indians and the Nepalese acknowledge the spiritual life many times a day with their eloquent greeting, 'Namaste'. Briefly the head is bowed; the palms are joined as though in prayer, and inclined towards the other in a salutation from the divine in me to the divine in you. This simple, perfect gesture establishes common ground. It is a fundamental meeting place, a pledge of connection, a deference to the spiritual in everyone, a salute to soul in the mundanity of everyday life. It transforms courteous connection into spirituality. After you have participated in *Namaste*, you are changed by it. In case you had forgotten, you are alerted to the presence of your own soul, and to that of the person whom you are encountering. *Namaste* is a momentary halting of time, in which the eternal breaks through. You have taken another sip from the deep.

My experience of this greeting came when I went trekking in the Himalayas in Nepal. With a group of other Australians, I was guided and cared for in this daunting environment by the distinguished mountain Sherpas. It was a revelation to encounter people so poor in material goods and natural resources, yet so rich in spirit. There was no limit to their service to visitors, but it was service graciously performed and devoid of servility, every act of care increasing their stature and integrity. In their culture, to give seems as natural as walking. On the most exhausting and challenging parts of the trail, there was always a Sherpa at your elbow or just behind, quietly ready to support, or to flash a brilliant, invigorating smile. Once or twice I saw a sudden eruption of argument between them, but never towards the people in their charge.

They invited us into their homes; they cooked for us; they taught us their songs and dances. Like parents with children, they took responsibility for our safety in the most hazardous conditions. They saw that, in the material sense, we were overburdened with more than anyone could need. We were festooned with cameras, lenses and binoculars, clothed in waterproof jackets stuffed with down, and beautifully shod in state-of-the-art climbing boots while many of them wore sandshoes. Our equipment and belongings bent their backs with enormous loads carried without complaint.

We climbed to 18,000 feet and, in the severe cold at great altitude, they saw our frailty, how we succumbed to altitude sickness and fatigue. They treated us with compassion, never with contempt. Although quick and resolute in their own activity, they were patient with the slow and kind to the sick. Keenly alive to the earthy humour of a situation, they were resourceful in the face of hardship and poverty, and absurdly energetic in the ferocious environment to which they had become conditioned over generations. They ran up steep pathways; they refused to be bowed by discomfort. And all was accomplished with grace, distinction and a lightness of being.

I allowed that trip to be marred by my reactions to fatigue, cold and physical pain. From the Sherpas I learned a valuable lesson for the future — not to let physical discomfort or the weather detract from an experience. I learned to detach from these distractions, rather than waste energy resisting them — to let them be and focus on the matter in hand.

As we became more closely acquainted, we heard the Sherpas' concerns about their children's health, education and future. Materially they were far less privileged than most children in my country, and yet I felt there was an additional element in their lives that was missing in mine. Their practice of Buddhism had become part of ordinary life. Loving kindness was not just a doctrine; it was second nature to them. Prayer flags, which they had planted in the hillsides behind their homes, blew with every gust of wind, like impossibly tall fronds of papyrus. And it was natural to them to spin the prayer wheels embedded in stone walls along the walking trails, wheels engraved with *Om mani padme hum*, a sacred religious formula which may be translated as 'the jewel is in the heart of the lotus'. The ubiquitous prayer wheels represent the wheel of life which symbolises the endless cycle of death and rebirth. This is one of the most important Buddhist symbols. To turn the wheel adds to that measure of credit which the Buddhist hopes to accumulate in this present life in order to escape the pain of rebirth.

It is a revelation to be in the presence of people of such transparent spirit. The visitor's life is changed forever by the privilege. I came down from the high mountains with an altered perspective on life and a sense of priorities rearranged.

For eight years on ABC radio I had the real gift of listening to Australians describing their spiritual quests. Lacking a commonly honoured spiritual life in their own community, some had gone to Greece to encounter the gods and goddesses of myth and found satisfaction and clarity there. They were looking for archetypes of their own experience, and legends in which the archetypes lived out their destiny. In doing this, they were seeking powerful guides and companions for the spiritual journey — just as the Christian falls into step with Jesus Christ and the Buddhist with the Buddha. Others told me they had gained access to their spirituality in the revelation of childbirth and the bond of love with their growing children. Some had experimented with drugs or gurus to alter their state of consciousness from the mundane. Some had studied and practised a variety of spiritual traditions from Tibetan Buddhism to Native American wisdom to Hinduism, Islam or Ba H'ai. Some were fulfilled in the religious tradition in which they were raised as children. Others found that their spirituality could be awakened and expressed adequately in humanism or social activism, without any reference to God or the transcendent. Some had found expansion of the soul through great suffering; some through wrestling with their God; some through redefining God as feminine, or the force, or higher power, or the void.

For the Aboriginal people I interviewed, spirituality seemed to be intrinsic, unquestioned, requiring no analysis, as total, natural and essential as breathing. Across the nation I found that, on the subjects of spirituality, soul and the search for meaning, Australians speak with passion and deep curiosity. These are issues of significant interest today, despite the fact that opinion leaders and the mainstream media ignore them or subject them to ridicule. Perhaps that is not so surprising in a population where more than 80 per cent acknowledge a belief in God.

I love to gaze at things, to give them my fullest attention, but I did not make a connection between gazing and spirituality until I happened on a notion expressed by the French philosopher Simone Weil in her work *Attente de Dieu*. Her idea that 'prayer is born from attention' offered me an interpretation of what had often been my potent experience. For instance, in church one morning, my attention was drawn to a brass vase flamboyantly filled with blue and mauve hydrangeas set on a stand beside a statue of Mary, the mother of Jesus. This statue is truly a depiction of Our Lady of Dolours, for whom this church is named. Every fold of her draped garment and the cowl covering her bent head speaks of unutterable sorrow. The hydrangeas, bright against the pale plaster, seemed an impulsive human gesture made to relieve the grief of centuries. It took another moment to notice that, beside the large vase, was an identical smaller one, spilling over with more hydrangea and a hectic spray of white daisies, as if the giver had succumbed to excess in a desire to revere and console. My gaze was compelled from the statue to the large vase to the smaller one and back to the statue, over and over. The scene held my full attention until it had relinquished its meaning to me and I had taken it into myself.

To put it rationally, I saw an arresting image of the eternal (Mary) in juxtaposition with the ephemeral (flowers) and related to it as a metaphor of my own human life. But it was primarily a meditation of the imagination which called my soul into awareness for the communal Mass in which I was about to participate, as effectively as any formal spoken prayer could have done. Something in my sensibility was alerted by the impulse of this morning's flower arranger.

No matter that later, when I spoke to her about it, she laughed and claimed that she had arrived late with too many flowers and 'had to stick them somewhere'. Our laughter did not diminish the quality of my own encounter with her flowers and the statue; and served as a reminder that meetings with the soul often begin in the absurdity of mundane life.

For many people today, church is not the setting for spiritual awareness. For those who have had an unhappy history in organised religion, it may be the last place. If you just gaze at the clouds, or the swirled pink and orange boughs of a snow gum, or a sleeping child, or a candle flame, or a shell, something like revelation can take place. Silently, a thin veil lifts between material reality and some coexisting dimension of which you may feel part, in union.

And then Dr Deepak Chopra speaks of the potential for spiritual awakening in sexual union, when self-absorption may be abandoned and replaced by an experience of unity in which boundaries dissolve and, for a time, one is part of another and of all that is.[5] Some spiritual traditions like Tantric Buddhism embrace this in their teaching. Modern Christianity is uncomfortable with the spirituality of sex, although it has the poetry for it in texts like *The Song of Songs* in the

Old Testament; and in the passionate outpourings of the mystics.

Deepak Chopra also speaks of a month he spent alone in the desert. He found that, as the days went on, without company, radio or books, he became aware of the tangible presence of space in a way that was new to him, and that drew him into a profound spiritual experience. I write more about the practice of making such a retreat in the next chapter.

Reading has always been a great solace and inspiration to me and I am eternally grateful to those many writers who have helped me to explore the complexity of human nature and given me language to express the way in which I experience my own life. One of my favourites is the American poet May Sarton who died in 1996. For long periods of her life, she lived alone with a beautiful and demanding garden, her pets and her writing. In her old age, most helpfully for me, she writes about her experience of solitude: 'Friends, even passionate love, are not my real life, unless there is time alone in which to explore and to discover what is happening.'[6] Other introverts may be as relieved as I was when first I read those words, while extroverts will be appalled. For them, the spiritual life is often nourished in relationship and community, in sharing talk and ideas.

But back to my mentor, May Sarton. She writes: 'I am furious at all the letters to answer when what I want to do is think and write. I long for open time, with no obligations, except toward the inner world and what is going on there.' That speaks to me exactly. I could ponder and gaze *ad infinitum*, to nourish my soul. I even have a special place for it — a big old pink armchair by the window, with a potted Iceberg rose and a pile of books beside it. However, May Sarton disciplined herself to answer the endless letters, perhaps because, like the contemplative monk Thomas Merton, she had won some wisdom from the solitude, and felt a responsibility to share it.

In concluding this chapter, I draw your attention to the quotation from Brenda Ueland at the beginning of the chapter. She makes the spiritual life seem easily accessible when she writes that 'it is when you are really living in the present, working, thinking, lost, absorbed in something you care about very much, that you are living spiritually'.

I invite you to ponder and to record in your journal some circumstances in which you have found yourself to be aware of your soul. It is important to identify them because they provide you with windows through which to glimpse the soul; evidence that you have a spiritual life; and situations in which to seek spiritual nourishment with some hope of success. As usual, if words get in the way, use cut-out pictures or diagrams or symbols or photographs or something collected, like a leaf you brought home from a bushwalk. The questions below may prompt you in this reflection.

The next chapter considers how to create more opportunity in your life for care of the soul.

For your Journal

* What are the situations in which you find sustenance for the soul?

* In what ways do people around you acknowledge their spirituality?

* When are you at peace with the world? Where do you find harmony?

* Where do you feel most whole, least fragmented, most yourself?

* When do you feel least whole, most fragmented, least yourself?

* Where are you accepted, just as you are?

* When have you felt loved, guided and supported in a most wholesome way

* Where are you in awe, aware of something much greater than yourself?

* When do you feel connection and compassion for other lives?

* Where do you most find meaning at the moment?

* When do you have a sense of rightness about your life?

* Do you have some new symbols to add to your 'name' page?

* Turn back to your statement of purpose. Are you fulfilling it? Does it need amending?

Endnotes

1 Thomas Moore, *Care of the Soul*, Harper Perennial, 1992.
2 Dorothy Ann Lovell, *In the Land of the Thinsies*, Faber and Faber, 1944.
3 Michael Leunig, *Common Prayer Collection*, Collins Dove, 1993.
4 *Common Prayer Collection*.
5 Deepak Chopra, *The Path to Love*, Harmony Books, New York, 1997.
6 May Sarton, *Journal of a Solitude*, The Women's Press, 1985.

6 SACRED TIME

Teach us to sit still.

T. S. Eliot[1]

God help us to live slowly:
To move simply:
To look softly:
To allow emptiness:
To let the heart create for us.
Amen.

Michael Leunig[2]

space

SOME SPACE HAS TO BE dedicated to accommodate the soul and the spiritual life that nourishes it. It is easy to neglect the need to withdraw from activity for periods of rest and renewal. Many people simply do not take this need into account. They have become habituated to living at an extraordinarily fast pace, with a tormenting complexity of commitments. Once this comes to seem normal, and then a virtue, they feel guilt at any slackening of their momentum. Time has been made into a commodity, of which there is never enough. This is illustrated by the fact that media interviewers now actually thank people for their *time*, rather than their expertise.

Time management has turned into a neurosis, in which it is a status symbol to suffer inordinate pressure of time. There is even rivalry in comparison of the overpacked schedules by which some friends and

110

work colleagues regulate their busy lives. This is exacerbated by a corporate expectation of longer and longer working hours by those few privileged to be in work. Living at top speed becomes an addiction, as painful to break as any other. It may be a stimulating way to live, for a limited period, but it is inhospitable to spirituality and it can hardly be healthy as a permanent way of life, physically, psychologically, emotionally or spiritually; nor a desirable ideal to demonstrate to your children or others for whom you are a model.

If shortage of time is a problem for you, if you have become expert at juggling multiple commitments, perhaps you need to block out some spaces in your schedule in which to attend to your peace of mind. Some busy people find that a daily time of prayer or meditation fulfils this need. One man told me that his suburban train journey is devoted to silent prayer. An executive on my ferry used to read his Bible during the journey. He would read a passage, then gaze out at the water for a time, then resume his reading.

Others are sustained spiritually by the familiar ritual of making a cup of tea and enjoying it in peace and contemplation. If tea is prepared calmly, with intention, this simple ceremony makes a welcome pause, refreshing to the spirit. Some go into reverie as they bend their heads over knitting or intricate needlework. Many men claim that time in their den or shed is essential to them. They may not use the term 'sacred time' but their determination to claim it suggests a stronger imperative than the need to do running repairs.

Thomas Moore's guide to cultivating depth and sacredness in everyday life, *Care of the Soul*, reminds the reader that small children paint almost every day, making images to reflect what's going on in their souls. As we grow up we abandon this expression of soul. He writes: 'We are then left with mere rational reasons for our lives, feelings of emptiness and confusion . . . and a compulsive attachment to pseudo-images such as shallow t.v. programs.' When our own images have no home, no 'personal museum', we drown our sense of loss in pale substitutes.

Thomas Moore writes that 'art captures the eternal in the everyday, and it is the eternal that feeds soul'. He means art of all kinds: poetry, painting, woodwork, craftwork, writing letters, recording images from our dreams, playing music, keeping a journal. He says that 'the point of art is not simply to express ourselves, but to create an external, concrete form in which the soul of our lives can be evoked and contained'.

Thomas Moore goes on:

> Art beckons us into contemplation, so that we have an intensified experience of the presence of the world. We see it more vividly and more deeply. The emptiness that many people complain dominates their lives comes in part from a failure to let the world in, to perceive it and engage it fully. Naturally, we'll feel empty if everything we do slides past without sticking ... Soul cannot thrive in a fast-paced life because being affected, taking things in and chewing on them requires time.[3]

Thomas Moore makes it clear that, as long as we leave care of the soul out of our daily lives, we will suffer loneliness. So we could consider that time devoted to care of the soul is sacred time.

The Blue Mountains artist John Ellison thinks along the same lines. He teaches people to see with the inner eye.[4] He suggests that you can make a start by looking through a book of great paintings, slowly, savouring. See how Van Gogh portrays the essential nature of a yellow chair; how Lloyd Rees is exalted to ecstasy by the quality of light over the Derwent; how Monet luxuriates, almost drowns, in the waterlilies of his Giverny garden. This exercise is designed to refresh your own eyes, to wash them clear in order to look at everyday things anew, to see them in more depth, to connect with them, to absorb something of their essence.

Fine photography can serve the same purpose. If you take the time to look through a book of the photographs of Max Dupain in the library, you will be arrested by the drama of light and shade, as he was. When I talked with him about what really mattered in life, he told me 'I adore the light'. And that adoration is communicated in his brilliant black and white images. He was first alerted to the quality of light in the paintings of the French Impressionists.[5] His photography gives the viewer new eyes with which to see the everyday world.

Traditional cultures believed that certain places had distinctive qualities and that one should spend time in such places, regardless of the time it took and the hardship of making the journey there. That is what lay behind the custom of pilgrimage to sacred places. It happens still today. Moslems strive to make a pilgrimage to Mecca, Christians to the holy places in Israel. In India and Bali, and in Europe, people visit holy wells, sacred mountains, great temples and cathedrals, holy rivers and springs and the shrines of saints. This belief in sacred places was suppressed in western culture at the time of the Reformation when there was a move to desacralise the world. In England the Protestants destroyed religious images in many of the holy places that were intrinsic to Catholicism and earlier religions, because they saw them as remnants of a superstitious belief to be exterminated. Later, many such holy places were restored to their former significance and became again places of pilgrimage.

The English biologist and author Rupert Sheldrake contends that if you come into a place where many people have gathered before for special activities, you will be stimulated in the same way that they were by that particular environment — by its smells, sights, the quality of light, even the very atmosphere.[6] Thus, the physical aspects of the place give you some of the same experiences as other people had in earlier times. These physical aspects, together with our knowledge of the events that happened there, can create a deep sense of connection to those events and experiences. Perhaps there is even more to it than physical place and intellectual knowledge. Could it be that the energy of all the thoughts and experiences still exists in that place?

Rupert Sheldrake believes that a place may indeed have a field, what he calls a 'morphic field', inherent in the place itself, so that some places make you feel uneasy — places like prisons, torture chambers or a house where people have been murdered or have suffered. In such places, there can be a sense of haunting by a negative presence. On the other hand, places where people have meditated or prayed over centuries will be imbued with a characteristic resonance. That's why you may find it easier to pray in a cathedral than in an airport lounge, which has a very different quality of place.

In some cultures, this understanding is taken for granted. Sheldrake points to the Chinese science of place, *Feng Shui*, which takes great pains to position buildings in appropriate relationship to the environment so that they enhance it rather than diminish it. In traditional Japan, temples and pagodas were situated in such a way that they lay harmoniously with the land and complemented the beauty of the landscape. Many old, settled landscapes have a beautiful sense of harmony between the buildings and the land; that's why we love to visit them as tourists. They resonate with our desire for inner harmony and beauty. Some places are held to be sacred in themselves, without any buildings — places like Mt Fuji or the Irish sacred mountain, Croagh Patrick. In the modern western world, little account is taken of such things. Land is bought and sold as real estate. Buildings are put where they are fed by roads or where there is some other utilitarian purpose for them, with the result that many modern landscapes are hideous, with the buildings disrupting the beauty of their situation.

Sheldrake argues that, at some level, we modern western people know these concepts of sacred time and sacred place but we have forgotten them. He takes the point further to suggest that much modern tourism is actually unconscious spiritual pilgrimage, a search for that quality which has been removed from modern western life but for which we still yearn.

Living with more care for the soul in everyday life might require something as simple as pausing more often, for a few moments of quiet reflection, for a period of *being* rather than doing. This can be achieved on a daily basis and may begin to nurture a more peaceful ambience in your life. People practise meditation for this purpose, so that a period of each day is dedicated just to being and to contacting the inner world.

One method of meditation, which I learned in a yoga class, is to sit upright but relaxed, with eyes closed, and to concentrate on the breath passing in and out of the nostrils. If thoughts come into your mind, don't fight them, just watch them floating past like clouds, and gently return your attention to feeling the breath passing in and out of your nostrils. This could be done for five minutes at a time, later working up to 20 minutes.

Or you could try lying on the grass under a tree and gazing up into its leaves. You will be surprised by the effect this has on you: the unaccustomed feeling of the ground beneath your back and grass under your hands; the change of perspective; the intricate silhouette of leaves on the brightness of the sky; the humility of it, the relief of it. Let the concerns of the day drop out of the back of your busy head into the earth. Feel your jaw slacken and your eyes fall back into their sockets and just be, like an animal flopped down, at rest. Remember how you used to roll down a grassy bank as a child, arms and legs loose like spaghetti. How carefree it was. How long is it since you have done something like that?

Without any sacred time, we are robbed of the possibility of peace. Most of us long for peace but have little guidance in how to attain it. We may like to think that peace can be achieved by having everything under control, but that is an illusion. Very little is under our control at any time. Similarly, we imagine that peace may come by keeping a distance in relationships, by not becoming too involved or committed. There is too much of the self or the ego in each of these approaches, whereas the way to peace is more likely to be found through unselfishness, the cultivation of a sense of meaning, and attention to the spiritual life. That sounds like a big commitment but it may be achieved in many small ways. If you will simply give full, benevolent attention to what is happening around you at this moment, you are building the possibility of peace for yourself and others. If you are quiet and attentive in the company of others, you are adding peace to the occasion. If you detach yourself slightly from your circumstances, rather than becoming emotionally embroiled in everything you encounter, you are adding to the possibility of peace. Or you could listen without judgment to a person confiding in you, or trying to teach you something, or asking for your help.

As an instrument of peace, listening is one of the most underrated of all human activities and, for that reason, I want to spend a little time exploring it. Listening is one of the most loving services that one person can offer another. We find out what another person's world is like by listening to them. And that greatly increases the possibility of understanding and peace between people. The problem is that very few people take the time to listen and this constitutes a serious barrier to peace, first for the individual and then on many levels, up to world peace.

Anyone knows that to be listened to without judgment is a liberating experience — and a rare one. When someone listens to me, I become much clearer about what I really think. I may even modify what I think at that moment when I hear myself speak it out, because in the accepting silence of being listened to I can hear whether or not it rings true. Whereas if someone argues with me, I become more preoccupied with defending my belief than subjecting it to re-examination.

When someone listens with benevolent interest and questions me only for the purpose of clarification, I can relax my guard and speak candidly. That is valuable, because in the process I am discovering more of who I am; I am defining my sense of values; I am attending to my spiritual life and therefore I am caring for my soul. The listener's lack of censure, advice or argument disarms the defences which I spend so much time and energy protecting. I can then reach in to retrieve deep feelings; I can confess my shame and sadness and, in doing so, relieve them; I can disclose my hopes and dreams and so enhance the possibility of their realisation. To articulate them and have them heard is a powerful step towards achieving them. The listener has created a safe enclosure of time and place in which that may happen.

For this reason I am inclined to think of listening as the creation of sacred time. As stories unfolded on *The Search for Meaning* programs, I felt that I was walking on holy ground, created not so much by my questions as by the listening — my own and that of the radio audience. As well, to prepare for the recorded interview, guests had been invited to reflect upon or listen to their own experience, over a period of time. They were then listened to as they revealed the fruit of that reflection.

To be listened to is to be taken seriously, to feel that one's story and ideas have legitimacy. This is affirming. It builds self-respect and a sense of authenticity. If I am worth listening to, then I feel that who I am has validity, that I am not alone or invisible or of little account.

Listening also brings a healing of loneliness for it makes a meaningful connection between people. If I am listened to with empathy, then I have the acceptance of my own kind, for communication through language is one of the distinguishing features of being human. We are able to reflect on our experience of life and communicate our insights to each other. We are curious about the mysterious odyssey of life on which we are embarked and communication about it is one of our greatest satisfactions. It is the foundation of all our learning and development. We are here not only to have an individual experience of life but to share it with interest and delight, and to help each other live life to the full. Listening to each other is a prerequisite to doing this well. Later on, we can enjoy the stimulation of discussion and challenging each other's ideas in argument. That too facilitates the search for meaning. But all too often the first stage of simply listening is left out.

If listening is so valuable in human relationships, why don't we do it for each other more readily? For one reason, it is quite difficult. The western mind is schooled to be individualistic, active and competitive; it is endlessly making decisions about what it likes and what it doesn't like. It is an effort for us to step aside from that powerful lifelong conditioning and open our minds to the concept that apparent opposites may be complementary; or merely to contemplate a statement without judging it. In other cultures, the conditioning of the mind is otherwise. In Aboriginal custom, and in many Pacific cultures, it is usual to make decisions through consensus rather than argument, so that all viewpoints are heard and considered, as though equally valid. Then, slowly, gradually, people agree to sufficient common ground to constitute an outcome — but not without a great deal of listening.

Differing cultural approaches cause conflict in communication. For instance, the Aborigine sees the western adversarial way as entrenched conflict, while the western mind may see the Aboriginal way as slow and tortuous. This divergence of views could be alleviated if the practice of listening and feedback was introduced to interrupt the impasse. This valuable process is taught as a method of conflict resolution. For example, in a discussion of apparently conflicting claims about land use, the traditional Aboriginal owner may make an opening statement: 'I know that you have a pastoral lease of that land, but it is important for me to have access to that land also because my ancestors lived there and are buried there. I feel a great spiritual connection to that land and I have spiritual duties to perform there.'

Ideally, instead of arguing, the pastoralist replies in a way that indicates firstly that he has been listening, and only secondly that he too has an important relationship to the land. He says: 'So, it is important for you to have access to that land because your ancestors lived there and are buried there and you feel a great spiritual connection to the place and you have spiritual duties to perform there. Have I understood you correctly?'

The Aboriginal owner says 'Yes'.

The pastoralist's listening has shown respect for the opinion of the other. It has also opened the way for him to express his own requirements. He says: 'The land is also important to me, because I want to run my cattle there, as my lease allows, and there is a bore which provides them with water and that is crucial to my livelihood. I must be certain that it is not interfered with.'

The Aboriginal owner returns the pastoralist's courtesy by showing that he too is listening. He responds: 'So this land is important to you too, because you run your cattle there, and there is a bore to give them water. The bore is crucial to you. You must be sure it is not interfered with.'

The pastoralist replies: 'Yes, that's right.'

At this point, each has demonstrated that he has heard the other's view. This creates an atmosphere of relationship rather than conflict. It has also become apparent that the needs defined by each of them are not in conflict, and that coexistence on the same piece of land could be achieved. This is indeed how many Aboriginals and pastoralists have come to creative and practical agreements about coexistence on land for the past 150 years. It is a wonderfully effective process that could be applied to other areas of national life.

It may take longer to conduct negotiation in this way but it is more likely to produce a mutually agreeable outcome to which both parties will subscribe. Clearly, such an agreement has more chance of holding than an imposed decision that favours the interests of the Aborigine above the interests of the pastoralist, and therefore leaves the pastoralist aggrieved. Such win/win strategies are widely taught in many areas of Australian life by the Conflict Resolution Network.[7] They are an effective way of coming to peace with issues at home, between neighbours, in the workplace or wherever differences arise, whether between two people or between nations.

Although I had been earning my living by listening for years, I remember the pleasure with which I first discovered how listening actually works, from psychologist Hugh Mackay. I had invited him to do a series of interviews on communication for the ABC radio program *City Extra*. He explained to me and a large audience that listening is an act of generosity, even something of a sacrifice. He explained that we spend a lifetime building a framework of meaning, plank by hard-won plank. It is precious to us. We do not want any plank dislodged. When I listen, I step temporarily out of my framework of meaning in order to contemplate your framework which is different from mine in many ways. This is uncomfortable and I resist it. But it can be done if I want to do it, first just for a brief time and then for longer. Listening takes time and we are parsimonious with our time. We think that we do not have enough of it, that we must keep moving on. Listening requires us to curb that compulsion. And the rewards for making that generous step are great.

I will come to know the person I listen to more fully. My gift of listening will gain their confidence and deepen the encounter between us. I need then to be faithful in not betraying the confidence won by my listening. I know that if I listen to someone I am giving them something of value, something they do not often receive, something that is freeing and life-enhancing and adds to their peace of mind and spirit. If there is any relationship in your life that you want to improve, then listening is a fine first step. Listening is a pathway to intimacy — in friendship, personal relationships, marriage, parenting, and working partnerships.

Listening requires self-discipline and practice and a readiness to put yourself in another person's shoes, even for three minutes. It's difficult to do because you are breaking the habits of a lifetime. It is important to think of fully opening your attention to another, without judging, without advising, without switching the subject to yourself by telling them a similar experience of your own. When they come to the end of one thought, don't jump in with your response. Leave a welcoming silence for them to continue. Or feed back your understanding of what they have just said and ask for confirmation that you have got it right, as the pastoralist did. Then you could inquire what happened next. Later, when the person has finished, it may be appropriate for you to offer optional ways to see the situation. This can be helpful, for it widens their perspective, but it must be an offer only, not a prescription. Quite often, people come to see their own solution, simply by being listened to.

When you listen, you are providing precious attentive silence in which a person may venture forth to show himself. At its best, this is soul hearkening to soul. When you listen, it may seem to you that you are not really doing anything, and that's hard for most of us because we want to be able to *do* something. No, you are just *being with* a person. And being with is compassion and, when you act with compassion, you act with love. And that is when you are indeed creating sacred time and contributing to a more meaningful world.

Of course, when you become an accomplished listener, you may find that everyone wants to tell you their life story because you have become one of a rare species and much in demand. Then, to sustain you, you need a good listener in your life. Sometimes people will take advantage of your listening ear but usually it is an honour to hear a chapter of their story. They are bestowing on you their most trusting offering. In turn, you are giving them the peace, respect and freedom of a safe enclosure in which they may be themselves and reveal their heart and soul. When you do this, you are adding to the peace of the world and gaining a little measure of serenity for your soul.

A publican friend of my father's, Stan Macauley, was fond of saying that happiness comes from within. Peace, too, needs to be cultivated within us. It flourishes in the presence of a meaningful creed or faith or guiding story by which to live. We need to discern what matters and what does not, in the light of that creed, so that in every situation we can be true to what we believe is right and act accordingly. In responding to an inner sense of truth, we are charting a course set by principles, and are not attached to a particular outcome. This is easier said than done, but isn't it better to have an ideal in mind, than to lurch from one crisis to the next, creating disturbance around us, with no underlying sense of integrity or fundamental purpose? We will have much more stomach and energy for a challenge if we really believe in what we are doing, and if it is congruent with our sense of values.

It seems to me that the soul of a community needs as much care as the souls of the individuals who live in it. While open discussion of issues is necessary, too much conflict is ravaging for the health of community life. We can reflect with some pride on the fact that the Conflict Resolution Network was founded here in Australia and that its principles are widely practised in many areas of the public and private sectors of our national life. The objective of conflict resolution is to find what is called a win/win situation, in which the needs of both parties in a conflict may be satisfied. In the justice system in Australia, the conventional adversarial process is being complemented by the use of mediation in some disputes. In mediation, the parties meet to articulate their needs, to be heard, and to search out a mutually agreeable solution. They are accompanied in this process by a trained mediator, not by lawyers or barristers with a vested interest in keeping them at loggerheads. In good mediation, justice is served and any agreement reached has a greater chance of enduring because it took the needs of both sides into account. The process may take more time than a traditional court case but, considering the outcome, it seems to be time well spent on the healing of serious rifts in human relationships.

Judge Dorothy Nelson, Senior Judge of the United States Court of Appeals, is an internationally recognised champion of mediation. While not claiming it as a panacea for all disputes, she has many exciting stories to tell of its success when used in appropriate situations. In one instance, youth gangs were causing havoc in her district each day after school, and the police were failing to contain the mischief. She called the police chief and the youth gang leaders into mediation. The atmosphere was tense as they sat side by side in her chambers. They were asked in turn to express their needs and to listen to each other. The youths said there was nothing for them to do after school closed in the afternoon; the police chief said that he lacked sufficient officers to police the streets. Their *common need* was identified as a requirement for school to remain open in the afternoon, and to provide a range of stimulating and constructive activities for youth to enjoy. And that is what happened.

Judge Nelson reported that, over time, there was significant relief of the problem and even some unforeseen benefits. She kept in touch with progress and, weeks later, one of the burly young gang leaders told her his personal story. He had taken home with him what he had learned during the mediation process and told his father, with whom he was constantly at loggerheads, that what they needed was conflict resolution. He taught his father how it worked and, as a result, he and his father had their first-ever civilised conversation.

We do not experience conflict only with other people. We experience conflict and contradiction within ourselves, in our feelings and thought processes. The principles of conflict resolution apply just the same. We can let the opposing feelings or thoughts talk to each other. Identify and list the needs behind each of them. It is most likely that this will indicate some common ground and a way forward.

When you come across someone who seems to enjoy a sense of peace, ask for their secret. The answer may be quite surprising. Sometimes a person experiencing powerlessness simply waits, and achieves a measure of peace in their acceptance. The prayer so dear to Alcoholics Anonymous lends words to this circumstance:

> God grant me the serenity to accept the things I cannot change, the courage to change the things I can, and the wisdom to know the difference.

Sometimes you hear a story that illuminates your own experience, bringing you a sense of peace. To my surprise, I found the Annunciation to be such a story, even though I encountered it well before I had made any religious commitment myself. I was invited to read this famous passage from the Christian gospels at the traditional Christmas Eve Festival of Lessons and Carols at St Andrew's Anglican Cathedral in Sydney. The honour of this invitation came to me several years in a row, and each time I was asked to do the same reading. It was a joy to be there, to feel my spirit lifted by the sublime music of Christmas performed by the renowned St Andrew's Choir. But that was not all. As the years went on, my appreciation of the story I was reading gradually deepened.

It offers an image of 'the eternal' breaking through into ordinary time, in the account of the angel Gabriel announcing to Mary that she will bear the son of God. You can read it in Luke 1, 26–38. What a terrifying prospect for a modest young Jewish girl. This dramatic turning point in history has been depicted by many painters because it is so rich in significance for the human condition. For Christians, this is what each one is called to do — nothing less — to give birth in themselves to the son of God — that is, to become more like Jesus Christ. The secular reader may prefer to think of it as realising the potential of their true self. Of course, the prospect is as daunting to us today as it was to Mary. Do we accept this challenge, in faith, and go where it leads us, or do we say 'No' and settle for making more money, having the next sexual adventure or playing another computer game?

In that crucial moment of sacred time, Mary chose acceptance. In her trust in God, she risked the scandal of pregnancy before marriage in a community of strict religious law. It led her into a life of worry, rejection, loneliness, sacrifice, grief and apparent failure. But it was also a life of love and absolute commitment. And it bore fruit that would nourish people down the ages. Against all appearances at the time, hers was a supremely successful life.

To my surprise, as a single, working woman with no children, I found this story had something to say to me personally. It illuminated my own experience of being faced with a challenge and having to work out a way to deal with it. Mary's story gave me a model of how to respond in difficult times. I saw that I had freedom to choose my attitude.

How can a story from 2000 years ago sustain a modern woman in the very different world of the 20th century? I don't know how it works exactly but I do know that, for me, it is effective. At a time of difficult challenge, I ponder Mary's story, let it seep into my consciousness. I have a print of Fra Angelico's painting of the Annunciation above my desk, given to me by a thoughtful young friend. I am especially touched by his gift because he is an atheist. Yet he was generous enough in spirit to acknowledge what this image means to me, and to take the extra step of finding a beautiful version of it, framing it and delivering it to me as a surprise. It was an exquisite gesture of friendship. As I work at my desk, Max's gift of Mary is there beside me, her slight body curved in apprehension as she accepts her destiny. She is making an act of faith in life and in her God, taking a trusting step into the unknown.

How many times each one of us is asked to do this, throughout life. I find it daunting every time and I am grateful every time for Mary's brave company because her story rang true to me as a valid way to respond to the mysterious choices that life presents. I was fascinated by my identification with Mary's story, not in any literal sense but as a metaphor whose meaning could help me, especially in acceptance of those things I could not change. Such circumstances may be crushing if you cannot find a viable attitude with which to endure them and still retain integrity.

At times, for instance, a feeling of duty towards others may be onerous and unwelcome. Dr David Reynolds would go the Zen way.[8] He would sidestep the thinking and the feeling and say, just do it ! Then your problem is overcome. This is certainly one way to act. Another is to find an attitude towards the situation that will free you to act generously, without feeling oppressed by your choice. To achieve this, you need to locate yourself in a bigger story which interprets the choice for you and invests it with some ultimate meaning. Such guiding stories call us into sacred time. They relieve us of that lonely autonomy in which we seem to be acting alone, guided only by meagre notions like 'my rights' or 'my choice'. 'My rights' and 'my choice' can be valid components of a way of thinking but alone they are too narrow to sustain valid decision-making. I am inclined to think it is the nature of the human person to need that sense of wider perspective and communal purpose that comes with feeling connected to all other life in a grand saga, be it Christianity, Islam, Buddhism, Hinduism, Aboriginal spirituality, Native American mythology, the deep ecology movement or transpersonal psychology.

When I first met Mary's story I could not have articulated any of this. I know only that it spoke to me and kept me company when I needed it. It is one of my many treasured stories; together they make up my framework of meaning and so they are precious to me. Patti Miller, author of *The Last One Who Remembers*[9] described this human anatomy of stories when she told me:

> If I could be held up to the light, it would shine through me in a dappled pattern, and looking closer it could be seen I was made of densely woven stories which blocked and let through the light in this intricate way. They make a near impenetrable story fabric of my being.[10]

She writes that the longing to be in a story is deep and strange and undeniable. She travelled across the globe in her effort to inhabit the 'told' world, the world of stories which her grandmother first gave her. She writes that stories of every kind cover the Earth:

> They sing in the air, buzz in the classrooms, wail in streets, murmur in bedrooms. They shape daily lives and nightly fears. Wars are begun on the strength of a good story and could not be started without one. If a people's stories are destroyed they wander dispossessed on the fringes of others' stories, and eventually dissolve into oblivion. Journeys are begun, colonies are founded, hearts are broken, souls inspired. If you're not in a story, you don't exist ...
>
> I'm caught in the weave of all stories ... but I don't yet dare relinquish any of them. Once, they were snatched away from me

overnight and although in the morning I knew everything had been taken from me, I could not name what had happened. I didn't know that stories could dissolve and leave disconnected terror'.[11]

Patti Miller's wonderful image of stories as the fabric of her being suggests the extraordinary potency that stories hold for us.

Another powerful contemporary story is that of Nelson Mandela, figurehead of the new South Africa. It is easy now to forget that he spent 27 years of his life in prison. He made the choice early to be true to his principles, no matter what the cost. His face today is inscribed with his suffering but also with an unmistakable serenity. He gives the impression of a man who is at home in himself. You could say that his life has been appallingly hard, but you must also say he has lived it with faith in what he believed to be right. It appears to have won him peace of mind.

Whether you are drawn to a religious image like that of Mary, or a more secular one, like Mandela, or both of them, these are powerful metaphors on which to meditate to sustain your own search. The error you can make at this point is to distance yourself from Mary and Mandela (or any other admired figure); to give them celebrity status. No, spend some sacred time with them; commune with them; let them show you the way. They too are human, figures of flesh and blood. Taste that flesh and blood, by which I mean meditate on their experience, allow it to speak to some suffering or disquiet of your own. Can the daily choices you need to make be illuminated by their choice, their endurance, their patience, their faith?

Another sensitive companion to meditation or prayer may be found in four little books by Sister Wendy Beckett: her meditations on *Love, Peace, Joy* and *Silence*, published by Doubleday. Wendy Beckett has spent a quarter of a century as a contemplative nun. She has a profound appreciation of the layers of sacred meaning to be found in art — and the teacher's skill in communication. Her books and her idiosyncratic television series have introduced her to a wide audience. Her work includes a book of prayers for children. She is a passionate, eloquent and lucid guide to the spiritual life and the cultivation of deep inner peace to support you beneath the inevitable turmoil of life. You might choose to spend ten minutes a day reflecting on a meditation in one of her books.

In some of your quiet time, you may like to become more familiar with the great spiritual traditions. When you wonder about the point of life, it is reassuring to know that people have puzzled over this question for thousands of years and have come up with a range of satisfying answers that can be found in the scriptures of the spiritual traditions. An excellent book to take you on a journey through the sacred wisdom of the world is *Universal Wisdom,* selected and introduced by Bede Griffiths.[12] It contains sections on Hinduism, Buddhism, the Chinese tradition, Sikhism, Islam, Judaism and Christianity. His life embodied the core teachings of the great religious traditions. His genius was to honour them all and to identify the deep connections between them.

Today, when spirituality is offered as a sort of smorgasbord, it is wise to go to a work of scholarship like *Universal Wisdom* as a starting point. It may save you from wasting time on questionable gurus and spiritual fads that lack integrity. Bede Griffiths writes in accessible language and the book will give you a solid basis of understanding from which to explore further. If later you are attracted to the Buddhist way, contact a centre of Buddhist studies and ask for guidance. Others will be interested in information from more modern sources like the Transpersonal Association or the C. G. Jung Society. Expense need not be a barrier to your search. If someone is seeking to charge you a fortune for spiritual insights, be wary. The library is a magnificent free resource available to everyone. If Islam draws your interest, or Zen, look up the subject in the catalogue and see what's available. One book will lead you to another and, as your interest waxes or wanes, you will know which direction to pursue. If you would like some prayers for your reflection time, seek them out in the same way.

In the Christian tradition, you can find the Lord's Prayer in the Bible, in the Gospel of Matthew, Chapter 6; and the Psalms will offer you many poetic prayers, especially for times of trouble. Two of my favourites are Psalm 139, and Psalm 121, which was introduced to me years ago, in a Seventh Day Adventist hospital. I awoke from an anaesthetic to find a handmade card at eye level on the bedside cabinet. There was a pen sketch of rolling hills with a cross on the highest, a promise of prayers for my recovery and the first verse of Psalm 121:

I will lift up mine eyes unto the hills, from whence cometh my help. My help cometh from the Lord, which made heaven and earth.

At that time, I did not think of myself as having any particular faith. I remember feeling very much alone. The only thing that seemed solid to me was my career. Feeling that I should be capable of looking after myself, I had admitted myself to hospital unaccompanied, and had not asked anyone to visit me. I was not hostile to Christianity or to religion in general but it seemed irrelevant to me. My religion at the time was journalism! However, excellent nursing and kindness were being offered to me in a Christian hospital, and I was grateful for that. So the card was congruent with my situation and I could accept the truth of its message because it was being acted out in my life. Nothing could have been more helpful to me at that time, and I am indebted to the anonymous nurse or chaplain who cared for my neglected soul in such a thoughtful way. The card is preserved in my journal. Today, it is common to have a pastoral care team in hospitals to attend to patients' emotional and spiritual needs and this constitutes a great advance in the understanding of the complexity of ill-health, and what is needed for healing.

A popular prayer that has sustained people through the centuries is the prayer of St Francis:

Lord, make me an instrument of your peace
Where there is hatred, let me sow love.
Where there is injury, pardon.
Where there is discord, unity.
Where there is doubt, faith.
Where there is error, truth.
Where there is despair, hope.

Where there is sadness, joy.
Where there is darkness, light.

O Divine Master, grant that I may not so much seek
To be consoled, as to console.
To be understood, as to understand.
To be loved, as to love.

For it is in giving that we receive.
It is in pardoning that we are pardoned.
It is in dying that we are born to eternal life.

Reading in sacred scriptures is a new experience for me and I was glad to have some guidance in how to go about it. I was told to try to discern how the scripture speaks to my own lived experience, rather than learning it as a lesson. With that in mind, I found a connection with this passage from the Christian Gospel of Matthew, Chapter 6:

Consider the lilies of the field, how they grow; they toil not, neither do they spin: And yet I say unto you, That even Solomon in all his glory was not arrayed like one of these.

I prefer to read the King James translation of the Bible because I appreciate the poetry of it.

This passage speaks in metaphor to my own experience. First, it gives permission to stop and look at flowers and contemplate them. That is a relief, and sheer pleasure. Next, it provides a balance to my natural melancholy and is an antidote to the torment of anxiety because it gives reassurance that, like the lilies, I am acceptable, even cherished, just as I am, without the need to toil and spin, which I take to be a symbol of all my work and busyness. For you, it may have other connotations. It is part of the Sermon on the Mount which is contained in Matthew, Chapters 5 and 6, and has been much quoted for the past 2000 years. Many of its admonitions have passed into secular language. People who deny being Christian may nevertheless claim the Christian ethic as a wholesome prescription for a life lived well, just as Jews who are not 'religious' may still gain solace, wisdom and forbearance from the Jewish tradition.

It was suggested to me that it's best if you read sacred scripture slowly and ruminate on it. Remember that you are dealing with a truth expressed in poetry and parable, and it is through your imagination that you will most readily engage with it. As you read, certain words and phrases will attract your attention more than others. Say them out loud. Allow them to speak to you, give them time to soak into your own experience. Ponder what light they can shine on your life. Sacred scriptures seek to free you to an abundance of life. They need not be read as a canon of literal laws to hobble you or whip you into submission.

In his *Biographia Literaria*, Coleridge wrote of the imagination as 'the living power and prime agent of all human perception, a repetition in the finite mind of the eternal act of creation in the infinite "I am"'. To put it another way, he is suggesting that our human imagination is a reflection of the imagination of the divine mind. And that the whole creation is an act of the imagination of the divine mind.

This is a profound insight on which to reflect. It carries the suggestion that imagination has the capacity to inform the totality of our being. This habit of seeking understanding through the imagination is easier for some than others. It is my preferred way. I am frustrated by what I perceive as the incompleteness of a television interview, say, which deals solely with a person's work, never delving into the depth of their motivation, never exploring the imagination and the spirit of their project. That is always what I want to know. Short of that, I feel cheated of comprehending anything significant about the person. For me, at least, to regard the world with the eye of the imagination is to have a fuller, deeper engagement with it.

In everyday life, I am constantly drifting back and forth between the literal and the symbolic, in search of meaning. If I see a lone sculler rowing on the pewter river below my window, I wonder, for a moment, whether it's man or woman, a professional training or an amateur relaxing. This interests me briefly. Next, I imagine myself into the experience. I have been in a kayak, so I know the exhilaration of self-propelled gliding on water, the adventure of it, the possibilities of the view beyond the headland, the expansion of river and sky all around, the slap of water on the skin of the shell, the pull on arm and stomach muscles. That stage of thought reminds me that this is something I would like to do again.

When I've finished with that physical appraisal, I change to yet another lens, as it were, to see a bigger perspective: I envisage the single sculler as metaphor of the human journey. This is the most profound level where thought deepens into contemplation, offering a window into the universal.

If I saw the sculler on a lonely day, it would be a piercing sight — an outward manifestation of a wistful inner feeling. It would sharpen that feeling, adding to the sight both poignancy and the solace of recognition. In recent years, since my loneliness has been transfigured into taking more pleasure in solitude, the image of the sculler becomes part of my wide-awake, continuous grateful meditation on the nature of life. This is how it is; I am intrinsically alone, with free will to steer a course and to embark on a grand adventure. I am also in possession of a means of travel, a frail boat which is my individual self. I am supported on a great body of water, mysterious, with life teeming in its depths — like Jung's collective unconscious. True, I am uncertain of my destination but, if I look around me, I discover that I am in company with many other little craft travelling in the same direction.

Anyone interested in delving more deeply into the influence of symbol, metaphor and myth in human affairs could read the works of the American scholar of myth, Joseph Campbell, especially *The Power of Myth*, available as a book and as an audiotape and videotape series in many libraries. In an accessible and engrossing way, Campbell discusses myths as stories with universal themes about the wisdom of life. For example, there are parallel myths in many cultures which explain what marriage really is — not a love affair, he points out, but a spiritual reunion of the separated male and female counterparts that together make up the image of the incarnate God.

The Chinese image of the Tao, with the dark and light interacting — that's the relationship of yang and yin, male and female, which is what a marriage is ... Marriage is not a simple love affair, it's an ordeal, and the ordeal is the sacrifice of ego to a relationship in which two have become one.[13]

Joseph Campbell says that marriages break up because couples misunderstand the true purpose of marriage. They think that its purpose has been served once the children are raised, whereas the myths indicate that the enduring task of marriage is a spiritual one.

Joseph Campbell also writes, very engagingly, about human life as the hero's adventure, in which the basic motif is death and resurrection — the leaving of one stage to find the source of life to bring you into a richer or more mature condition. The true hero is someone who has given their life, as it were, to something bigger than themselves. Using this image, he describes childbirth as a heroic deed in which the mother undergoes a great trial to bring forth new life. He also describes birth as the first heroic adventure of every human life, that dramatic process in which a tiny, helpless water creature is pushed out into another world of light and air to set forth on a journey of many trials. Campbell's work has much to offer about the significance of suffering in the human condition. Bill Moyers, the thoughtful American broadcaster who interviewed Joseph Campbell for the celebrated television series, *The Power of Myth*, came to understand that myths reveal what all human beings have in common. He said that Campbell's work in mythology liberated *his* faith 'from the cultural prisons to which it had been sentenced'.

I imagine that is the basis of the great popularity of Joseph Campbell's work. He has released into the modern world a storehouse of universal wisdom, translated into accessible language, which contemporary people are ready to hear now that they have become deaf to traditional religious doctrines. As well, when he indicates parallels and draws connections between all the great traditions, he frees us to think universally, which is compatible with the spirit of the times.

Reading to nourish the spirit need not be concerned exclusively with sacred tradition. Any literature of quality is sustaining, from *The Wind in the Willows* by Kenneth Grahame to the stories of Flannery O'Connor or the verse of our splendid Australian poets.

To facilitate spiritual exercise, some religious traditions have the custom of making a retreat into sacred time. This is a well-defined period of withdrawal from daily routine. It is usually spent in silence, contemplation and prayer, in a place where basic needs are met while the business of the world is kept at a distance. No radio, television, newspapers, books or small talk. When all the distractions of life are removed, you are faced with your own company and the state of your soul. It can be confronting. You may be surprised by joy; and sadness, anger and fear that you have buried for years may surface. For this reason, well-established retreat houses offer spiritual direction by people trained in accompanying the spiritual journey. The retreatant may spend one hour a day with the director so that there is supervision and companionship as one cautiously opens windows to the soul that may have been closed for many years.

St Mary's Towers Retreat Centre at Douglas Park, New South Wales, is run by the Missionaries of the Sacred Heart. It's set in 500 hectares of bush and pasture land, with lovely gardens surrounding an extended historic house. This was where I first discovered the possibility of taking sacred time. The sandstone walls of the old house were glowing in late afternoon sun as I made my way up a long, wide gravel driveway bordered with purple and white agapanthus. Venerable trees shaded pathways and gardens of fragrant summer roses. After a gracious welcome, I entered the silence as though coming home to a place for which I had been yearning in all my years of striving. Some guidance was given on the practice of silence: no writing of letters or reading; moving slowly; closing doors quietly; sitting and rising thoughtfully; eating calmly; using utensils quietly; keeping your eyes to yourself in the monastic tradition of custody of the eyes. The outer silence develops an inner silence. You become more perceptive; you notice what is around you. You are invited to leave behind yesterday, and to enter today.

Sit and enjoy, enter the experiences so present to you of bushland and nature. Look at colours, study shapes, patterns, trees, birds, rocks. Listen to the sounds of birdsong, wind in the trees, sheep. Touch trees, feeling the texture of bark, rocks, soil under bare feet, the warmth of sun as you lie on the lawns. Enjoy the warmth of your bed, taking a shower, and the taste of food. Take time to savour them, to enter into them in ways not usually possible in a busy life. Smell the flowers, fresh-mown grass, untainted air.[14]

The aim of these directions is to allow a reorientation from daily preoccupations towards attentiveness to the real issues of the heart and soul. It enables a shift from small talk to a deeper silent attention, 'holding the soul in peace' before God. It is the cultivation of a trusting, expectant patience that must be the experience of the sailor who, having set his sails, can only await the arrival of the winds. Naturally, in a religious retreat house, the waiting is for God, to console, to heal, to enlighten; to reveal or to fulfil the heart's desire. However, the person for whom God has no place in the picture may still enjoy a retreat as a rest and a chance to get in touch with a deeper reality.

At Stroud, 80 kilometres north of Newcastle, New South Wales, the Anglican Franciscan Sisters of St Clare welcome visitors to their mud-brick monastery on 12 hectares of scenic bushland. You can join the Community for daily prayer and Eucharist services. This is an especially beautiful experience when the prayers are sung in plainchant. There is accommodation for five in the guesthouse, a sitting room with an open fire and a small library. For a modest donation, food is provided and guests prepare their own meals in the guesthouse kitchen.

This place has a unique story. In the 1970s, volunteers came to Stroud from all over Australia to take part in making mud-bricks to build the monastery. It became a focus for the contemplative life in action, led by Sr Angela, full of the joy of living, in remission from cancer, and driving a tractor with exuberant style in her brown seer-sucker Franciscan habit. As news of the project spread round the country, people came to camp on the site and gave their labour in long, happy exhausting days of mud-mixing and brick-making. It was a soul-satisfying project to take part in, and it produced a powerhouse of essentially Australian spirituality.

Across the continent, there is Mirrilingki Centre where Catholic and Aboriginal spirituality are combined. This is a large property in the East Kimberley, adjacent to a remote Aboriginal community 200 kilometres south of Kununurra. Mirrilingki hosts a program of retreats and workshops, as well as short residential courses. At Chittering, in Western Australia, visitors are welcomed at the Peace Be Still Guesthouse, which is non-denominational. There is a variety of Buddhist retreat centres around the country, where vegetarian food is provided, together with instruction in Buddhism and meditation. The Satyananda Ashram at Mangrove Mountain, New South Wales, invites visitors to share the daily life of the community in dormitory accommodation, with vegetarian meals, and teaches meditation, yoga and health management.

South Australia has the Christian Feminist Sophia Centre in the Adelaide suburb of Cumberland. One feature of Sophia is the annual Daily Life Retreat, a week-long exploration of a person's spiritual journey that is designed to fit in around the normal working week at home. Tabgha Farm in the New South Wales Hunter Valley is a centre for spirituality centred on creation and ecology. It offers a number of courses focusing on such issues as the new cosmology, creativity, religious experience and the music of the universe.

You will find details and costs of these places (and many more) in a book called *A Quiet Place: The Australian Retreat Directory*, which contains references to 140 oases where the spiritual life is acknowledged and nurtured.[15]

Each time I have made a retreat, the silence, the shared ritual and the spiritual direction have revealed fresh insight and nourishment for the way ahead. I have not found it a lonely experience. On the contrary, I felt a deep companionship with other retreatants in our shared endeavour, and in the need to heighten attention to the needs of others — at mealtimes, for example, where silence prevents you asking someone to pass the salt. However, others have told me that they find the silence oppressive so it may not be an experience for everyone.

Each person will bring to a retreat the insights of their own tradition.

What they may find in common is a place of rest for reflection, reverie and listening, for attention to the heart, for care of the soul; a sanctuary in which to relish the world afresh through heightened awareness of the senses; a haven in which to explore the inner landscape; a place of invitation to encounter the eternal; a place to find sustenance for the next stage of the journey.

While the modest cost of a short retreat is within most people's budget, shortage of time and the press of responsibility make it difficult for many to take time out. So it's necessary to make some space, some sacred time for spiritual nourishment in the life you live every day. It might be as simple as pausing occasionally just to rest in the moment, to reflect or pray. People of many spiritual traditions gather in meditation groups. Among Catholics, the Christian Life Community (CLC) movement has been gathering strength in recent years.[16] Groups of about ten meet once a fortnight in members' homes to reflect on daily life in the light of the Christian gospels.

Members of CLC groups say they are grateful for the regular time out, for the depth of friendships which develop through the sharing of a common spiritual purpose, and for increased awareness of their own spirituality and of the needs of the world. CLC is an international movement.

Other churches and traditions have their practices of prayer and meditation which they are pleased to discuss with inquirers. One advantage of participating in a spiritual community or group is that you're more likely to keep your commitment when other people are involved and you're expected somewhere at a certain time.

Other spiritual exercises can easily be done alone. As I live in a small home unit, my garden consists of four pots on the balcony. Each November I plant them with petunia seedlings. It is a ritual I carry on from my father. I go to the nursery, peruse all the varieties on offer, and choose the same as last year. I buy plenty and I plant them close together. I water them and I contemplate them as they bunch up into a mass of green. Very soon, the first flower opens into purple velvet or frilly white or scarlet. And so the profusion of colour begins for another summer. They grow thick and high, and they spill out over the rims of the pots. When I water them in the evening, they answer with perfume. I dote on them and they are extravagant in their response. In these four flower pots I can worship all creation. They are my harbingers of Christmas. They see the New Year in with me. They are gentle and generous and, as I gaze at them and tend them, they call me directly into silent sacred time.

For your Journal

* How could you allow more time and opportunity for the nurturing of your spirituality?

* What are you reading at present to nourish your spirit?

* What else do you need to do to allow fullness and balance in your life?

* To whom in your life could you listen more carefully?

Endnotes

1 T. S. Eliot, 'Ash Wednesday', *Collected Poems 1909–1962*, Faber and Faber, 1974.
2 Michael Leunig, 'The Prayer Tree', *Common Prayer Collection*, Collins Dove, 1993.
3 Thomas Moore, *Care of the Soul*, Harper Perennial, 1992.
4 John Ellison, Tape 47, *The Search for Meaning Catalogue*, ABC Radio Tapes.
5 Max Dupain, Tape 183, *The Search for Meaning Catalogue*, ABC Radio Tapes.
6 Dr Rupert Sheldrake in *The Search for Meaning: Conversations with Caroline Jones*, ABC/ Collins Dove, 1992. Also Tape 137 in *The Search for Meaning Catalogue*, ABC Radio Tapes.
7 Conflict Resolution Network, P.O. Box 1016, Chatswood, NSW 2057. Tel: (02) 9419 8500.
8 David Reynolds talks with Stephanie Dowrick on an audiotape called *Living with Change*, ABC Radio Tapes.
9 Patti Miller, *The Last One Who Remembers*, Allen & Unwin, 1997.
10 Patti Miller, Tape 235, *The Search for Meaning Catalogue*, ABC Radio Tapes.
11 *The Last One Who Remembers*.
12 Bede Griffiths, *Universal Wisdom*, Fount, 1994.
13 Joseph Campbell with Bill Moyers, *The Power of Myth*, Doubleday, 1988.
14 Notes in leaflet for St Mary's Towers Retreat Centre, Douglas Park, NSW 2569.
15 *A Quiet Place: The Australian Retreat Directory*, Catholic Communications, P.O. Box 869, Crows Nest, NSW 2065.
16 Christian Life Community National Office, Saint Ignatius College, Riverview, NSW 2066.

7 AUSTRALIAN MYSTICS

... you're actually inside the surfboard ...
you're inside the landscape around you and the ocean
as it's surging, you get totally inside the
moment and it's so intense that time disappears,
you disappear ...

Nick Carroll, surfing champion and writer[1]

WHEN AT LAST it rained, I stood on the front balcony looking down at the glistening, wet canopy of the trees. It was heaving slowly, bending to the wind in deep, resilient swells. Wave upon wave of gleaming leaves beneath me and around me. Saturated mauve clusters of jacaranda hung in tatters among the green. The frangipani was shooting yellow-green spears from its archaic, seemingly dead branches, in a shocking display of resurrection. Long tendrils of wisteria whipped in the wind without snapping. Rain pelted on the sea of leaves.

And suddenly I stopped thinking about anything and became engrossed in the rain and the leaves. The soft staccato sound and the fresh, damp smell and the cold splash on my skin were enough, were everything. My awareness flowed out of me and into everything around me and back again like the figure-of-eight symbol of eternity. All anxiety ceased, held back somewhere in the net of time from which I had been cut loose. A veil had lifted between my everyday reality and some other dimension without boundaries.

I don't know how long I stayed there and I don't know why I ever returned, for there was nothing half as alluring to recall me from that luminous, oceanic state. Inside me, some compliant tethered creature slipped the harness, tossed its head and expanded, breathing deeply, drawing in unaccustomed great draughts of air, in and out, in and out. But it was as though the air was breathing me. Exaltation swelled, and it was a victory requiring no vanquished. The strain of conscious endeavour melted away, unnecessary now, for there was no separate self to try, nothing against which to struggle and nothing lacking. The tight tunnel of self-discipline opened out into spaciousness. Something inside stretched and yawned, relaxed and floated weightless in dense supporting airs. There was no obligation but to be aware without stress and to bathe in a tranquil reservoir of wellbeing.

My entry into this state and my exit from it were not chosen. When the experience was ready, it returned me to my customary reality in time and space. Everything was normal but everything was vivid. I came inside and put some water on to boil. I folded a willow-pattern tea towel onto the wooden inlaid tray that my father made during the long hours of tropical monsoon in wartime. I poured milk into a treasured pottery jug made by my mother. It is glazed cream and green and into its base she has etched her name and the date 1937. Often I struggle to bring an image of her to mind, trying too hard, but today, with that cool, solid, little jug between my palms, I can recall the squared shape of her hands and feel the firm strength of her fingers. It's a relief to remember something of flesh and bone. It happens too when I am sewing or making pastry and it is not going well. I remember the determination with which she set her jaw and coaxed the treadle machine foot around the awkward curve of an armhole, or patched the cracks in a pie crust.

The milk jug cover is crocheted cotton with glass beads around the edge. It clinks against the pottery. I poured hot water onto the tea in the china teapot. The fragrance rose into my head. The tea-cosy is one that I knitted years ago from scraps of wool left over from jumpers. On top it has a bunch of woollen flowers which Granny Pountney taught me to crochet when I was eight in Murrurundi. I carried the tray from the kitchen into the living room, translucent with green light in the stormy afternoon, and poured a cup of tea into the willow-pattern cup. The ritual followed the same form as ever, lending a sacred quality to a homely activity, and creating space for a few minutes' care of the soul.

As I drank my tea, I reflected on the numinous experience of the balcony in the rain. I savoured it and wondered at it and thought perhaps that's what it's like to die. Suddenly a curtain is drawn back, you stop being an entity and, instead, you become everything, in some ecstatic unity. In that case, could life and death really be so different from each other? Was death just a brilliantly vivid, oceanic elaboration of life? I wondered too if it was anything like poet Kevin Gilbert's description of Aboriginal consciousness, when he told me that 'whatever the substance around me, that creation flows to me, through me, within me; that the universe is part of me as I am a part of it'. He had also said, 'Once you know that, there is no fear ... there is complete belonging, and life and death is just a constant flowing ... a continual renewing.' Had I stumbled, one rainy afternoon, on something many Aboriginal people have always known as their daily reality?

This was familiar territory to the American philosopher and experimental psychologist William James. He wrote, in *The Varieties of Religious Experience*, that

> our normal waking consciousness, rational consciousness as we call it, is but one special type of consciousness, whilst all about it, parted from it by the filmiest of screens, there lie potential forms of consciousness entirely different.[2]

And he thought that no account of the universe in its totality could be final which left these other forms of consciousness quite disregarded. He also wrote that, while the mystical feeling of enlargement, union and emancipation had no specific intellectual content, and should not be invoked in favour of any particular belief, it may provide one of the truest of insights into the meaning of life.

Wondering what Australians would have to say about such experience in the 1990s, we invited contributions by telephone to *The Search for Meaning* program on the off-peak open line. There were many fascinating responses from all round the country. We edited some of them into an edition of the program which became a finalist in the religious category of the 1993 New York Festival's International Radio Competition.[3] The question I put to listeners was this: 'Have you had any moments in your life when everything changed and was never the same again; a moment when you learned something very deep, basic, that you had never understood before — something that is difficult to put into words perhaps?'

Here's an edited version of some of the responses:

Linda called in from a little coastal village:

It was only a fairly momentary experience. I was living in a house overlooking the sea on the cliff edge and I would go down early every morning for my swim. It was a beautiful day, I had a very nice swim and I was walking back up along the headland right on the sea's edge and I just had this experience of blending into everything, I guess. I was totally relaxed and I just felt that I'd become everything. I felt that I was part of the ocean, I was part of the trees, although I was moving, I must have been walking, although I wasn't conscious of still walking. I felt very still and then I was at the front gate and I came out of it and I went inside and realised that it must have been some fairly unusual experience.

It's the only thing that's really kept me going through some rather difficult times. I suffer from a chronic illness which I'm now recovering from, and I'm absolutely positive it's because I feel that I'm now able to connect with this energy that I'm getting well through it. And it certainly gives me optimism that I will be well. But even if one isn't well, and one dies or whatever, that there is more to it than that, that this is just a stage.

Richard had been prompted to telephone the program by Brisbane Archbishop Peter Hollingworth, a family friend. Richard recounted a powerful experience he had had while on holiday with two friends in Papua New Guinea:

For some unaccountable reason I had been quite depressed for the first week or so of the holiday. We were travelling on a rusty, old boat with two or three hundred nationals and there was only a handful of

Australians, on the way from Rabaul to Lae back on the mainland. It took over 24 hours, the journey. And there came a moment, during that trip, late one afternoon, when I was standing at the back of the boat, and I was literally surrounded, we were packed in like sardines, and I was overwhelmed by this feeling of — it's very hard to say anything concrete — but a feeling of oneness and of essential interrelatedness even though I was only one of a handful of whites. And colour meant almost nothing. It was as if the people I was with were, sort of, my people. It sounds very strange but it was such an overwhelming feeling and such a joyful feeling that I was sort of reduced to weeping and it reminded me a little bit of the man who weeps in one of Les Murray's famous poems, *An Absolutely Ordinary Rainbow.*[4]

But there was also a feeling that humanity was very close to achieving this sense of oneness that would not just be a fleeting thing that so many people have talked to you about, over the years, but a kind of permanent thing for all of humanity.

Andrew rang next to tell this story:

I was visiting Mt Emu with a friend who had a farm nearby ... we ascended to the top of the mountain and had our lunch up there. He decided he'd go down the way we came, and I chose the south-western side of the mountain which is a sheer granite bluff. I started to shimmy down and the further I got the steeper the mountain got and the more lichen was growing on that side, being the cool side, and the wetter it was.

And just as I realised that I'd made a mistake, I started to slip and began to slide down the side of the mountain with my feet in front of me and my hands behind, scrabbling to try and get a hold of the rock. I accelerated faster and faster and eventually saw coming up in front of me on my right-hand side a sheer drop to shattered rocks hundreds of feet below; on the left-hand side a drop of about 50 feet to the grassy paddock; and right in front of me a small promontory of rock with a little bit of soil in between it and the mountain, and a tiny little bush growing there ... time slowed down tremendously and I was able to collect my thoughts and try to steer towards this one ray of hope, and I eventually dropped the last 20 feet or so into the arms of that little bush and lay there on the ground next to it for some time, quite winded and stunned.

I was so grateful to this little bush and told it I was sorry that I had broken some of its branches. I was overcome with emotion and I couldn't express what had happened, to my friend, when I caught up with him ... that feeling that overcame me as I lay there looking up at where I'd slid down with not a scratch on me next to that dear little bush ... I had for a time certainly become part of the mountain ... and the thing that had saved me was also part of the mountain because it was growing on a tiny patch of soil that had eroded over many years off the mountain itself. So in a way the mountain had participated with me in an act and then saved me from the potential disaster of that act. So, yes, it was overwhelming gratitude ... this absolute self-awareness but there's no distinction made between yourself and whatever else is around you. And that's a very strong feeling.

Susan, aged 18, rang from Perth to describe an experience that happened in her final year at school:

I was suicidal and I was really depressed about my emerging into an adult world that to me seemed so pervasive with business and it was just horrible and I was really scared. I thought I'd really be a cog in a machine and everything seemed so final. I remember at one point, at school, I was talking to the psychologist and I was telling her about my fear of concrete and cold, and the feeling that I was becoming more distanced from something very natural in me and essential to my being. My experiences were becoming more distorted and my meanings so ultimately hopeless and the psychologist was listening to me and then she sent me to the sickroom. And it really made me sick. It seemed to represent all that could hurt me. It was cold and concrete, white and sterile. The windows were barred, there was paper on the beds, there was no warmth, no life, no opportunity for growth.

After a time, and I was quite distressed at this point, a teacher of mine came to see me. I was probably afraid of the loss of this teacher because she'd given me so much, guided me. She was really full of life and I was scared of the loss of someone so special. She came into the room and held me and she brought life and love and comfort to me and though those moments were tremendously painful they filled me with courage and hope that there is purpose in this struggle because that moment really stands out as a moment of deep realisation and change, that there is a divine connection between life forces and a deep need for communication, for understanding and most of all for compassion.

Susan went on to say that this had been a crucial turning point with an enduring effect on her confidence and her attitude to suffering. She had come to realise that suffering may be survived through love because, with love, there is always healing. She had also identified a living image of hope in those tiny green plants which insinuate themselves in a most unlikely way through cracks in concrete.

By this time, we were fascinated by the response from all round Australia, and still the calls kept coming, this one from David:

In 1970 I was on my way to Australia. I was travelling through India and I stopped off in a place on the east coast. I got up just before dawn to go for a swim in the ocean. In India people throw flowers on the water at dawn, as a form of ceremony. I saw women in saris throwing flowers on the water. I walked past them into the water and they probably thought I was crazy because most people don't go swimming in India. I swam out towards the sunrise. As I swam, on the horizon the sun was starting to rise, and just at that moment it was as if all time disappeared. I wasn't swimming. I was just in the eternal at one moment, and I had this tremendous feeling, which is very hard to express, a feeling of total at-one-ment with everything, that I was a part of everything, and as if a voice said to me, 'All is well, all will be well, everything is going according to plan and everything is right.'

And for that brief timeless moment, I felt completely at peace, at one with everything. And the moment passed, I swam back to the shore and I've always remembered. Of course, now it's a memory of that feeling. The memory is never quite the same as the actual moment, but from then onwards I knew for certain that there was some divine creative energy in the universe — God, if you like. I know I'd call it God. I suppose from then I started to analyse it and intellectualise it and try and understand it but the experience never quite left me.

Next, Alison called from Bundaberg in Queensland:

Caroline, I'm going to describe an experience I had on Lizard Island about 17 years ago when I was working there as a marine biologist. It happened at a time when I was very depressed and alone, because my partner and I were in the process of separating. I lay down to rest and my mind drifted to the little things I wanted to do for people that I loved. This imperceptibly fused into a greater and greater flood of love and expanded to fill my whole being. If I read from my diary it might put it in words more clearly:

'It felt so pure, like a radiant white fire, like the very essence of the universe and like what might be left after death removed all other conflicting awareness. It was a sense of love that was coming both from within me and from outside of me and for that time I just felt as if I was in the heart of God.'

And I'm not a religious person but it was a very intense spiritual experience. I really felt that every man and every creature was my friend at that time and it's only when we cease to love that we create a sort of barrier around ourselves; and it was a tremendous sense of belonging.

Alison said that her experience had made a difference to her professional, as well as to her personal life. She explained it like this:

I believe that science would do well to pay attention to some of our more spiritual values. I became a little disillusioned because people were starting to use computer models to plan the Great Barrier Reef Marine Park, and I felt that if you approached it in a different way — with a sense of respect and love for the environment you were working with — you'd probably make better judgments. I'm not saying that scientific method should be discarded at all but I believe that if we were able to bring some of these other values into making decisions, that would be a really good thing also.

Judy called in from Melbourne to tell her story.

My story and my experience of the infinite began when I was about 13. I lived in Communist Hungary and I was a really convinced atheist. I began to study physics and found it fascinating. I used to ask the teacher all sorts of questions after class; when we were studying gravitation, it led me to the ultimate question of why, and I asked her how come these laws are the way they are, and what is it that makes gravity and holds the whole universe together. And she said to me that some people call it nature, some people call it God.

Having said that, she risked being put into jail. But it opened a door for me and it began a journey which has lasted for 40 years. It was a wonderful revelation to me to see things falling into place with a new meaning because I had been convinced that religion was really only the opiate of the people and a crutch for weaklings, and I was very proud of the fact that I was an atheist and could stand on my own.

But after being told that some people call it God, I began to search — is there such a thing as God? — and that led me within a year to becoming a Catholic. I was a nun, a Dominican sister, for five years and during that time my faith deepened very much. When I came out I completed my degree in physics and married and had three children and they are all grown up. And now I've come full circle and I'm painting. I'm working as a full-time artist and I'm painting about physics and religion.

And the greatest thing is that in my reading of modern physics I find this unity between understanding the universe in a scientific and in an intuitive and religious way. We can't just analyse and understand things by cutting them up and trying to put them together again, because the whole is a lot more than its parts.

The call that came from Jan was quite brief but it, too, told of a life-changing experience:

This is Jan speaking. I'm from Sydney and I want to tell you about an incident that happened to me at a time when I was very, very depressed and feeling almost full of despair, not knowing how to keep on going, and just willing myself to put one foot after the other. You know, 'Now I pick up the spoon, now I get the lunch, now I get out the plates, now I set the table . . .'. It was like crawling, really, through the day. I had just washed some cherries to put on the table and I picked one up and I put it in my mouth, to eat it. But the cherry exploded in my mouth is all I can say; and it was like an explosion all through my body; it was as if the juice went all through my whole body and out through my hands.

I asked Jan if it was a frightening feeling but she said that, on the contrary, it was absolutely ecstatic.

It was just so blissful. I suppose it was so extraordinary because I didn't really ever feel very much in my body and so this was just so amazing and wondrous and sacred and the whole day just turned completely. My whole life changed after that.

Another Sydney call came from Shirley:

About eight years ago I had dropped my daughter at her gymnastics class and I had some time to wait to collect her and it was about dusk and I was at the edge of the water in Cronulla. There was a beautiful sunset. I walked out along the pier and I was just standing quietly watching the sunset. Quite suddenly I became aware that everything had changed. It was almost as if there was a split in the universe and I had slipped into it. It was just a most peculiar feeling. Until that time I'd always had a dream of visiting Paris and I'd always wanted to acquire wisdom. They were my dreams in life. And at that point in time I realised that I was Paris and I already had the wisdom of the ages. It was most peculiar. And I don't know how long it lasted, maybe three seconds, maybe 0.3 of a second, I don't know. But as soon as I tried to grasp it, it disappeared. But it was a feeling of total connection with everything, I knew that I was part of everything and there was nothing on earth to worry about because I was a part of everything.

Afterwards I was walking back along the sand and I found a key with a plastic child's toy and for me it became the symbol of having stumbled upon the key to everything. And then I had a swing on the swings in the park and I thought I was totally free. And that was the end of it. But it made me more free to take chances. It made me realise that God wasn't something up there, up in heaven, that God was everywhere and that I was a part of God.

The mention of God seemed to come rather abruptly into Shirley's description, and I asked her why she brought God into it. She explained:

147

Because until that point I'd been searching for a way back to my spiritual source and I hadn't found it. I'd been brought up a Catholic and I hadn't found anything in my religious upbringing to satisfy that spiritual seeking of wholeness. And suddenly I realised that was the answer, that's where God lies for me.

Loma telephoned from Tasmania. From her voice, I judged that she was probably the oldest of the callers so far. Her story was of a slightly different order to the others since she was describing a decision, rather than an involuntary experience. I included it because it was a decision to embrace a mystery and because she said it gave her a feeling of homecoming:

Yes, not terribly exciting, I suppose. It's just when I decided to embrace Christianity and embrace Christ as my personal saviour. Since then my life has changed. I'm afraid I've not always been perfectly happy or perfectly holy, but my Lord is always there, He's always there to come back to, to forgive. Oh, yes, it's much happier. I've heard people say God is only a crutch, but my word, what a wonderful crutch, what a wonderful support He is. God is my father and I feel that I can trust Him, now that I'm getting on in years, we have to face passing over sooner or later. And I have no fear or doubt that God will look after me, that I will have a friend when I cross the river, when I come to cross the bar.

I think Loma was referring to Tennyson's poem, Crossing the Bar, *set to music for a hymn by Joseph Barnby, of which the last two lines are:*

I hope to see my Pilot face to face
When I have crossed the bar.

And we concluded the program with this memory from Michael:

But I do remember one winter, sitting out on the front lawn at night and we had this thing we used to call a tulip tree. It has since been dug out and when I went back I was so — it was like they had dug my soul out, with this tree. So I'm with the Greenies in that. But we had this beautiful tree which had nothing on it, no branches, but it was kind of reaching up to the heavens. And for some reason, that evening, after doing a lot of study and reading and a whole lot of things, I must say at that moment I knew that I belonged to the tree, and I belonged to the sky, and I belonged to the earth and I think I've never lost that feeling.

There were more telephone responses than we could accommodate in one program and listeners also wrote to me with their experiences. Some referred to them as being 'peak' experiences. There were other occasions in *The Search for Meaning* programs when people recounted powerful incidents of a similar nature. The great Methodist churchman and preacher, the Reverend Dr Sir Alan Walker told me this story:

I had been appointed by the Methodist Church of Australasia to lead the Mission to the Nation, the largest evangelical undertaking any church in this country has ever attempted and it was to be launched in Melbourne on 6 April. I went away for a week to get ready. On the evening before I flew to Melbourne I was overwhelmed with the responsibility. Who was I to be the spokesman of the Methodist Church for three years? I went up after the evening meal and lay on the warm grass under two big gum trees and tried to pray. And suddenly I was transported in thought away to Jerusalem and I could see Jesus talking to Nicodemus, trying to explain the mystery of the Holy Spirit and how he could bring new life to people. Nicodemus couldn't understand so Jesus took him over to the window, and there was an olive tree outside and the wind was blowing it and Jesus said, 'Look, Nicodemus, you can't see where the wind comes from and where it's going, but it's there — look at the sign of it.'

And then I was back in Australia, and by that time the wind had sprung up in the gum trees above me and I could hear the rustle of the leaves and I suddenly heard a phrase come into my mind, 'the wind is in the gum trees'.

The wind was in the gum trees! The Holy Spirit's going to blow across Australia! And I had an experience of the Holy Spirit that absolutely transformed my ministry. I think I was of some use to God before that but afterwards there was so much more happening; and so my life can be divided into two parts and the line runs through that experience in 5 April 1953.[5]

And the surfing champion and writer, Nick Carroll, gave us this magnificent description of what happens in the most exalted moments of riding a surfboard in the ocean:

> You get moments where your whole body, soul and mind are just concentrated on doing something in the surf. You have to just get up, trust your instinct and fall into the wave. It's during seconds like that that you seem to just totally disappear, you as a being don't really exist at that moment. It's hard to express, you throw yourself into the moment so heavily that you're actually inside the surfboard and what it's doing. You're inside the landscape around you and the ocean as it's surging. You get totally inside the moment and it's so intense that time disappears, everything disappears. You disappear, you're not thinking of you, Nick Carroll, or whoever. It's way beyond that.
>
> If you're going to make a very big wave, you have to be totally unified with everything that's happening. You have to know absolutely everything about what the board's doing, what's happening with the wave, where the water is on the wave, how fast the water's moving up the face of the wave, what's happening with the wind, where there might be a couple of people in the way. And I don't think you can know about all that if you choose to take the form of thinking that we do in our everyday lives. Your brain just can't handle it, it has to throw stuff away to fit it all in. And so it throws away the useless stuff, the ego, the 'I'm Nick Carroll, I've got fears, worries, doubts etc' — all very useless stuff. Maybe in the moment of having to know everything all at once you burst through the barriers of trying to put things in order. [6]

I found all these stories moving and fascinating. They were remarkable and yet they were told so simply it did not occur to me to doubt their authenticity. People used ordinary words to describe something out of the ordinary. Their descriptions were calmly spoken. There was no coercion in them, no desperation to persuade. The volume of calls hints that such incidents may be common in human experience.

I was interested that no one conjectured what might have caused these events, but several recalled they had been depressed at the time.

And none of them gave their experience a negative connotation. This surprised me because some of the descriptions could apply just as well to a nervous breakdown: 'Suddenly, I wasn't there any longer' could be very alarming, you would think. But, no, all were grateful. It is of peace that they spoke, purity, radiance, light, love and a tremendous sense of belonging. Becoming part of everything else was interpreted not as a loss of oneself but as an expansion of self, and a connection into a unified state of energy and wellbeing. You will also notice that several people, but not all, made an unsolicited link between their oceanic experience and some divine creative energy or God. I noticed another curious conclusion. More than one of the participants said that, because they were part of everything, there was nothing to worry about.

The temporary disappearance of time seemed to give people the idea that they had somehow slipped through into 'the eternal', as though that idea had some practical reality for them. And two spoke of a sudden access to all knowledge. Another common feature of these remarkable stories is that they have had a continuing effect in people's lives; the memory is easily recalled to give inspiration or help during difficult times.

They are described as life-altering events. It seems that, once you have had such an interlude, you think differently about the nature of your existence. There has been a reorientation of your perspective. If you are connected into the spirit of all that is, then you are endowed with increased awareness and compassion for all that is. Your sense of solitary individualism has been exposed as an illusion. As a result, your isolation is relieved and loneliness seems to dissolve.

William James was very interested in these occurrences and in his classic work, *The Varieties of Religious Experience*, he wrote:

> Looking back on my own experiences, they all converge towards a kind of insight to which I cannot help ascribing some metaphysical significance. The keynote of it is invariably a reconciliation. It is as if the opposites of the world, whose contradictoriness and conflict make all our difficulties and troubles, were melted into unity.[7]

Apart from his own experiences, most of the cases he collected took place outdoors. He wrote that 'certain aspects of nature seem to have a peculiar power of awakening such mystical moods'. He came to the conclusion that mystical experiences have four characteristics. First, they are ineffable, that is, they almost defy description. Secondly, they have a noetic quality, that is to say they seem to be a state of knowledge — as he put it, a state of 'insight into depths of truth unplumbed by the discursive intellect'. He considered them to be revelations of insight or truth full of significance and carrying with them an enduring sense of authority. He felt their third characteristic was that they are transient, lasting from a few seconds to half an hour or, at most, an hour. And finally, they are characterised by passivity, that is, 'the mystic feels as if his own will were in abeyance, and indeed sometimes as if he were grasped and held by a superior power'.

Not everyone who has had a peak or oceanic or mystical experience brings God into the picture. On the other hand, mysticism has been cultivated methodically as an element of the religious life. In India, training in mystical insight has long been carried out under the practice of yoga, whose original intention was the union of the individual with the divine. In the Muslim world, the Sufi sect and various dervish bodies possess the mystical tradition, the ultimate aim of Sufism being total absorption in God. There is a strong tradition of mysticism in the Christian church; some of the most magnificent descriptions of mystical union with God may be found in the writings of Dame Julian of Norwich, Meister Eckhart, St John of the Cross, St Teresa of Avila and St Ignatius of Loyola.

William James considered that the great achievement of mystical experience was the overcoming of all the usual barriers between the individual and the Absolute.

In mystic states we both become one with the Absolute and we become aware of our oneness. This is the everlasting and triumphant mystical tradition, hardly altered by differences of clime or creed. In Hinduism, in Neoplatonism, in Sufism, in Christian mysticism, in Whitmanism, we find the same recurring note, so that there is about mystical utterances an eternal unanimity . . . [8]

Can we go so far as to take the merging of ego into unity as a metaphor of death? If so, and if it is so blissful, should fear of death perhaps be replaced by serene anticipation or even excitement? Is it possible that these moments of mystical awareness, although so brief and so occasional, reveal the nature of life itself? In their glimpse of 'all that is', are they pinpricks of light from an eternal dimension to remind us of the grandeur and proximity of its existence? Could it be that, in such moments, outside time, or somehow coexistent with time, we remember what reality is and what life is and what God is and what consciousness is, and the way in which we are part of it all? For a fleeting moment, do we remember and re-enter that ecstatic state that is always there — and then forget again? It is tempting to think so.

Whether or not you have had experiences similar to those described, you may like to reflect on this phenomenon to see what it suggests to you about the nature of existence.

Endnotes

1 Nick Carroll in *The Search for Meaning Collection*, Caroline Jones, ABC/Harper Collins, 1995. Also Tape 10 in *The Search for Meaning Catalogue*, ABC Radio Tapes.
2 William James, *The Varieties of Religious Experience*, The Modern Library, 1902.
3 Audio-cassette entitled 'Numinous' in *The Search for Meaning Catalogue*, ABC Radio Tapes.
4 *Anthology of Australian Religious Poetry* selected by Les Murray, Collins Dove, 1986.
5 Reverend Dr Sir Alan Walker, Tape 141, *The Search for Meaning Catalogue*, ABC Radio Tapes.
6 Nick Carroll in *The Search for Meaning Collection*. Also Tape 10 in *The Search for Meaning Catalogue*.
7 *The Varieties of Religious Experience*.
8 *The Varieties of Religious Experience*.

8 BUT WHO AM I?

Ask, and it will be given to you;
search, and you will find;
knock, and the door will be opened to you.

Matthew 7:7

You cannot build a nation
until there is a national spirit.

Kevin Gilbert[1]

IN THE LATE 1970s, when Gerald Stone was putting together his first team for *Sixty Minutes*, he asked me to come on board as one of the original reporters. I had worked well with him when he was a producer at ABC TV on *This Day Tonight*, and I would have been happy to work with him again. However, at that time I was fully extended at the ABC with daily live morning radio (1977–81) as well as presenting *Four Corners* (1972–81), and I decided to stay put. I missed out on a big adventure, a glamorous salary and the well-known Channel 9 care for its presenters. But at that time it seemed idealistic to stay where I was, and certainly I was happy there.

Had I known how carelessly the ABC would shed me, a few years on, perhaps I would have gone to *Sixty Minutes*. But then I may never have done *The Search for Meaning* programs. As my father says, every decision brings pluses and minuses and I am quite philosophical about my choice. The interesting point is that, for better or worse, my decision to say no opened a door for Jana Wendt at *Sixty Minutes*. And I was excited to see how beautifully she walked through it, into her own impressive career, for one of my hopes was to lay a foundation, by example, for more women to be invited into current affairs reporting.

It was interesting to be in a position to turn down such high-profile work as the *Sixty Minutes* offer, and it may sound odd when I tell you that my own sense of identity has been elusive for most of my life. When I say that, I am usually met with disbelief. People think that to become well known in public guarantees a high degree of self-confidence. Not in my experience.

I am recognised in public life only because I happened to work in the media, and media workers are often given inappropriate prominence, out of all proportion to their wisdom or contribution to society. I tried to get into journalism when I first left school but, in spite of trooping round all the newspapers, I was unable to obtain a cadetship. It was not until several years later that I was recommended to the ABC in Canberra by a thoughtful friend, Ines Truse, who was a presentation announcer on television, newly established in the national capital. At the time I was working as a receptionist at the Hotel Acton for one of the famous Commonwealth Hostels managers, Mr Jim Neilson. When I got my chance at the ABC, Mr Neilson was generous enough to let me alter my working hours so that I could take advantage of the part-time opening at the ABC that would develop into my new career. How many people help us on our way!

I spent several years in training at the ABC in Canberra on both radio and television. From the late sixties, Australians who watched television and listened to radio came to know me as a young current affairs reporter. I worked on *This Day Tonight* from the beginning, at first in Canberra, then in Sydney. After five years with *TDT*, I presented *Four Corners* for nine years. My job was to question public officials, to report on events at home and internationally, to interview representatives of various interest groups, and to draw out people's stories. When I was given the chance to do this work, I was amazed by my good fortune and threw myself into it with full concentration.

I watched and listened and learned from the people I worked with. We had good researchers to do the groundwork.

Although the reporters take the limelight on television, it is the camera crews who collect the pictures and sounds that bring reporting to life. They are underacknowledged. I worked with men (exclusively in the 1960s, 70s and 80s) who were brilliant in their craft, their professionalism and their general capability. They were also patient and generous, and made many of us reporters look much better than we merited. I am grateful to all those with whom I worked and travelled and brought back reports for *This Day Tonight* and *Four Corners*. Equally skilful film editors and producers completed the creative task.

On overseas assignments, I was given the nickname 'Matron' for checking to see whether my crew had taken their daily malaria tablets and assorted compulsory medications. These epithets last for ever. In 1997 we had a *TDT* reunion on Peter Luck's *Where are They Now?* show on Channel 7, and Mike Carlton greeted me immediately as 'Matron'. Thinking back over all our adventures, the nickname could have been much worse.

When out on assignments, we all basked in Bill Peach's reflected glory. People would peer over our shoulders looking for Bill, and were often quite disappointed that he hadn't come in person to film them. You couldn't blame them. Bill had complete identification with *This Day Tonight*. As far as viewers were concerned, he was the program.

Many things happened to keep our feet on the ground. Once, when I was out filming in the city, a passer-by approached me deferentially and seemed almost overawed to meet me. After a few minutes when I had to get back to filming, he said, 'Well, it's been so wonderful to meet you. You can't imagine how excited my wife and daughters will be tonight when I go home and tell them that I have actually met Anne Deveson in person.'

I dined out on this story. I was proud to be confused with Anne Deveson, whom I admired, but the incident warned me that media celebrity may be very insubstantial. The job gave me an education and a vantage point from which to learn how the world worked. At all times I knew it was a privilege and a responsibility. I had several mentors, all men, for they were the ones in charge of everything; and much encouragement, especially from my father, who is a keen observer of life, and my mother, who had reported for her father's country newspaper, *The Quirindi Advocate*. The night I won a Logie award for special contribution to television journalism in 1971, I was accompanied to the ceremony by Peg McGrath, secretary to the *This Day Tonight* unit. I could not have been in better company. Apart from being great fun, she had offered me friendship and hospitality when I was new in Sydney. Her husband, Jim, a meat inspector, was a fine cook and they kept a generous 'open house'. I could never repay their kindness but I enshrine it here in my story.

I was a rare bird, in those days. Not until later, when there were more women reporters involved, did I encounter the readiness of some insecure men to use the killer instinct against what they saw as the unwelcome competition of women in the media. I was happily engrossed in my work, and I rarely stopped to think about anything except the next story. It was a peculiarly extroverted job in which one was trained in the observation of facts and warned to give no credence to feelings. My increasing public recognition gave me a lively sense that I was part of something exciting, but I had little time or taste for introspection.

For many years, it was a great adventure. Then, one day, without warning, the excitement turned into a precarious high-wire act without a net. Suddenly, everything seemed to depend on my capacity to keep performing. It was as though some vital source of energy had dried up, and I was stranded in peril. I confided in no one. Somehow I kept the act going but any sense of my own true identity was disturbingly hazy. Have you ever had the feeling of knowing what you were doing without being sure who was doing it? Perhaps I was just exhausted. When you're young, you don't always recognise fatigue. You burn the candle at both ends in the illusion that you're invincible.

This was an experience of disorientation. When I looked in the mirror I would see the reflection of Caroline and wonder exactly who she was. She looked sad and rather lost. A lot of other people seemed to know who Caroline Jones was, and so did I, from reading magazine articles, but I was quite uncertain just who was inside the image. It was a feeling of haziness rather than panic. I had no way of knowing if it was abnormal. Perhaps everyone felt like this and just put on an act of identity, as I did.

Certainly, I had been working very hard, with *Four Corners* on television and, simultaneously, the daily live morning radio program, *City Extra.* With such a heavy commitment, the concentration was intense. The radio program was not just chat: we were striving to maintain a high standard of current affairs reporting. I could do up to ten interviews in a morning. It got to the stage where I would turn up the volume of music in my headphones to top level in order to shock myself out of one interview into readiness for the next.

Eventually, the whispered undertone 'but who am I?' broke through all the questions I was asking other people. I didn't like to admit it to anyone else, yet it became so demanding of attention that I went in search of answers. But where to search? I had taken journalism as my creed and it had revealed to me the fallibility of every institution in our society. I had no religious affiliation and little sense of spirituality. Now I was being confronted with the lack of attention to any inner life. I hardly knew where to turn. I pored over books on psychology, Buddhism and other spiritual traditions. I went to New Age personal development courses. In search of a deeper sense of purpose, I pestered charitable institutions to work as a volunteer alongside their professionals. Suddenly exhausted by my own work, still I had energy for this searching because I was in urgent need of answers. I had fallen into an abyss. Whoever I was felt, by turns, lost, depressed, angry and sad.

No solution came quickly, yet every effort I made yielded some crack of light and opened the way to another avenue of possibility.  Over several hard, questing years I came upon a crucial insight that I had never before considered. It was the possibility of forgiveness, and it would prove to be a threshold to deeper discovery of my identity, and of peace of mind.

For 40 years I had thought that life required you to carry the weight of your experience with you; that, as your emotional baggage grew heavier, you simply had to bear its load, with occasional forays into oblivion for temporary relief. I had an image of life as a tough race to run, a struggle in which the fittest survived and others succumbed, and I felt this was a matter of chance, no matter how hard you tried. As for the future, I had no sense of it at all. Every ounce of energy was consumed staying alive in the present. For this cul-de-sac of understanding, I suppose I can thank Charles Darwin, or perhaps those who decided that his brutal theory of natural selection could be applied to human society. It had never occurred to me that experience could be redeemed, guilt dissolved, spiritual pain alleviated, that broken relationships and even memories could be healed, that personal wretchedness could be transformed into peaceful self-acceptance.

The beginnings of this understanding came to me first in personal counselling with a clinical psychologist. I went to a counsellor very reluctantly, appalled that I could not solve my own problems. The symptoms I presented to the counsellor were severe loneliness, exhaustion, a sense of fragmentation, and fear of being unable to continue the work on which my very survival seemed to depend. The counsellor asked me about my life and listened to my story.

For several weeks, we met for one hour a week. She identified grief as my underlying problem — the grief of several losses that had never been dealt with, buried sadness and anger that had not been expressed. We set to work: the work was a series of conversations. It was an extraordinary relief to have someone else ask the questions for a change. It was even better to have someone listen to me. And for once I was doing something that came naturally rather than striving. My daily professional work required constant, intensive study of a great variety of subjects. I felt harnessed and driven by it. I experienced it as an enormous discipline but I presumed that was the price of the job, and I paid it.

This subject, however — my own life — required no homework. I knew it and, as I began to tell my story, I realised that the story was my self, my buried self, all stored up inside, ready to be released by someone's questioning. I told my story and I felt my story. The pent-up emotions of years were released in that safe place. The counsellor listened to me with full attention and somehow that gave me a mirror in which gradually I could see myself more and more clearly. The more I brought chapters of my story into the open, and the more I named my hurts and failures, the more I knew myself. It was as though the speaking of my story out loud to another person began to make me real and to set me free.

The process also cleared away some long-held misunderstandings that I had carried heavily for many years. This was done in an astonishing way under guidance from the counsellor and in her presence. First, I was invited to express an issue that was painful for me. I had to say it to the person it concerned, addressing them directly as though they were sitting in the chair opposite. I then had to move into that chair facing my own, and give a reply.

When first invited to do this, I could not imagine how I would carry it out. Stating the painful problem out loud was hard enough, but how could I possibly know someone else's reply? The extraordinary thing was that I did know. It came to me directly. I could speak it out loud, and it sounded convincing. I remember, for instance, expressing deep shame to a person I thought that I had failed to care for sufficiently, and who was long since gone. Prompt and definite the response came back:

'God damn it, I had my chance, and I did it my way. Now stop wasting precious time and get on with your own life!'

The characteristic idiom and the edge of exasperation were unmistakably authentic, almost comically so, and I accepted their rightness without hesitation. That is exactly what she would have said. It was a profound relief. The sadness of her going remained but shame dissolved, pain was alleviated, memory healed, and a burden lifted from the soul.

Revealing exchanges like that one released me from a miasma of faulty perceptions in which I had been shrouded, obscuring and distorting a clear view of the present. They freed me from my restricted tunnel vision to offer me alternative ways of seeing my situation and an unforeseen choice of ways in which to act.

What was happening seemed to me like self-revelation, self-forgiveness and self-acceptance. I suppose in fact it was a dramatic reorientation of my picture of the world. It was a transforming process that opened up the possibility of change. It felt like unhooking myself from a load of wretchedness that I no longer had to carry. I saw that I did not have to go on and on punishing myself for failures, real or imagined. I saw that, without forgetting, condoning or justifying a mistake, I could be deeply sad that it had happened (speaking out the shame and sorrow was important), but then let it go.

I came to see, as well, that lack of self-forgiveness sometimes causes you to blame other people or circumstances for your difficulties — that you judge and criticise in others what you cannot acknowledge or forgive in yourself. This was a sobering thought and I had to re-examine myself and my work in the light of it. Of course, a reporter is ideally placed to hunt for scapegoats. That's what you get paid for. But, before putting my own personal house in order, how unconsciously jaundiced was the professional eye I turned upon the world?

Similarly, I began to see that, while I might resent what someone had done to me, I had to give up wishing that person ill because my wish was a binding from which I needed release. However, this process was not achieved so quickly. It happened rarely but, when I felt wronged, I was a pretty good hater, brooding over the events, imagining vengeance. Striving to forgive someone else was different in nature from being forgiven myself. It was more coldly rational, more an exercise of will than the emotional relief of being forgiven. Forgiving someone who had wronged me did not bring any rush of loving kindness towards them, as perhaps it should. It was more like being able to detach myself from paying mental attention to them anymore. It was like seeing that the wrong was theirs to live with, theirs to carry, theirs to answer for, not mine. Achieving that detachment is still a struggle for me today, but it takes less time than it used to. If someone asks for my forgiveness I give it because I know, from experience, what it costs to ask. I forgive; I go through the mental exercise of transferring responsibility back to them for what they have done; in time, I detach myself from it, emotionally, but somehow I never quite forget.

As these powerful insights slowly became real for me, I was conscious first of massive physical relief, like tense muscles relaxing and stress dissolving. Tears were the currency of these discoveries; and long, deep sleep, and a new impression of lightness. These were engrossing experiences. They changed me. They shifted the focus of my attention. They altered my perspective and diminished the energy I had to expend on pursuing police and political corruption, which, by the early eighties, had become something of a specialty in my broadcasting work. Was this partly because, having stopped punishing myself, I no longer needed an external enemy, nor had the drive to blame and punish others? I am not sure, but it began to seem to me that too much of my reporting was adding to community anxiety, rather than offering solutions. I still knew that the job was important but it began to look like a task I could leave to someone else. This was a dramatic change for me.

In her analysis of forgiveness, psychotherapist and author Stephanie Dowrick suggests that new wisdom may well surface from an episode of forgiveness, including an improved ability to set boundaries on personal behaviour, one's own and that of others.[2] This is a helpful observation which explains to me what I could not articulate to myself or anyone else at the time: at the peak of my broadcasting work in current affairs on radio and television, I gave it all up. I felt that I had to take the road less travelled, without knowing where it might lead. This unaccountable decision marked the start of a long, slow healing of grief, loneliness, fatigue, fragmentation and overdependence on work and my own resources.

I went, for a year, to work with Hugh Mackay at his prestigious Centre for Communication Studies at Bathurst, where I learned a great deal. As a psychologist, Hugh recognised my situation. He and his family, with whom I stayed, were enormously helpful to me at that time.

In retrospect, I think that leaving all my broadcasting work was too dramatic a change. But because I could not imagine a compromise, I did not ask for it. I notice that, these days, some people are able to design job-sharing for themselves, or take long periods of leave, but

I think these options were not available then. It seemed to me that either you were up to a high-profile job, with all its demands, or you got out. In spite of my professional success, I was still not sufficiently confident in myself to ask for a job to be redesigned for me. Somehow I had not been able to take in my achievement, to be nourished by it and to make it part of me. As well, I did not want to show any weakness as a woman. I wanted my work record to stand as proof that a woman could do those two jobs, on radio and television, as well as a man, for the sake of those women who came after me.

When, after a few months, my counsellor returned to her native Canada, I still had a long way to go. My next powerful experiences of forgiveness came through personal development courses at the Self-Transformations Centre in Sydney, in the early eighties. Gita and Walter Bellin were the principals of a teaching centre that synthesised the insights of several popular New Age psychologies and practices, including transcendental meditation. People flocked to the Centre in their hundreds, cheerfully submitting to the Californian corniness of having their watches removed and being kept awake and 'aware' and 'sharing' until the early hours of the morning. Wide-eyed, we revelled in the jargon of our newly disclosed psychological types — 'Are you an oral? Well, he says I'm definitely schizoid and I know he's right!' — and inflicted on each other details of our 'breakthroughs'. Encouraged into excesses of candour, we participants publicly acknowledged our desires and shames, our fears and frailties in front of large groups. At these confessions, a mass intake of breath at such risky self-exposure was often followed by a relieved bellow of laughter which recognised that deeply guarded personal secrets were also held by many others. We were all fools of the human condition.

It was a touching and sometimes humorous process which helped us to break out of our restricted individualism into a more energetic, expanded, positive, connected understanding of life. The teaching of meditation gave many their first encounter with an inner life, the possibility of spirituality and the transcendence of everyday concerns. At the very least, it offered the safety valve of a regular daily quiet time. The teaching also allowed for the inclusion of some creative source in the scheme of things. This was referred to as a higher power, an acceptably non-specific term for the many who were on the run from an organised religion that had hurt them, or come to seem irrelevant to their contemporary lives.

Some graduates look back on those Self-Transformations days with scepticism or even declare that they were unhelpful. Many others claim that the courses brought improvement to their personal and working lives. For me, there were certainly benefits. One of many insights came when Walter Bellin interrupted his smooth delivery in the course of a lecture to several hundred people to tell me, 'And, Caroline Jones, you do not have to keep smiling all the time.' Not until that moment did I realise that I was always politely on professional listening duty, even in a paid public lecture, reassuring the speaker that he was being heard. Embarrassed, I obeyed Walter Bellin's instruction and felt the muscles of my face relax. It was a great relief.

One of the numerous Transformations 'processes' was that of 'making completions'. We had to recall unresolved situations in our lives, and imagine focusing on them with love rather than bitterness. It took some doing but, having been initiated into the concept of forgiveness with my counsellor, I was willing to explore it further. After many imaginary exercises in our small group sessions, we were invited to try it out in the real world by revisiting an unhappy situation and making our peace with it by asking forgiveness.

For my exercise, I chose a very difficult relationship, one I believed to be intractable. However, the Self-Transformations Centre gave us a prescription for every occasion. This time, following an admonition to 'feel the fear and do it anyway', I encountered the person with whom I had been at loggerheads over a long period. I asked pardon for any hurt I had caused and declared a desire for a happier situation between us. The effect was almost electric. Her body shuddered and she turned to give me an unaccustomed direct look. Her eyes filled with tears. She, too, asked forgiveness and, as if to seal the compact for a better relationship, was soon showing me some of her family treasures. From that day, although we still had our occasional tense outbursts of conflict, the original incident was potent enough to bring each of us back to the conference table with the intention of making peace. For me, it was another powerful turning point.

While the Self-Transformations Centre was an important place of personal development for me, it was not a final destination. It opened me to the religious experience that would take the potential of forgiveness, self-knowledge and self-acceptance to an even deeper level. At Easter, 1985, I was received into the community of the Catholic church. The formal practices of the church which encourage and support forgiveness were a major factor in my conversion. Part of the preparation in the year preceding confirmation was to receive the Sacrament of Reconciliation. This involves making a confession to a priest of all the things you're sorry for, and the areas of your life that need attention. At my age, there was plenty to tell. It was a fearful task, almost impossible to face another human being with so much shame, to hear my voice speak things that had lain like secret stones in my heart, things never before told, things I had done and things I had failed to do. There was not even the camouflage of a confessional box, as in the movies. But this was the price of entry into a beckoning spiritual sanctuary and I chose to pay it. It was also the opportunity to be authentically unburdened, to be absolved by another human being in the name of a God who promised forgiveness.

The genius was in the listening, a calm hearing without judgment or reproach. Somehow, I managed to say it all, reluctant, dreading to see contempt or revulsion in the eyes of the priest, but determined to reveal the brokenness of my life and to embrace the promise of a fresh start. The solace for this deep humiliation came at last with the laying of a dispassionate hand on my bowed head and the unimaginable relief of hearing the words, 'I absolve you of your sins in the name of the Father, and of the Son and of the Holy Spirit. Go in the peace of Christ and God bless you.'

In that moment, I felt that I had joined the human race; no longer striving to pass an impossible examination that I had failed long ago; no longer hobbled by remorse. Just a human being struggling like everyone else to do my best, but fallible like everyone else, falling down and getting up again. In subsequent experiences of the Sacrament of Reconciliation, I was encouraged not to be unduly hard on myself, to be more grateful for my life and my gifts; and to feel more deeply a sense of being loved and cared for.

At last I was gaining the capacity to take good experience into myself to become part of me. It was another building block in the long, slow construction of my sense of inner legitimacy. In the months that followed, I contacted several people with whom I had broken relationships in the past, to ask their forgiveness and seek reconciliation with them. To my amazement, each approach was welcomed and peace was created between us. I believe my action was made possible, in every instance, because I had been forgiven and affirmed in a context that had deep spiritual validity for me. These encounters were unforeseen and their possibility of success remote — and yet they happened. The peaceful relief they brought was visceral, the untying of knots in the stomach.

I still have more reconciliations to make, with myself and with others. I suppose it is a lifelong process. What I find extraordinary is that there is now an ongoing reorientation in me which allows forgiveness to become an option in challenging situations. I do not feel that I am the author of it. Rather, it rises from the depths, like the deepest note in Tibetan Buddhist chanting which, gathering intensity, produces a harmonic accompaniment in the high register.

It was a profound revelation to discover that the past is not set in concrete, that I am not its prisoner, that I am at liberty to break it open, to have a change of heart, to see it afresh. Even memories may be healed, opening a free way forward. The experience of forgiveness made a revolution in my life. It was as though my attention was redirected towards hope. Not only was my individual experience transfigured but I gained a sense of connection with other people that I had not felt before. The image of a private, beleaguered struggle gave way to a metaphor of 'companions of the way', all of us frail, vulnerable and prone to error, but travelling together with the promise of redemption, and in the hope of support and mercy from each other.

My experiences of forgiveness increased my sense of personal identity or authenticity. I now had more information about myself and I had been able to incorporate it: I was a person capable of forgiveness and a person worth forgiving. With this came a new conviction that there is some intrinsic value in my *being* as distinct from what I *do*. This was a very important shift for someone who had always relied on performance for approval.

I am frequently questioned about why I became a Catholic. To some it is inexplicable that a sceptical journalist should take such a step into religious faith. Even to some cradle Catholics, it is a puzzle that anyone would seek to join an institution which sometimes disappoints them and tries their loyalty. Often I am still surprised myself that I have become a Catholic. How did it happen?

I suppose we all hope to find a trustworthy ideal, someone to live up to, an exemplar who will not turn out to have the clay feet from which we know we suffer ourselves. As a journalist and a young woman of the sixties, I was a product of my times. In a community of dissolving values, people of my generation were cast adrift on a sea of uncertainty, self-indulgence and lack of boundaries. I had a lot of experience of the world and I had become rather lost in it. After turning 40, I was looking for more depth of meaning in life. My work brought me into contact with a great variety of people and philosophies of life. I saw that some lived in a way that had integrity and purpose, and I wanted to discover the source of their motivation — if possible, to have it for myself. When I encountered wisdom or goodness in people, I was attracted to fall into step beside them for a while, be they Aborigines, Jews, Hindus, Moslems or Buddhists. At the time of my searching for faith and meaning in life, I happened to encounter Catholic Christians.

One of many influential encounters occurred at Seton Villa, where the Daughters of Charity have made a home for intellectually impaired women. I was invited to open an exhibition of the residents' art. When I visited the Villa during the final weeks of preparation of the art works, the warm, cheerful care of the nuns for their residents brought to life for me the illustrated passages from Christ's teaching hanging on the walls of the art room. I recall the dramatic impact of looking from the framed written word to the human action being played out in front of it:

Love one another as I have loved you.
For I was thirsty and you gave me to drink.
Inasmuch as you do for one of these little ones, you do for me.

What I saw at Seton Villa was not martyred service. It was relationship, and there was an unaffected naturalness about it. I was attracted by the nuns, and very curious about the motivation for their life and the source of their happiness.

I wondered what might happen if I attempted to live, as they did, in the example of Jesus Christ. When I did try, I found that it encouraged the better traits in my character, restrained the worst and made me happier. Left to my own devices I would succumb to my introversion. I would probably read books and ride ferries, dance, eat, go to movies and daydream. I still do those things but Christian teaching gave me an expanded picture of life to be lived to the full in a relationship of love and service. The Christian story gave me a chart by which to steer my course, a faith community for support, and companions with whom I shared common values.

By nature and training I am suspicious of dogma, whether religious, political or scientific. I trust experience first and foremost. Then, if I find a compatible context for my experience, I am open to contemplate the validity of that context. Like many Australians, I look for local images and fresh language in which to express my spirituality. I was delighted to discover, in the beautiful Mary MacKillop Chapel in North Sydney, a tall candlestick engraved with a motif of death-and-resurrection. The artist has depicted this pivotal Christian theme by showing that, in order to germinate its seeds, the native Australian banksia needs the scorching heat of bushfire.

When I saw this, I understood that new life can come from apparent devastation. The engraving spoke with immediate appeal to my Australian sensibility. The Mary MacKillop shrine contains many touching images of the quintessentially Australian faith and work of the Sisters of St Joseph, founded by that remarkable Australian pioneer, Blessed Mary MacKillop.

We Australians seem determined not to walk without question in the well-worn tracks of traditional religion but to take our own sense of spirituality as a starting point and then to see which elements of the old traditions might support it. The Catholic faith gave me a vocabulary and a ritual in which to situate my transforming experiences of forgiveness and growing self-acceptance. I was then ready to listen to other aspects of Catholic teaching — to consider, for example, that I am made in the image and likeness of God, fallible but forgivable, unique and loved for myself. These beliefs did not immediately become incontrovertible doctrine for me. They were attractive ideas on which I ruminated and which I continue to test against the evidence of my experience and my observation of the world around me. At times I am easily in accord with them. At other times I doubt.

And then sometimes a religious symbol floods some aspect of my experience with understanding, and I embrace it with recognition and gratitude. I will explain later how the cross of Christ crucified gave me, for the first time, a satisfying way to contemplate suffering.

The practice of Christianity in everyday life did not come easily to me. I was often aware of an argument between my sophisticated, worldly self and my spiritual nature, and sometimes the former won. But, in other ways, my attempt to follow Christian teaching made life easier. It increased my capacity to distinguish wise directions from foolish ones. It set boundaries on my behaviour, giving me a more secure sense of integrity. It pushed me to make commitments in an unaccustomed way, to try to go the extra mile. It nurtured my self-respect and refashioned my response to others. It also shook me out of the pseudo-objectivity of journalism where I had no need to form an opinion on any issue. It forced me to think things through and to decide where I stand. This brought a greater depth, honesty and judgment to my journalism while objectivity took second place to that sense of justice which grows out of the Christian belief in the intrinsic dignity of each life.

Unexpectedly, I found a deep richness of thought in the Christian gospels. I suppose it is because the whole scripture is set out in story form that much of it is readily accessible. The stories are about ordinary recognisable people to whom I can relate. Time and again, I find myself in these stories. They intertwine with my life today and interrogate it and help me to make decisions about it.

In the story of the good Samaritan, am I the one who passes by the man fallen ill in the roadway, or do I stop to help him? In the story of Martha and Mary, am I the one who keeps so very busy, or the one who pauses to hear some wisdom? In the story of the prodigal son, am I the wastrel son returned home, for unmerited help; the merciful father who welcomes and forgives; or the second son, the dutiful one, who resents that prodigality should be rewarded with acceptance and a feast? Am I the rich man who recognises sadly that he cannot detach himself from his possessions in order to follow Jesus? Am I the blind, the lame or the leper in need of healing? What is it that I will not see? What is the mile that I will not walk? What is eating away at me? (You can find all these stories by browsing through the gospels of Matthew and Luke.)

When did I visit the prisoner, give a drink to the thirsty, feed the hungry, clothe the destitute? Do I love my neighbour? Who is my neighbour? Do I blame others instead of examining myself? On the Via Dolorosa, am I black Simon of Cyrene who shouldered Christ's tormenting cross for part of the way; Veronica who wiped his brow; or am I one of the disciples who melted into the crowd, frightened to be identified with my friend the revolutionary who had promised a kingdom but delivered instead a terrifying crucifixion?

They are questions from 2000 years ago. They are also questions that go to the heart of contemporary life and challenge me in the most incisive way. Do I live for myself or take care also for others, including the man in the gutter, the unemployed, the frail, the disadvantaged, the one who is different? Do I spend my life in hyperactivity or pause sometimes to reflect, to nourish the spirit, to be grateful for my life? Do I give a full day's work for a full day's pay? Do I condemn someone who's gone wrong or give them a hand

and a second chance? Am I so attached to amassing possessions that deeper values are obscured? Do I live in my own snug cocoon or am I awake to the needs of the people around me, in the family and in my community? Do I care about the plight of people in other countries? Do I avoid products whose manufacture oppresses people or harms the environment? Do I speak out against unjust actions by government or business or the media, or do I melt into the anonymity of the conforming crowd? Am I too quick with blame, too lazy to discern my own motives and set my own house in order? How do I use my power, at home and at work? Have I the courage of my convictions, regardless of the cost, or do I follow the trend-setters?

The story of the Samaritan woman at the well is another that is deeply relevant to me. She was a spiritually alienated, worldly experienced, culturally foreign woman who was nonetheless accepted by Jesus. He saw exactly what she was and how needy she was and, regardless of her reputation, he offered her the living water of his spirit and his way of life. She was claimed by this experience of unconditional love which she happened upon, one lonely day at the well, and through it she came to new life (John 4, 1–26). It is our profound human need to know such generous love, and it is sweet for me to rediscover it as an adult in the faith story of my childhood.

The example of Jesus Christ challenged me to be realistic, rather than sentimental, about the world in which I live. It is important to me that Christianity acknowledges the real power and presence of evil in the world — at the end of the violent 20th century, how could we doubt it? — and requires me to put up some fight against it, both within myself and outside. Sometimes I perceive evil as an active force — I think, for instance, of child abuse or the terrible purges of the early 1990s in the former Yugoslavia. At other times, I experience evil as being an absence of love or compassion or generosity. This can be a confronting personal experience.

Christ's teaching requires followers to love God, not in some ethereal way, but in working to fulfil the needs and relieve the suffering of people. His injunction to 'love one another' is no easy thing. He calls you to account for meanness; for being self-righteous;

for failing to protect a child or failing to forgive; for being envious, for gossiping, for not trying hard enough; for failing to nurture life or to make peace; for falling asleep when wakefulness is needed.

There is a sense of rightness for me about the spiritual path I have chosen to follow because it tests me and extends me. The Christian church was founded for sinners, not for the comfortably self-righteous, and a temperament like mine needs spiritual discipline. As people have found for 2000 years, Jesus Christ is a supremely inspiring model and his invitation is not, I think, to be perfect, rather to keep trying to love and to give to the utmost of your capacity. Then, on those rare occasions when you manage to do it for just a minute or two, by the grace of God, the reward is peace, the pearl beyond price — before you retreat, inevitably, into human fallibility once again.

For some reason I felt at home in the Catholic culture and intrigued, even entertained, by the Catholic mythology. And perhaps it's the Irish heritage in Australian Catholicism that produces a cheerful approach to religious faith that suits me. It is a good counter to my natural wistfulness. Although the teaching is profound, in the practice of it there's an absence of anything sombre or self-righteous, and a ready acknowledgement that we're all in the company of sinners but doing our best, with the help of God, and enjoying life along the way. Catholics are good at being involved and they're good at sociability. There's never a prayer meeting without supper and a good yarn afterwards. 'Spirituality in the Pub' gatherings are preceded and followed by a drink, as you would expect. People feel free to come to Mass in their casual clothes on the way to a bushwalk, or after sailing, so that church attendance — the desire for God — is integrated into everyday life.

The sense of being received into a big, traditional family was very welcome to a rather solitary person like myself, and perhaps the shared Celtic ancestry was appealing. On my mother's side, I am descended from Flora MacDonald and the MacDonald Lords of the Isles who were great patrons of the church and of the arts. It was in the 14th century, when Good John of Islay was Lord of the Isles (1330–86), that there began on Iona the tradition of monumental stone-carving that is one of the treasures of Scotland. The endurance of Scots Catholicism is also commemorated at South Uist, where an eight-metre-high granite statue of Our Lady of the Isles, by sculptor Hew Lorimer, stands as a memorial to the faithfulness of Catholics of the Isles and Western Highlands who never surrendered to the Protestant Reformers. Who knows what lies latent in the race memory, waiting to be met in a later generation?

I love to walk into a Catholic church anywhere in the world and know that I am walking into the heart of European historical tradition; to know that I will feel at home and be able to participate in the Mass. It is all so curiously familiar. I feel that I am accepted into the extended Catholic family, not for anything I have done, but just for myself and my desire to be there. This allows me to be myself, and to be natural. I cannot overstate the liberating effect of this after the confusing fragmentation of 'celebrity'. My conversion was not so much that I had suddenly come to believe in God, but rather I had come to contemplate the fact that some all-encompassing benevolent Other might believe in me.

I'm not sure that I can claim a personal relationship with God as yet, but the line of a hymn, based on Psalm 27, caught my imagination: 'Do not be afraid, I am with you, I have called you by your name, you are mine.'[3] I suppose one reason we want God is that we long for someone who truly knows us. And if there is God, and if God made me, then God knows me as well or better than I know myself. And if this is true, then it satisfies my human yearning to believe that I exist, that I am real, that I am known.

I was encouraged by the congruence I found in all my experiences of church. First, there were many reassuring echoes to validate the childhood Christian example of beloved figures like my grandmother. Then the liturgy of the Mass, the music, the seasonal ritual, the decoration of the church nourished my imagination and answered my desire for beauty, artistry, order and an emotional life for the soul. The moving ritual of the Eucharist continued to provide its mysterious but undeniable nourishment. Preaching informed by scholarship and wisdom brought the scriptures alive to make sense of my own experience, and regularly articulated a solid sense of values and an appropriate way to respond to events in an uncertain world. The church's practical, compassionate work in every area of need in society is extraordinary in its reach and effectiveness, not only in Australia but internationally; this provided me with a trustworthy avenue through which to contribute.

I happened to enter the church in a Jesuit parish so I was fortunate to encounter a far deeper intellectual climate than I had experienced ever before. Here, it seemed to me, people were giving intelligent and practical attention to questions that really mattered, like social justice and how the individual was to live a worthwhile and contributing life on a daily basis. Catholic thinking has been formulated and refined over many centuries. It satisfies both faith and reason; the totality of issues is examined; the deepest sources of motivation are called into question. No matter where it ends up, every argument begins with the sanctity of life. Catholic thinking goes way beyond the merely ideological, psychological or economic to matters of universal and ultimate significance.

From this vantage point, I could see the framework in which the media commonly operate as being threadbare, and I got my first glimmering of a more comprehensive approach to public enlightenment. After much searching, the Catholic church was the most coherent and satisfying attempt I had found to make sense of life and to show a way to live, both as an individual and a member of the human race.

Adult education associated with the church is of a high intellectual order. Living in Sydney, there is much from which to choose. I was challenged by Dr Michael Whelan's Christian Life Formation seminars at the Catholic Theological Union — brilliant lectures in which literature, philosophy, history and theology were plumbed in a *tour de force* exploration of the human condition.[4] Aquinas Academy offered the latest learning in depth psychology, spirituality and theology, embracing traditions other than the Christian. Dr Noel Rowe and Dr Erin White offered a brilliant series on Australian Religious Imagination which shifted me to a new level of religious understanding through exploration of my own experience in the contexts of landscape, poetry and theology.

This education was crucial in developing a sense of intellectual inquiry, morality and values to which previously I had given insufficient attention. And, importantly, for someone trained to question, there was a lively movement for reform of some of the church's teaching, structure and administration among progressive thinkers determined to work for change from within. I consider this to be a position of integrity.

For the most personal and convincing aspect of my conversion, it is difficult to find words. I can say that it is somehow a homecoming to myself, and to a pervading sense of being faithfully accompanied and continually challenged in ways that feel authentic to me. It is the discovery of a guiding story in which I can locate myself and which helps me to make sense of life. I have an increased sense of my inner legitimacy and therefore of my personal identity. For much of the time, I have a conviction of being accepted and cared for which frees me to look out beyond myself to the needs of others. I have an intuition of the peace and support of some mystery known as God beneath difficult circumstances; and the understanding that I alone am not responsible for everything.

I have a wider perspective on life, a sense of connection with others, an exhilaration in living the present day and a consciousness that it is I who am doing so. This is what is called the gift of faith. The term seems appropriate to me because I first came to faith by gift or grace, while I stay with it by commitment, through the exercise of will and reason; and for love of it, with all its perplexities. After all, you do not remain in your family because it is perfect but because it is your family. Hitherto, I had thought of myself as someone to whom things happened. But this new orientation gave me a new sense of myself as an active participant in my destiny, as one who could freely make choices and decisions that would, in large part, determine how I would live.

Although some people appear to be very confident in their identity, it is still not like that for me. The quest to discover 'who I am' is more like a continuing unfolding than a finite goal to be achieved once and for all. Sometimes I lose my sense of faith and find myself back in that solitary struggle where identity disintegrates into a neurotic isolation, and anxiety and vertigo prevail; back in a place where I seem weakened yet responsible for everything; and where meaning shatters into a thousand volatile fragments like spilled quicksilver.

These episodes are demoralising. They have their own conviction and cannot easily be resisted or denied. They are marked by a feeling of desolation. I have been told that this is the time to pray for help, and I believe it, but sometimes I forget or feel that I cannot. It seems to me that I am recalled from such desolate interludes not by an act of will, but by grace, of which I write in the next chapter. Something I read or an apparently chance encounter calls me back. Hope slips a hand into mine. I detach myself from the clinging remnants of the bad dream and I am returned again into that polyglot, struggling band of travellers who are gambling on the promise that we are on some purposeful journey and that someone has indeed prepared a place for us.

I am not ingenuous about religion or the church. Indeed, I am struck dumb by the horrors that men have perpetrated in the name of their church and their religions. I am equally appalled by the cruelties committed in the name of ideology, science or medicine. This does not prevent me from following the progress of religion, science, ideology and medicine with great interest. I respect the efforts of all men and women who strive to make things better in the world, whatever their religion or philosophy of life. I admire the independent courage of the atheist and I honour the dedication of the humanist. I am relieved to notice that finding faith and a spiritual home has increased my curiosity about all the great traditions. From my own instinct, and, as it happens, in accordance with Catholic teaching, I respect what is true in each of them.

This new-found peace of mind freed me from personal preoccupation and revealed a wider perception. With a more outward orientation, I could seek a way to make a contribution again to community life. When the invitation came from Dr David

Millikan, Head of Religious Programs for the ABC, to join his broadcasting team, I was ready to accept. Together we formulated *The Search for Meaning* format which would deal with human affairs in the more profound way I had been seeking. The program produced eight years of generous revelation of the lives of Australian men and women. My role was to listen, to provide a space in which it was safe for people to describe what they had discovered, through the experience of life, to be sustaining. It made for deeply interesting programs, as guests detailed the wisdom they had gleaned from life, how they had made their choices and what they most cared about. For me, the new congruence between my personal convictions and my professional work provided a welcome fullness of life, an unexpected source of energy and a more secure sense of identity.

The quest for personal identity or authenticity is often synonymous with the search for the divine. Reviewing my recollection of childhood, only now do I see that it contains several images or reflections of what might be God. One is that of my father, continuing to love and support me through the war years of my childhood, although he was absent on military service. This image helps me to contemplate the idea that God may be both hidden and loving. Important too because it allows me to redeem the image of 'absent father'. After that long separation in my childhood, my father and I have been able to accompany each other through tragedy and testing emotional challenges to find a deep mutual trust, love and loyalty that is one of the treasures of my life.

And there are many other images of what might be God in my childhood recollection — all the loving, companionable, capable women; the sustaining relationships of country life; the shelter of our modest cottage; the flowers and trees in my grandmother's garden; and my excellent early teachers at Murrurundi Public School.

Was God in the church too? I suppose so, but church seemed more of a social than a religious occasion. Now I see that it can be both. Some of the most potent early images require more contemplation. Did the wild thunderstorms conjure, as well as fear, the exciting possibility that this small world could be opened up, that there might

be adventure waiting to be claimed in a wider sphere, beyond the
mountains, or at the other end of the valley; that moving out might
give a refreshed view of this safe enclosure? And what of the indifferent, awesome atmosphere of Paradise Park, Murrurundi? Was God
there too? No tame God, certainly. Perhaps the Aboriginal God
Biami; or the God Moses met on Sinai who would answer only 'I am
who I am.'[5] And perhaps they are one and the same?

Over the years I have talked with many people about their understanding of God, and been fascinated by the variety of interpretations
expressed. Each one expanded my own religious imagination and
gave me a new area for contemplation. In this scientific age, we are
unsatisfied by the traditional language of religion, yet reluctant to
abandon its insights, for they speak to a need that is still very real for
us: we remain intensely curious about the nature of the universe,
about who we are, what might be our source or author and why we
are here. But we are looking for fresh ways of talking about these
questions, ways that can claim some currency in the modern world.

Nick Carroll, speaking of the intense relationship that surfers have
with the sea, told me:

> There's definitely a religious aspect although I don't know whether
> religion is the right word — it's probably more spiritual. I would
> hesitate to put a particular name on it like 'God' or 'Buddha' or
> 'Mohammed'. I think it's more an awareness of the pulse of life on
> Earth, and if God's inherent in that, then they [surfers] learn about
> God too.[6]

Nick Carroll's metaphor of 'the pulse of life on Earth' is a powerful
one. Like many younger people, he does not want to personalise God
or situate the divine in any one religious tradition, but prefers to
encounter it as a sort of universal presence riding the waves, or
schussing down a ski slope, or immanent in the bush.

Influenced by Jungian and Sufi understanding, Barbara Blackman
told me that 'there is an area that is unconditioned, and the human
spirit, the human psyche, can sometimes dip into it. That's what the

innocent, unselfconscious child and the committed artist do — like diving deep and bringing up the fish.'

She continued:

My understanding is that's what Jesus did with his healing. He did nothing. He just *was* there, part of that 'unconditioned'. So He was able to take the wounded, the unwhole person, and dip them into it, in an instant ... I think also that the 'me' that is unique, that is in every person, is part of that 'unconditioned' — whether you call it divinity, eternity, the collective unconscious.'[7]

Many people are unprepared to define God and surely that's appropriate when God is, above all, mystery; and when words can so easily render ideas impotent. But most people I spoke to were happy to wonder aloud about God, to search out some elements of that supernatural dimension that is part of their reality, even though it may be difficult to put into words.

When I asked Judge Marcus Einfeld if he had a faith in God he said:

Yes. I don't know that I could define precisely what God was, or is, but I certainly have a faith that there is a divine, superhuman entity which has a significant role to play in guiding our lives. I certainly don't believe that he or she is directing everything we do or think, but I think there is a moral guidance, divine guidance, yes.[8]

Since many people are bewildered about how they can legitimately incorporate religion or spirituality into contemporary life, it is enlightening to find a thinker who shows the way. For Dr John Polkinghorne, science and religion stand together, as concepts of equal validity, not at war with each other. This is a relief to the western mind which is constantly badgered into an adversarial view of the world. As President of Queen's College, Cambridge, Dr Polkinghorne has the advantage of being both scientist and minister of religion.

Western science, he suggests, gives us the 'how' and religion the 'why'. Science explores the universe in which we find ourselves; religion offers some reasons for our purpose here. He asks why we need to set the two in confrontation with each other. Why confuse the language of prose (science) with the language of poetry (religion)? When the poet Burns says, 'O, my love's like a red, red rose', we do not conclude that the woman has green leaves, thorns and a mass of red petals. We know that he is inferring something, attributing a certain quality to a woman.

When people complain that there is no proof for religious belief, Dr Polkinghorne points out that no one has proved the existence of quarks either, yet his reason is satisfied, by the arguments and methods of science, that quarks exist; just as his reason is satisfied, by the methods of religion, that there is a 'why' for our existence.

It is clarifying to hear such a polymath at work — someone who does not set different streams of knowledge into contradiction with each other, but discerns how they may illuminate each other. Professor Charles Birch, one of our great Australian thinkers, also has that gift of broad intelligence which allows him to cross academic boundaries and to offer a more expansive view of life as a result. Emeritus Professor Birch is a doctor of science, and the author of a number of authoritative books. He says:

> I think the important approach is to start with yourself because, after all, you are the entity that you know best in this universe.
>
> I have a profound feeling that there is a source for my experiences of love, of forgiveness and so on, all those qualities in human life. There is a reality which contributes to my life and I call that reality, that entity 'God', but that same reality receives a contribution from me. I think that's the meaning of 'God is love'; God not only gives but God also receives.[9]

Charles Birch's idea of my contributing something to God came as a surprising possibility. It's a thought that brings a new sense of creative responsibility to everyday life. It suggests that everything we do has some significance, for better or worse. Charles Birch refines that idea when he goes on to say:

> Nothing that *we* think important matters, unless it matters ultimately, that is unless it matters to the one who is everlasting, God. People

want to think of themselves as persisting for ever, if not in this world, well hopefully in some other world. I think that is irrational . . . what persists is our contribution to the life of God.[10]

This allows an optimistic approach to life in the here and now, which I find practical and attractive. It seems attainable. Perhaps, in order to live a good life, all I have to do is to respond, as well as I can, with love and generosity to what I encounter around me each day. This view also promises immortality, not through graduation to some uncertain afterlife, but through the simple kind deeds of this one, which make a contribution to the common good and affect the lives of others in an ongoing way.

Phillip Adams has probably done more than anyone in Australian public life to keep the subject of God alive — by proclaiming his own atheism ad infinitum and very entertainingly. I have heard him discussing it with Robert Dessaix, on radio, and he spoke with me for *The Search for Meaning* program. He is modest and witty enough to address only a single listener on his *Late Night Live* Radio National program, but his long-running newspaper columns suggest a devoted constituency. Perhaps that is because he represents quintessential Millennium Man, a zealous disciple of scepticism, rationality and science.

To me the universe is meaningless. There is no destiny, there's no author to creation. To me life is just a brief flash in infinite darkness. No one wanted to believe more in a cosmic father than I did, given the absence of a real father but my prayers were never answered. I know the universe is cold and meaningless and whatever meaning life has is a subjective meaning, something that you give or you project on life.[11]

For some readers, this will provoke intriguing questions: How do human beings come to possess the capacity to 'give' meaning, to 'project' meaning on life? What is the source of that capacity? And how does Phillip Adams arrive at the conclusion that the universe is 'cold and meaningless', that life is 'just a brief flash in infinite darkness'? Is that knowledge deduced from science or from the imagination or from a dream? And where is the human capacity for love to be sourced ... merely in biology? And, if so, where in biology?

With no sense of divine protection or ultimate meaning or guiding story for his spirit, Phillip set out on a desperate search for meaning. And he found it, in teenage, when he picked up his first novel by John Steinbeck. In *The Grapes of Wrath*, he found a cause that answered the awful need of a child who lived in fear of a violent stepfather and who felt himself to be abandoned. That cause was a generalised rage against injustice; and the Steinbeck novel became his gospel for what he describes as a lifelong commitment to activism. Each time he encounters fresh evidence of injustice, his life purpose is renewed. He speaks of the 'exhilaration' of his anger at injustice.

It is typical of the atheist that he feels himself to be alone in his endeavour. Unlike Charles Birch, Phillip Adams does not have the company of God to share the burden of injustice, nor to shoulder it for him. I can readily identify with this frame of mind because I spent some years of my life there. The drive and the loneliness of it are familiar to me. I found it very uncomfortable and I return to it occasionally, albeit unwillingly.

I have interviewed a number of atheist crusaders. They each had a terrifying experience in their early childhood. Perhaps a psychologist would be tempted to make a connection. If you are threatened with extinction when you are tiny and helpless, and no one comes to your aid, is it difficult ever after to believe in an omnipotent carer who will be there for you? Or have you been robbed of the capacity to imagine it? It could be that Phillip Adams is aggravated by religious believers because not one of them has been able to convince his clever, logical mind of the existence of the cosmic father for whom he longed as a child.

He told me that, in childhood, when the chaos of a frightening domestic life threatened to engulf him, he set out to build his own imaginary universe. He covered his walls with cut-out pictures of far-away places and reassuring images of antiquity, and began to read and write in order to construct a framework of reality. It was his therapy then and he says it is still, today.

When he was a child, Phillip's fragile fortress was a galvanised iron sleepout, separate from the house. Today he's still writing and broadcasting from his isolation, still 'outside', as he puts it. But the antiquities, which his prosperity converted from cut-out pictures in childhood to the real thing when he grew up, have played a trick on him. He paid big money for them, so he thought he owned them, but now he realises that they are just on short-term loan to him, that they will survive long after he has been snuffed out. To some, they may seem sentinels of eternity, but for him they have become conquistadors. As he puts it, 'The antiquities have won.' Phillip Adams hears the urgent ticking of the biological clock. He has calculated how many hours of life remain to him and he counts them down, reluctant to waste any of this fast-fleeing time. His conviction of the brevity of life sharpens his appreciation of a treat that will be over all too soon. Who would not go along with that, whatever their belief system?

As Phillip's faithful following indicates, the 'big questions' are endlessly interesting and people have been asking them, in a continuum of changing systems of thought, since self-consciousness began. One of the paradigms in which the search for meaning is being pursued today is deep ecology. A prominent advocate of this perspective is Ian Cohen, who represents the Greens in the New South Wales Parliament. He has adopted a belief system based on wilderness as the ground of all being. Clearly his faith is reinforced by his own convincing experience:

> Civilisation has moved so far from its origin. I think we're part of the earth. The concept of the rainforest being the womb of life is something I believe in ... the value system must get back to the environment as it was originally, the magnificence from where we emerged. I believe we carry certain seeds in our genes that connect us to that time. We're not people of concrete.
>
> To feel a real love for and an empathy with the environment I had to overcome a lot of 'city kid' fears like leeches, ticks, snakes, but now I feel the energy emanating from those environments. There's something there that gives me the incentive to act, to work, and it's something that has never come to me before in my life.

I've looked at all the ideologies. I've travelled and looked at the various religions, because I was always so off-balance and wondered why. And I really have something to believe in now, something above and beyond the often male intellectual gymnastics of humanity. It's real. It's a way and it sustains, and it's so unbelievably beautiful to be able to draw from and merge into that environment and I wish more political leaders and others would enjoy and understand, and open themselves to a change of consciousness.

Education in many instances can move us right away from the very things that are important in life. I'm so often working out of the intellect, and what I've got to learn, as a male in this society, is to get down to the heart level and down to the gut level and start feeling my emotions. We must start understanding other cultures, such as the Aboriginal culture. They have a harmony with the Earth and from that harmony has grown a certain spirituality.

The whole environment out there is a living, breathing, almost conscious being that is saying something to us human beings. The forests can't act but they can inspire us and they inspire people like myself and many others in the conservation movement to act on their behalf.[12]

Ian Cohen intends this claim to be taken literally. He identifies former New South Wales Premier Neville Wran's walk through a rainforest as being the crucial factor in his government's decision to review rainforest logging. While demonstrations and intellectual argument may have been persuasive, Cohen believes that Wran was most deeply touched by his personal experience in the forest.

The environmental movement has provided an identity, a creed and a conviction for many people unfulfilled by traditional organised religion yet still in search of a valid, meaningful expression of their spirituality.

The search for personal and spiritual identity is also affected by our sense of group and national identity. In Australia we seem to be on a perennial unsatisfied quest for this — except in times of national disaster, like the Newcastle earthquake, and Port Arthur and Thredbo, and bushfires, when the heroic effort of rescue workers, many of them voluntary, reminds us that we are people of practical ingenuity and generous compassion.

The day on which we come closest to knowing national identity is Anzac Day. For one day of the year the majority of Australians are reassured that we belong to a tradition of noble service and sacrifice — and newcomers are given a display of that tradition in our most significant national spiritual ritual. For one day of the year we let ourselves off the guard-duty of existential loneliness and escape into the psychological relief of communal ritual. The neurosis of our striving, competitive individualism can relax for once into the comfortable anonymity of the crowd.[13]

Not a moment of this sacred day is wasted. Before dawn the devotees assemble in sombre purpose and the day-long ceremonial begins to unfold. As with any ritual, its meaning lies in faithful adherence to an established form. Reiteration of the familiar words swells the breast and lifts the hand to the heart. Only speak the time-honoured exhortation and our fallen heroes will be conjured out of the darkness:

> They shall grow not old, as we that are left grow old. Age shall not weary them, nor the years condemn. At the going down of the sun, and in the morning, we will remember them.[14]

As the first rays of sun pierce the dawn, the solemn incantation calls our immortal gods from their 12-month slumber. The ghostly young heroes march again from the shearing sheds of Barcaldine and the Mallee, from the cattle runs of the Top End and the Diamantina. The backs of their necks clean-shaven, they stream out of the school-rooms and collar-proud city offices and hasten with self-conscious smiles to the recruiting centres. Crows' feet of irreverent laughter crease the corners of their eyes as they accept lightly the slouch hat and tunic of their mission — only two sizes: too large and too small. They climb the gangplanks of the great ships that will carry them Over There. Our nurses, gallant in starched white, volunteer to accompany the troops to unknown battlefields.

Cockade feathers blowing in the breeze, the Light Horse rides again in Egypt. Weary diggers in muddy trenches suck the last drag of a bumper before going over the top on the Somme. Red poppies glow like gobs of blood on Flanders Field. The 2nd AIF lay down their lives in jungle and rubber plantation. Our boys are carried to safety down precipitous mountain trails by the angels of Timor.

In the full sunlight of mid-morning, the veterans of Crete and the Western Desert march in step again with the middle-aged veterans of Korea and the grown-up boys we balloted off to Vietnam who returned with a look in their eyes we could not fathom. They are dressed for the ritual in the polyglot uniform of unaccustomed suits, tighter than this time last year, seasoned with medals and sprigs of rosemary. They have donned the ceremonial mask of an expression that hides sacred secrets and reveals for a day the confidence of initiated manhood.

The names of the theatres of battle are proclaimed on pennants that dignify the ranks of diminishing numbers marching beneath them. They announce where men have been, what they have done and, best of all, who they are, just when they had almost forgotten.

'O valiant hearts . . .'

For one day of the year it is legitimate for men to cry in public. For all of us watching, quiet for a change, a few more tears may be shed from what grief counsellor Mal McKissock described to me as the deep reservoir of unresolved grief on which the nation is founded: from convict transport and Aboriginal dispossession through successive waves of migration from an old world reluctantly farewelled.

It is possible to be profoundly nourished by this great ritual and to put on the mantle of its national identity. As you watch the Anzac Day march, you can let the faces of those marching men and women enter into your imagination, to sustain you and keep you company on the road ahead. For they are flesh-and-blood people, but they are more than that. Some of them, in enlisting, may have simply desired adventure, or escape from limiting or unpleasant domestic lives. As individuals they had numerous reasons for going to war, not all of them clearly thought out or noble, by any means, but as a group they are imbued with a quality with which we can commune and which can strengthen our resolve. Even if we see the Anzacs only as victims of injustice — as cannon fodder sacrificed for Empire — they can lend us the strength of endurance. These are men and women who have known fear and helplessness; and lived in dirty, uncomfortable conditions; and gone without sleep and cried secretly in homesickness and wondered if it would ever end, and if they had the guts to see it through.

And they saw it through. They gave witness that the challenge of life is not to be perfect, but to be fully human, to respond, as generously as you can, in all your frailty, to what is asked of you; to contribute to the common good. Their limps, their walking sticks, their weathered faces, the variety of their appearance, race and personality opens a place for every one of us in their ranks. Whatever took them to war, we know, through their example, that we are people whose history is adorned with the nobility of service.

They also provide the answer to one of the burning questions in a society fearful of death: 'What happens after I die?' They provide evidence that, whether or not there is an afterlife, you live on in spirit, in memory, in example, in the contribution you have made to the lives around you. Everything you do matters. It is all foundation for the next generation, to give them hope and faith. You do not know the names of the men and women who march past you on Anzac Day but you can embrace their spirit and invite their example into your own everyday life. You can be aware of them at your elbow when you strike the next rough patch. Many Australians use Anzac Day as just another public holiday and may end the day entertained but with a vague sensation of emptiness. Those who enter into the observance of the ritual are likely to conclude the day with their spirit enlivened and their sense of meaning expanded.

For one day of the year the haunting notes of the Last Post command us into a welcome communal silence, *Lest We Forget*. Only the bark of a dog breaks the hush of a quiet we have neglected and which releases us to reflect, as we rarely do, and to feel for a hallowed minute, the breathing of our common humanity.

The trumpet call of reveille rallies us, renewed as by sleep. The bag-pipes skirl and stir old instincts and for once it is easy to honour heroes rather than subvert them; natural to wave an Australian flag without questioning its relevance.

By afternoon the men are fulfilling the obligation of recounting the old campaign stories in an intoxication only partly due to alcohol. After nightfall, we seal the ceremony of the day by watching it all again on television, as if to make it real, as if to hold its glamour to the last moment.

Once again, ritual will have performed its cohesive function, as it has always done for humankind. Once again, we understand that the whole is greater than the sum of its parts; that we are embarked not on a solitary odyssey but on a mass evolutionary human journey. The destination may be uncertain, but for one day of the year we are reminded that the challenge is to be, for each other, trustworthy companions of the way.

For your Journal

* How clear are you in your sense of identity and authenticity? Perhaps write a list or draw a diagram of what forms your sense of identity, your sense of being you.

* How would you describe your purpose?

* Is forgiveness alive in your life, forgiveness of both yourself and others?

* Have you a satisfying spiritual home and a story in which to situate your spiritual life?

* Is your spiritual life a private matter or does it find some expression as well in community life?

* In what ways are you able to express your spiritual values in your occupation or career?

* What are your images of God?

* If God is not part of your picture, have you reflected on the source of your life, love and wellbeing?

Endnotes

1 Kevin Gilbert, *The Search for Meaning Collection*, Caroline Jones, ABC/Harper Collins, 1995.

2 Stephanie Dowrick, *Forgiveness and other Acts of Love*, Penguin, 1997.

3 Hymn by Christopher Willcock SJ, 1975. Dove Communications, 203 Darling Road, East Malvern, Victoria 3145.

4 A recent book by Michael Whelan is *Living Strings: An Introduction to Biblical Spirituality*, E. J. Dwyer, 1994.

5 'I am who I am', Exodus, Chapter 3, Verse 14.

6 Nick Carroll in *The Search for Meaning Collection*, Caroline Jones, ABC/Harper Collins, 1995.

7 Barbara Blackman in *The Search for Meaning Collection*, Caroline Jones, ABC/Harper Collins, 1995.

8 Judge Marcus Einfeld in *The Search for Meaning*, Caroline Jones, ABC/Collins Dove, 1989.

9 Professor Charles Birch in *The Search for Meaning*, Caroline Jones, ABC/Collins Dove, 1989. Also Tapes 27 and Tape 109 in *The Search for Meaning Catalogue*, ABC Radio Tapes.

10 Professor Charles Birch in *The Search for Meaning*.

11 Phillip Adams in *The Search for Meaning*, Caroline Jones, ABC/Collins Dove, 1989.

12 Ian Cohen in *The Search for Meaning*, Caroline Jones, ABC/Collins Dove, 1989.

13 Part of this reflection on Anzac Day was first published in *The Sydney Morning Herald*, 25 April 1996.

14 'For the Fallen' by Laurence Binyon.

9 GRACE

Happiness is not a state to arrive at,
but a manner of travelling.

Margaret Lee Runbeck, 20th-century American writer

Gratitude is a sign of noble souls.

Aesop

IT WAS THE first Sunday after Easter 1995. I was in an unfamiliar
district and I found my way to the local Catholic church. It was only
four months since *The Search for Meaning* program had been terminated
on ABC radio. I was still shocked from the loss and struggling to
come to terms with sudden, unexpected unemployment. Among the
capacity crowd flowing into the church, I noticed several people from a
nearby residence for women with Down syndrome, run by a religious
congregation of nuns. When it was time to go forward in long, slow
rows for communion, one of the women with Down syndrome fell
into line directly in front of me. Her hair was white and I thought
she could be older than me. She received the host but, when she
turned to go back, could not remember where she had been sitting.
I was almost past her before I realised her bewilderment. Someone
asked her, 'Where did you come from?' But she didn't know.

I held out my hand. Immediately, she put her hand in mine. It felt
warm and gentle. Slowly we wove our way back down the aisle against
the tide of people still coming forward. I did not know where she

had been sitting, but she trusted me to accompany her. Eventually a young woman near the back of the church came smiling towards us with recognition and the interlude drew to a calm conclusion. I returned to my place, puzzled that I felt moved by the brief encounter.

To me, chaos always seems quite near, just the other side of a thin partition, ready to break through. Order is hard-won and precarious. We appear to know where we are going. We put one foot in front of the other. We greet each other. We take it for granted that we will remember names. Some foolishness has convinced us that we are in control of our lives but, at any moment, that illusion can be breached. Suddenly, something is not where we left it; or toothache floods the jaw; or we're made redundant. When I lost my work, I lost some of my sense of order and meaning. My spirit felt crushed and I doubted my own worth. And then, one morning in church, the small, gentle hand of another perplexed person put it all into perspective: I am in control of nothing but as long as there's someone who will give me a hand in trust, there is dignity and purpose for me as a human being, whether or not I have paid work.

This is sheer grace. I do nothing to earn it. I cannot will an experience such as this. It has no explanation in logic or science. I cannot buy it. It is not material. Like every breath I draw, it is a gift, to which the only valid response is gratitude, and curiosity about its source.

Grace intervenes in human affairs in the most unexpected ways. In a moment, it can lift the yoke of a burden from the shoulders, restoring a lightness of being one thought had gone forever. Grace alone has enabled me to survive unbearable situations. At times, it has transformed my fear or resentment into gentler behaviour which I could never have achieved unaided. Dr M. Scott Peck writes that experiences of grace are 'manifestations of a powerful force originating outside of human consciousness which nurtures the spiritual growth of human beings'. He discusses the subject at length in *The Road Less Travelled*.[1]

I believe in grace because I experience it. It suggests to me an ultimate sensibility so far beyond my own capacity that I can only marvel at it and hope it may be a kindly intervention of the divine.

Whether or not you want to consider the question of God, life is enriched if you are open to experiences of grace — to recognise them, reflect on them and perhaps wonder at their origin. This may necessitate the cultivation of a new habit of gratitude which requires a relaxation of judgment. If you carry with you a rigid formula of expectation — for how things should be and how people should behave — you are limiting your experience of life, excluding the possibility of surprise. Strict preferences can narrow the horizon so that life becomes a disappointing process of mere categorisation.

Emma Pierce, whom I interviewed for *The Search for Meaning*, told me that 'misplaced importance' was a significant contributing factor to mental illness, and I find that a very useful insight.[2] I have felt a significant improvement in my peace of mind since I relinquished most expectations of people and circumstances. If you have not locked yourself into an ironclad picture of what a holiday must be, you are free to enjoy whatever that holiday may offer. If you hold no firm opinion of what another person should do, you save yourself from disillusion and you are open to being pleasantly surprised. After all, the only behaviour you can control is your own.

It's also possible to load too much anticipation onto some great day in the future when everything will come right. This can create a mirage that robs you of peace and enjoyment in the present. The only time you can actually live is the present, though certainly with hope and prudent plans for the future and, ideally, without regret for the past. But to attend to the present day with full awareness and a generous heart offers the best hope we have of living a good life in this world or the next, should that eventuate. Things seldom turn out exactly as we've imagined them, but the unforeseen can be a bonus if you're in the habit of entertaining that possibility. We have a choice. We can pine for the great day when happiness will arrive with a fanfare; or we can enjoy the travelling and contribute to its richness. The best way to achieve that is to greet your ordinary, daily reality with a sense of gratitude and in the hope of grace. When you allow life to flow around you rather than locking it into a set of compartments, you are constantly startled into fresh wonder.

In my experience, it is grace rather than will alone which enables some of our noblest achievements and our most sublime moments. I have just been rewarded by seeing again a drama produced for television in 1969 by the innovative English film director, Ken Russell. In black and white, it depicts the last few years of the English composer Frederick Delius and those around him. The film portrays an embittered Delius self-exiled in France, blind, paralysed, increasingly in pain and wasting from the effects of syphilis. He is aggrieved that his music is played only rarely in his homeland and disparaging of other English composers.

A young music scholar, Eric Fenby, leaves his home in the north of England to become Delius's amanuensis for the last five years of his life. It's a disturbing period for Fenby, isolated with the eccentric Delius household in rural France, devoid of any recreation or company of his own age. At first he is awed by Delius and intimidated by his imperious manner. Almost every hour of the day is regulated by the old composer's needs. A manservant carries him and feeds him. His wife Jelka devotes her life to him as she has done for years. He is a tyrant, and she allows it. He demands to be read to for hours on end. He is frequently rude and impatient. Sometimes he wants to listen to recordings of his own music and they sit together round the phonograph, relieved to see him transported for a few minutes out of his wretched physical state into the exaltation of his art.

Over four years, Delius relies on Fenby to take down his final compositions. Musically, it is a fruitful time but exhausting in its intensity as the irascible genius shouts and sings his instructions and the names of chords in a maddeningly nasal voice.

The drama raises many questions and leaves them for the viewer to answer. Why did Fenby stay in this painful situation? Was he more damaged or ennobled by it? Were he and Jelka right to bear Delius's ungracious selfishness for the sake of his music? Was their sacrifice grand or foolish or worse? How can appalling personal behaviour be reconciled with the creation of great art? Does the one diminish the other? What is the source of art like the music of Delius?

What I found most engrossing was the fact that young Eric Fenby stayed. In the face of much that he deplored, he found the courage to endure in the service of music and, ultimately, in the service of the cantankerous, helpless composer, long after the music had stopped. Many people who care for invalids or the frail elderly may relate to this tormenting dilemma, as they try to distinguish the boundary between compassionate duty and inappropriate self-sacrifice.

It seems to me that a sort of grace made this possible for Fenby. He could have left for a calmer life back in England doing his own work, yet some imperative called him to sacrifice four or five stressful years to enable the last of Delius's inspiration to be expressed. His personal happiness became secondary to more compelling values: reverence for art; pity for Jelka; and compassion for Delius as mortally wounded artist.

Although Fenby undoubtedly suffered himself during this period, surely he made a significant personal achievement. Difficult as it was, it must have been a maturing rite of passage for an unsophisticated young man, and fulfilling in its altruism and artistic creativity. In a shocking situation, he found new depth of character in himself. He saw a huge challenge honourably through to the end. How different his life might have been if he had taken flight as soon as his personality and sense of values came into collision with those of Delius.

In suggesting the possible contribution of grace to his achievement, I would not want to diminish Fenby's personal effort of will and character, as though the magic wand of grace dispelled the struggle of his ordeal. Not at all. What is arresting is his decision to surrender to the hardship and incompatibility of his commitment because it seemed right and decent. We are so unfamiliar today with the concepts of surrender, obedience and humility that they scarcely have meaning. Yet they suggest a cooperation between divine grace and human willpower which an earlier generation would have found natural, not demeaning, and which we could choose to validate today if we were prepared to withstand the tide of fashionable thinking. But that would run the risk of causing acute embarrassment. Today it is common to claim autonomy and the right to personal choice above all other values. All issues, including matters of life and death, are argued from that standpoint, as though we were the authors of the universe, and there were no such notion as responsibility to each other, to the wider society, or to any higher authority.

Grace is a mysterious quality that comes unbidden and never on demand. But one can become more aware of its possibility through gratitude. If you look back each evening over the events of the day, you will find much to appreciate. You may recall a pleasant encounter, a small problem solved, something beautiful in your surroundings, even the good health you enjoyed. Look for the simplest and the smallest evidence of grace and you will find it in abundance. It is always there. We just fail to notice it. Identifying gracious instances gives them validity and increases a positive approach to life that becomes its own reward. A habit of gratitude gradually strengthens a sense of benevolent order that will be an invaluable resource in times of trouble. We are inclined to magnify the significance of setbacks, to give them maximum, instant attention. A well-developed sense of the positive will provide a healthy antidote to this and a more realistic foundation from which to seek solutions.

Many of us will have a dim memory of Grace being the spoken prelude to a family meal. It was a gentle summons to be present, a ritual of connection between those seated around the table, and an acknowledgement of the providence of food and drink. It required the bowing of the head, a gesture of humility and respect now almost lost to western culture — like kneeling.

There are things you can do to introduce grace into your life. You might design your own small ceremony of gratitude to start the day. It could precede your exposure to the outside world in the form of radio, television or conversation. Be still; be present; give thanks for waking to another day, for your every breath and your eyesight, for fingers that move, for the blessing of a roof over your head, for the people who care about you, for your freedom . . . I am sure you will think of many other benefits to add to this list. You might like to ask for guidance (from your inner self, your higher power, God, the universe or virtual reality, if you like) to live this day with integrity and kindness; ask for inspiration to be of service to those you will encounter. Add your own favourite prayer, verse or affirmation, and sing a song in the shower, remembering to be grateful for running hot and cold water — unavailable to most people in the world. You may be surprised at the difference this prelude makes to your day.

Consider also the particular presence you will carry into the day. Could it be described as a gracious presence? Much more than we realise, we all carry with us a pervasive ambience. Deportment, expression, voice, manner, even clothes are all outward indicators of the state of your spirit. It is challenging to ponder what quality of spirit you bring to your environment, the shops, at work, and especially to your own home.

Your home is a revealing symbol of your inner state. It reflects your character in its decor, its state of order, and the space allocated to various activities. What does your home tell you about the condition of your inner self?

Where people share a house, interests and priorities compete for attention and the achievement of harmony becomes a challenge for all. What is your contribution to that harmony? On a daily basis, how do you make home more beautiful, more peaceful, more compatible for everyone who lives with you? Do you bring tension home, or the preoccupation of your work? Do you use home as a convenient hotel or staging post for your next foray into the real world outside? Do you bring home your best or what's left over? How does your arrival affect the atmosphere? What qualities do you carry over the threshold — gentleness or friction, self-absorption or readiness to share, praise or criticism, discontent or optimism, anxiety or serenity, dogmatism or willingness to listen, dullness or fun?

What was the most significant recent contribution you made to the happiness of your home? What do you do to make home a sacred place of nurture, respect, trust, security and faith in life for all who live there? Is there a place at your table for the unexpected guest? Do you live in tune with your natural environment, and with local bird and animal life?

Each day 14 lorikeets land screeching on my small balcony. Their electric-green flight is suddenly arrested in a pulsating hover of wing beats. Once landed, they lose their swift eloquence. They waddle to the two shallow bowls of water I keep filled for them, in the shade of the petunia pots. They sip the water; they loll and roll in it; they splash each other with widespread wings; they push each other and scream with satisfaction when one falls in. Most of the water is spilt during their raucous sortie. During the day they return in various combinations. Sometimes just a pair will come to play quietly, making soft sounds and preening each other.

They are confident in their sovereignty. They greet me with shrieks when I come to replenish their water, apparently pleased by my service to them. If I extend an arm, they will climb onto it and give it an exploratory nip. They peck my toenails and nibble the lip of the jug. Their presence is a source of wonder to me. I did not create them. I do not control them. I can only invite them with water but can never ensure they will come. Their visits are sheer grace. They are the very essence of lorikeetness. They remind me of the need to relax into my own nature, to be comfortable in my own skin.

Sometimes when I am worried, I remember them. I conjure the brilliant clash of their colouring, purple, green, red and yellow. I hear their screeching; I see them playing. Their spontaneity relieves my intensity; it makes me smile; it reminds me not to try so hard, reminds me that I am just a human whose obligation is just to be a human.

The lorikeets are not my only visitors. Pigeons come bearing a different quality. They step in quick, nervous jerks around the small space of the balcony. Their heads are in constant nodding movement. They peck ineffectually at the water and fail to get a drink. They are restless, anxious, ever-ready for escape. They climb carelessly onto the potplants and tread seedlings into the soil. They present a perfect mirror of my own occasional resort to anxiety and I'm relieved when they go in a startling whirr of wings.

Now a small, brush-tailed possum has come to spend its days curled up behind the potplants. I put an old mohair jumper down on the concrete, and the possum arranged it into a nest which she lined with a supple, perforated leaf of monstera deliciosa carried up from the garden, I cannot imagine how. I leave out pieces of fruit before I go to bed and I have seen the possum wake up at times during the day to nibble a piece of apple held in both paws, peering eyes unsighted by the light. The unlikeliness of this visitation is sheer grace.

I am reflecting on simple, accessible things — chance encounters, birds on the balcony, a television documentary. They are all around us, commonplace. But they are illuminated when regarded with the eye of gratitude. Like waking to a new day, they are all a gift if we choose to see them that way. And I suppose everyone has met one or two unusually graceful people and been uplifted by their quality. On the day Fr Richard Harris SJ said his last Mass in public, I knew that I was in a gracious presence.

Father had decided at the age of 92 to move from the retirement complex where he had been chaplain for ten years into a Jesuit community. Richard Harris was born in Ireland in 1903. After losing his mother when only a boy, he joined the Jesuits before fully understanding who they were. Later, after long years of education, he helped to train many young men for the priesthood in China, and suffered under the Japanese occupation of Hong Kong. In Australia, his service included a period at St Mary's parish, North Sydney. It was there that I first saw him, 14 years ago, standing at the back of the church after Mass, greeting people as they left. Tall and straight, he was dressed immaculately in clerical black topped with a cream jacket that suggested tropical kit in the Far East.

His ascetic demeanour was enlivened by a gentle Irish brogue and a readiness for laughter. People queued to see him, especially women. He remembered your name and asked how you were, and the warmth of his undivided attention for 30 seconds could give you hope and courage for the week ahead. He was one of the great mentors of Catholicism who attracted me to the church. He had a tremor and so, as he gave you a hug and then held your upper arms with kind bony hands, you were locked with him into a trembling embrace. When first I met him, I mistook the tremor for a shiver and bought him a warm singlet. Later I learned that he gave it away immediately to someone in need.

In this week of his farewell, he would accept nothing material in the way of a gift. 'I have taken a vow of poverty,' he would say, and you were startled into realising that he meant it. He demonstrated that in poverty there is a great freedom. He was attached to nothing but his lifelong faith. His final Mass was a test for the many of us who knew how much we would miss him, his honesty, and the absolute conviction with which he celebrated the sacrament.

Standing frail and trembling at the little altar in the chapel, he negotiated every move in the consecration of bread and wine with customary intention. It seemed miraculous that his shaking hands did not send the host scattering across the cloth or knock the chalice flying. But nothing could detract from his dignity.

Earlier, struggling to see the text, he had held the Lectionary up at an angle to focus on the words and capture them one by one before they slid sideways into a blur, escaping him. You could not take your eyes off him. He was translucent, ephemeral, more spirit than matter. He wore the lucidity of a long habit of truth in his face. And now, after a lifetime of devotion to his ideal, Fr Harris seemed to be looking beyond us, as though he had caught a glimpse of someone beckoning over our shoulder, and was eager to respond.

He assured us that, where he was going, he would not forget us and that he would continue to pray for us. Our sadness muted by awe for his sense of destination, we parted to let him pass. Our spattering of applause seemed puny in its attempt to honour a man who had walked faithfully in the steps of his master, no matter what the cost. We were in the presence of an authentic, humble holiness that had been 92 years in the making. We ended by singing one of his favourite hymns:

Oh, breathe on me, breath of God,
Fill me with life anew.
That I may love what Thou dost love
And do what Thou wouldst do.

Edwin Hatch and J. Harker

I have learned most of the important things I know about living not from textbooks but from gracious people. They are seldom prominent, instead living modestly and bringing a certain radiance to their small daily round. I have one friend who lives his life in considerable discomfort in a wheelchair. He is a distinguished poet, lecturer and translator whose speech, cruelly, has been scattered by stroke. Yet he has not turned to self-absorption. His former public life has been transmuted to a creative private life and, to describe his attitude to the change, one could borrow from George Eliot's *Middlemarch*, in which she wrote of the debt owed to those 'who lived faithfully a hidden life'; and described her heroine Dorothea's effect on those around her as 'incalculably diffusive: for the growing good of the world is partly dependent on unhistoric acts'.[3]

I find magnificent example in my friend's patience, the quick flashes of wit evident in his expression for long moments before he is able to give voice to them, the generous empathy of his listening, so ready to cry or laugh with me as I tell him what is happening in my life. Still excommunicated, as he recovers, from his own muse, yet he is ready to hear and respond to my struggles as a writer. I am in awe of the tenderness with which he and his loving wife regard each other. After a day spent with them I am grateful for their nourishment of my spirit. I am blessed by the stimulation of their company and the grace of their friendship.

My mother, too, had a remarkable capacity to make people welcome in her presence. She had a way of giving them her full attention and drawing them out that created an easy, hospitable atmosphere. You could see people relax safely into her ambience, glad to be near her. I suppose it was because she accorded each one their dignity. The tidiness of the house mattered far less to her than welcoming a visitor's arrival graciously. As she was neither extrovert nor gregarious by nature, I consider this to be an especially creative act of will and character. Whenever I see this quality emulated, I appreciate it deeply.

And I am repelled by its antithesis which was parodied to hilarious effect in the television situation comedy, *Keeping up Appearances*. The star chararacter, Hyacinth Bucket (pronounced 'Bouquet'), was immaculate in her portrayal of preoccupation with snobbery, status, belongings, the right clothes and grotesquely contrived candlelight suppers. Her affectation of a distinguished family background was regularly and delightfully punctured by the arrival of her unkempt, disreputable and far more appealing sisters.

Although we laughed at her, Hyacinth was a chilling character. She allowed no one else their integrity or humanity. Everyone was an object for manipulation to her own desires. She listened to no one and her sentimentality barely concealed a selfish cruelty. Consider her adulation of Daddy as a war hero whom she would gladly have to live with her 'if only he didn't dribble'. Quite unconsciously, she had the capacity to reduce everyone around her to clumsiness, fear, invisibility or weary resignation. Everyone, that is, except her son, Sheridan, conspicuous by his absence and a hereditary adeptness at manipulating regular loans by long-distance telephone call.

All the world's a mirror, if you're ready to peer honestly at your own reflection. I was chastened recently when an elderly friend chided me gently for 'getting everything done so quickly'. We were in her kitchen preparing a meal and I realised with regret that I had made her uncomfortable as she worked alongside me at the slower pace of age and infirmity.

I have always remembered a gracious colleague with whom I once worked. She was the least paid in the section and, in spite of her maturity, the most junior in professional status. Yet her presence brought to a tense workplace an air of courtesy, gentleness and humanity from which everyone benefited. She had brought up a large family and nursed a beloved husband to his death. She had a listening ear; she gave everyone the benefit of the doubt; she could do seven things at once with quiet competence and she remembered all our birthdays. She was a woman of devout faith who lived out all the human virtues, without ever preaching them, in ordinary daily life. Each afternoon when she left to catch the crowded suburban train home, she took with her an element of serenity that would be missed until her return next day. No doubt her gentleness was equally treasured in her own home. Like most gracious people, she seemed quite unconscious of her effect. Perhaps that is part of the gift.

When *The Search for Meaning* program began at ABC Radio in

1987, I worked with a number of different technical operators to record the interviews. They were all helpful and competent, but one of them went the extra mile. Brian Mattison was immediately in tune with the aim of the program. It was his inspiration to try to create an atmosphere conducive to the telling of a personal story. From somewhere in the inhospitable, spartan, rabbit warren of ancient studios, he found two armchairs which he placed facing each other at such an angle as to suggest conversation rather than confrontation. He would arrange two standing microphones on long arms in the most unobtrusive positions possible, to avoid any barrier to communication. Then he would purloin, possibly from the office of an executive puzzled by its regular disappearances, a large Benjamina figtree in a pot. It looked extremely heavy and it must have cost him enormous effort to manhandle it from place to place each time we had a studio booking.

My guest and I would sit sheltered from the glaring neon by this greenery, and furnished with a jug of water and two good glasses on a low table. I never asked about the source of these unwonted luxuries as I felt sure it would involve a bending of ABC regulations which Brian may prefer not to discuss. At any rate, we never began our talk until he had arranged us to his satisfaction, as though he were doing a vase of flowers.

I was so grateful to him for the thoughtful attention he gave to his work, well beyond the call of duty. Undoubtedly, he helped to relax guests in an unfamiliar situation and reassure them they were being taken seriously. When Brian was made redundant, in one of the regular purges inflicted by the ABC management upon its staff, his grief was a foreshadowing of my own, to come some months later. Casually, the organisation had dispensed with yet another talented worker, but nothing could expunge the grace of his contribution to *The Search for Meaning* programs.

Seeking to isolate the qualities of gracious behaviour that I have encountered, I can identify naturalness; lack of pretension; lack of guile; unselfconsciousness; kindliness; lack of pride; a habit of humility and considering others first; humour, especially the ability to laugh at oneself; capacity to listen; composure, serenity, even a certain detachment; wisdom; a sense of fairness; gentleness and patience. Perhaps adding to my list and amending it may be a place to begin your reflection on the presence of grace in your own life.

For your Journal

* Who are some of the graceful people in your life?
  What are the graceful characteristics of the way they live?

* Could you adopt any of these characteristics?

* Start a new page to make a list of all the things you're good at. Leave space to add to it. Include everything from listening to laughing to tying bows to ploughing a paddock. Who taught you these things?

* Consider the contribution that grace has made to your accomplishments.

* Reflect on your day. Identify those things for which you are grateful.

* Contemplate those aspects of your life that are pure gift.

* Is there room to increase your practice of being grateful?

* Design a short ritual for yourself to start each day with gratitude.

* What might be the source of grace?

* Recall instances of grace in your life, times when a burden was lifted; when you were enabled to do the seemingly impossible; when suddenly you were unaccountably light-hearted.

* Has your character been strengthened by persevering through a difficult time as Eric Fenby did?

* Which bird or animal expresses the way you feel yourself to be in the world?

* Have you a sense of being content in your own nature?

* What attributes do you bring to your environment, especially your home?

* What else could you bring?

* Do you concentrate on destinations rather than enjoy the travelling?

Endnotes

1 M. Scott Peck, *The Road Less Travelled: A New Psychology of Love, Traditional Values and Spiritual Growth*, Arrow Books, 1983.

2 Emma Pierce in *The Search for Meaning Collection*, Caroline Jones, ABC/Harper Collins 1995. Also an audiotape, *Making Sense of Life Vol. 2*, ABC shops. Books by Emma Pierce are available from the author: P.O. Box Q93, Queen Victoria Building, Sydney 2000.

3 George Eliot, *Middlemarch*, Oxford University Press, 1986, p. 682.

10 SUFFERING

*Your pain is the breaking of
the shell that encloses your understanding.*

Kahlil Gibran[1]

ONE OF THE MOST important aspects of life to come to terms with is suffering. Yet we do everything to avoid it. Earlier generations may have had a more realistic acceptance of the integral place of suffering in life, but in modern western society the prevailing message is that suffering can be anaesthetised with fun, sex, excitement, drugs, alcohol, taking risks, shopping, the amassing of information, or overwork; or ended with suicide or euthanasia. This carries the assumption that the only proper goal of life is pleasure — that suffering is an aberration. Armed with this misunderstanding, we venture into the world ill-equipped to deal with setbacks and missing the point of human experience altogether. To find some coherent and hopeful way to deal with suffering is one of the crucial keys to a life of meaning.

The truth of our own lived experience is that it contains much suffering, starting with the relatively slight problems of everyday life. To help develop a sense of proportion, consider the long procession of challenges that characterise every human life. First, we are pushed, howling, into the world; for many months we remain helpless and dependent; later, we have to separate from our mothers; then we are wrenched from the familiarity of home to go to school; we are pricked with immunisation needles; we are bullied in the playground; we can't have everything we want; we fail a test; we lose a race; a girlfriend or boyfriend leaves us; circumstances at work are difficult; we lose a job; we get sick; in marriage, we sacrifice our beloved individuality into the discipline of partnership; women give birth to children in the grinding pain of labour; we cede much of our freedom to look after our children.

In small and large ways, every life is marked by the milestones of suffering. And it comes in many forms — physical, emotional, psychological and spiritual. Whether we like it or not, it is a fact of the human condition. Whatever modern pretence we have entertained about the perfectability of human life through the enlightenment of rationality and science, we must acknowledge that suffering has been more hideously demonstrated in the 20th century than ever before. To ignore this is to sell ourselves short with a counterfeit scheme of meaning.

Suffering happens, and it can touch us at the very deepest level of our being. What matters is what we do with it. And what we do with it will grow to some extent out of how we think about it. Dr M. Scott Peck, in *The Road Less Travelled*, takes suffering as his starting point. He says that 'it is in this whole process of meeting and solving problems that life has its meaning . . . it is only because of problems that we grow mentally and spiritually'.[2]

Much of the popularity of his best-selling book can be attributed to its first sentence — 'Life is difficult'. I imagine the truth of this statement is such a relief to readers that they cannot wait to see where he will go with it. He has won our confidence and collaboration. So we read on, and the journey with him through the book turns out to be a rewarding one.

For it is our experience that life is difficult, and before accepting any solutions to that proposition we are pleased merely to have the fact acknowledged. When times of suffering come, physical pain, emotional pain, a bereavement, or the loss of a job, it is difficult to think about anything but the suffering. It engulfs you and all you can do is hope and pray that it will come to an end, and that you will survive it. While you are in the midst of it, it can be terribly destructive and demoralising. Scott Peck's acknowledgement of the difficulty of life and the fact of suffering validates our own experience. It gives the impression that someone understands; that someone is listening to us and actually hearing what we are saying. We are greatly encouraged by this, because the absence of a generously listening ear is one of our principal sources of suffering.

Scott Peck, who is a psychiatrist, goes on to say that the tendency to avoid difficulty is the primary basis of all mental illness. This arresting statement immediately invests difficulty and suffering with great potential and purpose, for none of us wishes to court mental illness. By the end of the second page, he has given the reader a strong motivation not to avoid difficulty. He has redefined difficulty as a gateway rather than a dead end or a punishment. He has moved life's difficulty from an isolated personal affliction to a general fact of the human condition. He has suggested self-discipline as a means of dealing creatively with it, and offered the incentives of growth and wisdom as likely outcomes of the struggle.

Paradoxical as it is, suffering often brings out the nobility in us. At our best, when we can manage it, we follow something like Scott Peck's suggestion. We accept the challenge of our difficulty and suffering, bear it with courage, accept help, try to find solutions, and learn and grow from it. Similarly, we do our best to alleviate or comfort the suffering of others. When a sister becomes ill, we care for her; a friend gets into strife — we stand by him. When we are told about starving people, we respond with generous donations. Because we feel the injustice of it, we strive to lessen the suffering in society.

There are many people living faithful, unsung and sometimes desperate lives of devotion caring for frail or incapacitated relatives or friends. Most of these things are done privately and we may think they make little difference in the grand scheme of things. But every such action has its own intrinsic worth. It is something of lasting or ultimate importance, whether it is acknowledged or not. Whatever you may do to bear your own suffering with hope or to alleviate the suffering of others is an encouraging inspiration to those around you. In a way that is often hard to see, it nurtures the spiritual life of the giver, the recipient and the whole community.

Sometimes the response to suffering becomes more publicly visible, when there is a tragedy involving numbers of people. Then we all learn something significant about the place of suffering in human life. The devoted nursing and care of HIV/AIDS patients is a case in point. Led by the gay community, people from all sections of society created a new benchmark for compassion and practical care. In that experience, our community discovered what we are capable of. It was a revelation and there is no turning back from it. This is not to say that the suffering was a good thing, but rather that people won some goodness from it. There are numerous stories of patients, families and carers being changed by a dreadfully testing experience which nonetheless provided opportunities for reconciliation. These stories also offer a new understanding of what matters in a life well lived, and what constitutes a good death. That new comprehension was hard-won through the anguish of those involved but it taught us that one legitimate version of a good death is a death supported by effective palliative care, and the love and company of family, friends and carers.

Gradually, through experience, we may learn that almost every episode of suffering is not only painful but also maturing: that it takes us to a new stage of understanding and leaves us with more resources and courage than we had before, often with more wisdom. This is a significant insight that we need to take in and carry with us. Then it becomes a sustaining inner knowledge that an upset is not an impasse, but an experience with various layers of testing, some of which may contain the possibilities of personal growth. But I doubt that this insight into suffering is born in us. We need to be taught about it, to experience it personally and see it demonstrated by influential figures like parents, teachers and community leaders.

One approach to suffering is to decide what, for you, constitutes a good life. Does life have some intrinsic purpose? Is it perhaps a journey of learning, or does it have no aim but the maximisation of pleasure and the minimisation of pain? In a consumer society, we are conditioned to think of life as a commodity to be enjoyed while it is in good working order and disposed of, like a faulty electric toaster, when it develops defects. A society like ours, which is frightened of illness and death, does not want to be confronted with its own frailty or mortality. We do not want to be reminded that, in spite of the many triumphs of science, illness and death have not been conquered, and that they will come to each of us. In a society that prizes personal autonomy we are fearful of the dependence that suffering may bring, yet the reality is that we are dependent on each other all through life, in many ways. My every action and decision impinges on those around me, as their decisions and actions affect my life. That is the way it is, yet so often we insist on the illusion of our independence, preferring denial to the truth.

Could it be that fear of dependence is bound up with fear of intimacy? In caring for a sick or suffering person, you come close to them, and enter into the minutiae of their life. This can be threatening on both sides, for secrets and foolishness and vulnerabilities are revealed in the process. Have you noticed how sometimes, when you have unburdened yourself to someone, or achieved an unusual closeness with them, you then avoid them for a while as though to avoid the risk of giving any more of yourself away into that intimacy? There can be a seesawing contradiction in our behaviour in this area. While we long for intimacy, we may also push it away because we treasure our autonomy. At the same time our longing for love draws us into closeness, and that leads to interdependence that will produce both the rewards and the tensions of intimacy. One way to find a measure of peace with this subject is to go back to your basic belief about life, and work from there.

A common view in western society today is that I 'own' my life, and therefore I control my life, and it is my right to make decisions and choices accordingly. We are conditioned to think in this way and it has some strengths because it may breed initiative. The autonomous view of life is fostered especially in men who are rewarded for independent toughness and competitiveness. Suffering of any kind may be especially difficult for the person who holds this belief because it forces him to realise that everything is not, after all, under his control. The experience may shake him to the foundations because it reveals a vulnerability he had denied. He may experience it as a humiliating weakness. He may say that he 'can't handle it'. He will resist his need for help and perhaps find it difficult to believe that such help would be available to him. Taken to an extreme, he may even opt to end his own life rather than submit to the process of suffering. On the other hand, if he can submit to it, he may be changed by that humbling experience of dependence to see that he does indeed need help from others, that they are willing to give it to him, and that the acceptance of their help has some unexpected rewards. To feel that experience and reflect on it, take it in and be enlightened by it, can lead to an enriching breakthrough that may facilitate his endurance of suffering in future.

Another view is that life is a gift from God and that our role is to cooperate with God in the unfolding of our destiny, even when that includes suffering. This does not mean that God inflicts suffering but that, however difficult things become, there is a purpose in life that only God can know fully, and one has faith in that purpose even when it seems inexplicable. This is a less lonely framework in which to encounter suffering than that of the person who holds personal autonomy as the highest value. The Christian, for instance, has God as creator, guide and companion; and also a hope of reward in an afterlife.

Similarly, a Buddhist may persevere with suffering because her deepest belief is that there is meaning in this suffering; that it represents a lesson she needs to learn; an atonement for some ignorance in her past history; an attachment or a desire she needs to let go; a river she needs to cross on the long ascent to Nirvana. Since Nirvana is her goal, her suffering becomes invested with meaning. It has a purpose and this will give her physical, psychological, intellectual, emotional and spiritual fortitude with which to endure the experience; and ritual, like meditation, through which to negotiate the rite of passage. Buddhism and other spiritual traditions also believe in the power of prayer and meditation to support people in their suffering.

Others may not acknowledge any role for God, but might argue: 'I need to live by right action. All my actions and decisions affect those around me. My life is inextricably linked with other lives in a complex web of interdependence. Therefore I nominate the common good as the prevailing value and recognise the capacity for basic goodness in people.' This too gives a lucid way to think about suffering. It holds the alleviation of suffering as an ideal. It is a way that relieves loneliness for it relies on the giving and receiving of help as a predictable characteristic of an essentially communal life in which we accept responsibility for each other.

Another person's basic belief about the nature of life may be principally influenced by the insights of science. He may consider himself to be a random assembly of biochemical elements activated by electrical impulses. In the absence of measurable evidence for any intrinsic meaning to life, he may conclude that it is up to the individual to create meaning for himself. In this framework of understanding, he may feel perfectly justified in the avoidance of suffering because it is an exercise in futility. His picture of life simply does not admit any sense beyond the material, visible, tangible and measurable. He is not on his way to Nirvana or Heaven or any other destination. His body and mind are the only realities of his personal existence, and suffering merely a sign that one or other of them is experiencing a systems failure.

As for his soul, he may repudiate the notion, or he may agree with Nobel laureate Francis Crick's hypothesis that the soul is no more than the behaviour of a 'vast assembly of nerve cells'.[3] Severe illness, accompanied by pain, indignity and dependence, might signal to him that he has become a burden to himself and those around him and that there is no point in prolonging life because he sees no way of being productive or happy. He can envisage his suffering in only one light. It is evidence of decay with no potential for enlightenment for himself or others. It will seem humane to him to put an end to human suffering, including his own, as one would put down an injured dog.

He may still lead a good and generous life with this approach. Indeed, he may feel an urgency to contribute to the betterment of that society to which he will belong so briefly and inexplicably. But he will live in that society with a different understanding from that of the Buddhist. And of course he will bring very different arguments to any conversation about suffering.

This view, which is related to the autonomous view described earlier, may be quite acceptable and satisfying to the individual who holds it. Yet, if he proposes it as a proper view for society as a whole, another question arises for reflection. Do we want a society in which some lives are judged to be not worth living *solely because of the suffering they contain*? If so, who will make that judgment in which it is considered merciful to end the suffering of the terminally ill, the physically disabled or the mentally incapacitated?

It is important to think about suffering because it comes to us all, and our ideas about it give us a basis on which to start to deal with it, both as individuals and as citizens of a humane society. However, there are many complexities and subtleties in this peculiarly challenging aspect of life. Each person's suffering is unique and all the thinking we do about it will be tempered by the actual experience of it, in our own lives and the lives of those around us.

One of my friends, Veronica, has served the wide community for almost half a century in religious life, as a Sister of Mercy, and is now suffering a most debilitating form of cancer whose effects check her every move. Before her body was claimed by this disease, she was very active, practising Hatha yoga and Tai Chi, long-distance walking and circle dancing; and she led groups of people on demanding journeys to some of the great spiritual centres of the world. Now, damaged bones have reduced her physical stature and left her body in a perpetual state of discomfort.

When the cancer was first discovered, she was shocked by some of the painful, invasive procedures used in diagnosis and treatment. Now she has learned to question everything the doctors propose and to get as much information as possible before agreeing to the next round of therapy. Having information about the drugs used in treatment is very important to her.

Her life today is a roller-coaster ride. Even in such frail health, she is sometimes out and about participating in social justice issues, attending gatherings and petitioning government ministers. Then, when another onerous course of treatment begins, she is flattened again. Patient with the suffering, she doesn't pretend it is not happening and, if you ask, she will search for words to describe it, seeming surprised at times that she is still alive to discuss something so severe in its effects.

Occasionally, she feels well enough to type for a while on the computer, reflecting with passion and humour on the experiences of a rich life. Veronica is a radical who has lived for many years outside the institutional structures of both church and religious order. An innovative thinker and communicator, she has studied Creation Spirituality in depth with the American theologian Matthew Fox, and it was she who first made its principles more widely known across Australia. With the Christian mystics, she believes that the Via Negativa is often the way through to the Via Positiva. She thinks of suffering not as a subject to be analysed but as something that flows in our blood, as does joy — in no way separate from the rest of life.

When I asked if prayer was any help in her difficult situation, the reply was that her prayer now is very simple: 'Lord, please help me to sit up in bed and achieve the few steps to the bathroom.' Faith in the Giver of life has taught her to depend, in suffering as in all else, on the compassionate challenge of the Christ of the scriptures; on the extraordinary fidelity and caring of her family and many, many friends; on the calming gift of nature; and on the skill of her doctors and other healing practitioners. Reading the lives of others who have suffered strengthens her courage. One recent inspiration was a memoir by American Cardinal Bernadin relating the ordeal of his own suffering and his reconciliation with those who had falsely accused him of wrongdoing.

Veronica lives in a tiny unit which has become a mecca for visitors. She bestows on them the great gift of her listening and her insights. Even at times when she is far from well, and in pain, her presence is strong. In learning how to live with suffering, by trial and error, and through faith, she is teaching everyone who meets her some powerful lessons. Young friends studying overseas have just named their new baby after her. They wrote to her: 'Our daughter will always remind us of you and if she captures some of the strength, love and freedom of spirit that you possess, she will be very fortunate.'

I accompanied another friend through her process of dying. She was an intuitive woman whose life was guided by the insights of transpersonal psychology. She thought that people attract into their lives the lessons they need to learn, on a pathway to self-actualisation. She ran a successful small business and, in both her professional and personal life, she placed a high value on being of service to others. She believed in reincarnation and in the influence of past lives on the present. When she was diagnosed with cancer, she had a preference for the therapies of complementary medicine and the practices of meditation and visualisation, but she accepted the treatment of conventional medicine as well.

As time went on, the disfigurement of her illness was grotesque and pitiable, yet she seemed to be sustained by her inner resources. Palliative care gave her relief from pain most of the time, but it would have shocked no one if she had asked for death. I expect that we would have been relieved. Yet she did not. Patiently she lived through her last days, meeting people with whom she needed to make peace, loving her family, even choosing the poems she would like read at her funeral. I have a happy memory of the day when she decided to do that. She asked me to bring some anthologies of poetry, and she sat on her hospital bed wearing a turban to cover the baldness of chemotherapy, and hunted through the books to find her favourite verses.

The process of her dying was undeniably ravaging yet never for a moment did it seem futile. She was disappointed by her terminal illness, and very sad to leave her family and friends, but somehow she was not defeated by it. While still able, she was interested in trying to discern some purpose in it, to do it as thoughtfully as she could, to learn from the experience of her life, right to the end. She used her last weeks to set her life in order and those close to her had time to say their goodbyes and thank her for all that she had meant to them.

In her last days she seemed unconscious but we continued to talk to her. I was grateful that she had let me accompany her dying. Even though at times I found it excruciating, it was a beautiful acknowl-edgement of her trust in me as a friend and it enabled me to bear something I had thought to be beyond me. It was the last of many kind and generous things she did for me.

One evening, calmly, as if by choice, she took her last breath and lay still and serene. Her mother, husband, two sons and I were gathered round her bed. It was a moment of heightened significance, almost excitement, certainly sacred. Her continuing presence was palpable. The sense was of a long, rigorous rite of passage safely traversed.

I am grateful for what I learned from these friends. Each one taught me more about the puzzle of suffering, about how to endure, how to ask for help and how to receive it. Each one expanded my understanding of what it is to be human, and what might be meant by a good life and a good death. I was learning that you cannot judge anyone else in how they choose to deal with their suffering. People will do what they can manage and they will do their best.

Not everyone can find a sustaining way to interpret and bear their suffering. For some, years of patient endurance and stoic struggle may end in apparent defeat. I wrote earlier about the tragedy of a member of my own family who took her life. I cannot know the full truth of her plight for there is always part of a person's story that remains cloistered in the sanctuary of the soul. I can only celebrate her life and search sadly for clues to the causes of her despair. She belonged to a generation in which women's work was principally homemaking, at which she excelled. Being homemaker and wife and mother is a vital and honourable endeavour but for some it is not a complete lifework. They yearn for a role in the wider world and, in this longing, she reflected the frustration of her generation. The men and women of her age had their youth conditioned by World War I and the poverty of the Depression, and their young married lives dislocated by World War II. Their values were shaped accordingly. Uppermost, for the majority, were thrift, caution and self-sacrifice for the wellbeing of the group. Most men got what work training they could rather than being able to follow a preferred personal calling, while women stayed at home to support men and children and took last priority in developing their own vocation.

By the time she was in her fifties, there was an epidemic of women presenting at doctors' surgeries with depression. The doctors had no answers for them. Community support groups had not yet been established. But the drug companies responded shrewdly with a plethora of mind-altering chemical preparations skilfully promoted to a nonplussed medical profession, to relieve *their* anxiety about this phenomenon. The advertising worked, and the legitimate sadness and frustration of countless women was tranquillised with chemicals. Deprived of their autonomy and without support to relieve the condition underlying their symptoms, their suffering was terrible and some did not survive.

For all my grieving over what had happened in my own family, I could not identify all its causes. Indeed, it would be arrogant to do so. You cannot come to conclusions about someone else's story and you can never know it in full. You can only reflect respectfully on their circumstances and see if there is something there for you to learn. What I did know was that she had lived her life in hard-working service to those around her and that she had a genius for encouraging others, including me, to reach their full potential. Part of her tragedy may have been that she did not realise her own.

She was intensely creative without adequate opportunity to express her creativity. She was loved and appreciated by many people yet she seemed unable to take this in, to receive love and be nourished by it. She seemed to lack a solid sense of her own inner authenticity — that she was unique, worthwhile, amusing and attractive in herself. In the absence of a purpose true to her own need, it is possible that she felt no legitimate cause for happiness and perhaps suffered a terrible loneliness, to which she could envisage no end.

Another real lack was that she did not find a spiritual home. For an artistic and sensitive person, this must have seemed a severe deprivation. It is a great testament to her courage and loyalty that she endured, for as long as she did, a life visited too often by a depression for which no remedy could be found. There is no doubt in my mind that it was her suffering and death that gave birth to my own search for a spiritual home and my desire to accompany others in their search for meaning. It was only one of her many gifts to me. I pray for her to rest in peace and I look forward with hope to our reunion.

It is difficult to know what to do in the presence of another person's grief or suffering. Most of us have been lost for words at a funeral. The things that were helpful to me in my own loss were rather simple. As we drove down the main street behind the hearse, an elderly man stopped on the footpath, removed his hat and held it over his heart as he watched us go by. I found it very touching that he did not know us and yet he showed his respect for our situation. It gave me a feeling of belonging to a society that shares important common values. It was a bleak, windy August and I recall how chilled I felt in my unsuitable black mini-dress at the edge of the grave, which was surrounded surprisingly by strips of synthetic green lawn. I was uncertain when and where to place my little bunch of violets as the coffin was lowered. I left it too late and had to throw them. They landed with a soft thump on the polished wood. It was all wrong.

I could not think how to cater for the gathering afterwards, so we bought fish and chips wrapped in big sheets of white paper with wedges of lemon, and went home and ate it on the front verandah in watery sunshine that had no solace in it. My aunts made pots of tea. It helped me when people expressed their own sorrow at her death. I remember one of our friends who couldn't stop crying. She was overcome with sadness and even though she talked and ate pieces of fish with her fingers and shared memories and even laughed at some of them, tears were coursing down her face. I was grateful to her, as though she were doing my crying for me when, at that stage, I could not.

The next day the Presbyterian minister came, which was an act of kindness since our family did not go to church. He seemed at a loss for anything to say except that he was sorry, which I appreciated. He asked if we would like to pray. Since conversation had dried up and we did not have any better suggestion, it seemed polite to kneel on the lounge room carpet with him while he said a few things to God. This was many years before I had any sense of religious conviction and I could not imagine God having any role in our scenario. Insofar as I had thought about it, which was very little, there were only two possibilities relating to God. Either He did not exist or He had abandoned us. The first possibility seemed preferable, for what sort of God would be absent when so desperately needed?

Other people gave comfort by writing a letter, by telephoning, or just by being there. It was wonderful that Bruce Buchanan, my boss at work, drove 80 kilometres to visit for a few kind hours. It helped when someone was ready to talk about her, or listen to how I felt. Just those few thoughtful gestures meant a great deal to me. Now, in the presence of someone else's grief, I imagine myself back into that time and try to reproduce those remembered acts of kindness.

People down the centuries have had coherent traditions to help them with their suffering, in all its manifestations. The earliest tribal religions had practices to incorporate suffering into their rites of passage and invest it with significance. All the great spiritual traditions give suffering a context that is ultimately purposeful, in a cycle of death and rebirth interpreted in various ways. But because modern people have discarded these formal traditions and found no satisfying substitute, we are in a bind that leads us into cul-de-sacs of avoidance, cynicism and despair, the most wretched of human conditions. At the start of the third millennium, where are we to look for guidance?

One of the most sustaining sources of meaning is to be found in the stories of suffering told by our contemporaries. In my *Search for Meaning* years on ABC radio, I was privileged to hear the life stories of many men and women and it was possible to discern a pattern in them. Often there was an early stage of unreflective living, a time of consuming, striving and achieving. Then some crisis, accident or illness led to a period of confinement that some called 'the dark night of the soul'. Many people recounted that this was followed by an awakening to fresh insight and a new sense of direction and purpose. This cycle was sometimes repeated many times in the course of a lifetime.

As I listened to these hundreds of revealing experiences, I remembered the lifecycle of the butterfly, learned at primary school. I had been fascinated by the four distinct stages: egg, caterpillar, chrysalis-in-cocoon, butterfly. We were encouraged to collect caterpillars and keep them supplied with leaves which they ate voraciously. The next stage was utterly mysterious, when the caterpillar wove itself into a cocoon, trussed, immobile, hanging in limbo, presumably living on stored food, and making a dramatic, secret transformation.

One day when the right flowers were in bloom and the temperature was hospitable, some instinct split open the shiny casing of the cocoon, and out climbed a vision of exquisite fragility. For a few moments it trembled on its former prison before taking gentle flight, a new creation with the victory of wings. I saw the magic of it but it didn't occur to me to see it as a metaphor of life, a blueprint of the journey on which I was embarking, all those years ago, at Murrurundi Primary School. Yet isn't the cocoon an apt symbol for times of suffering — those dry, dark passages of desolation when you are ill, anxious or uncertain; when you feel trapped or immobilised; when you feel lonely, rejected, grieving the loss of a relationship or a job; times when you are out of step with the world?

For the butterfly, the cocoon is not only a prison but also a place of transformation. Could it be that the cocoon of suffering is not only painful but also a creative place where you are evolving into the next stage of being human? Frequently, those who told me their stories on *The Search for Meaning* programs acknowledged the link between suffering and the new sense of life that followed, and found hope and satisfaction in the idea. Many felt that this gave them a new way to approach suffering and to bear it in future. As these stories were told to me, I found many encouraging elements in them about the place of suffering in human life.

I knew Yami Lester by reputation as one of the activists seeking recognition and compensation for people whose health had been affected by the British nuclear testing at Maralinga, but I had never met him before. On a visit to Sydney from Central Australia, he agreed to come to the ABC studios to record an interview with me. I was looking forward to our meeting.

Yami was a striking figure. He had a dark youthful face under a surprising shock of white hair. He described the sickness that had come like a pestilence upon his people in the desert after the nuclear testing and how he himself had gone blind. The loss of sight was devastating for a young rural worker with no qualification other than working cattle on the great outback holdings. The worst thing was having to leave his home and family to live far away among strangers in Adelaide, to learn how to manage as a blind person. It was a lonely, frightening time, but it turned him into a well-educated stirrer with new vision and purpose on behalf of his people. His suffering had transformed his life. I could detect no bitterness in him but only an intelligent determination that had proved very effective in gaining recompense for his afflicted people.[4]

I have been told by many people that rock bottom is the turning point. Many an Alcoholics Anonymous meeting has heard this theme repeated: that the moment of admitting helplessness was the first step on the road to hope and recovery.

Father Con Keogh told me quite frankly that, years ago, he had gone mad but no one explained it to him. He had thought he must be in hell. Eventually, a brother priest told him the truth of his condition and that was the turning point. Everything he learned on his long struggle back to health would produce the 12-step Grow program which has assisted countless people suffering mental anguish. It was an inspiration to meet him and to contemplate with him all that had grown out of his suffering. He had developed, through his own hard experience, a knowledge and understanding of mental breakdown and recovery that could not have been learned from textbooks. However I looked at it, I could not avoid making the connection between Fr Keogh's personal suffering and his great gift to the mentally ill.[5]

A similar equation presented itself when I met Paul Stevens. Two years before our meeting, he had been devastated by losing his job. After a period of depression, he set himself a simple task that he had never done before. He made a list of his skills. He looked at them and shuffled them like a pack of cards and put them into different combinations. He was analysing exactly what he had in the way of resources and how they could be employed. To his surprise, there were several viable possibilities, but his best inspiration came from the exercise he had just done. If he could identify new directions for himself in such a way, then he could do it for others. And so he did. He established the Centre for Worklife Counselling. Through his own painful experience, he was able to show other people how to see new possibilities for employment and, in doing so, created an authentic and satisfying job for himself.[6]

Over the years, I was told hundreds of stories about the experience and consequences of suffering. There was no mistaking the pain of them and yet I was inspired, time and again, by the strength, patience and faith people had found in order to endure. I could not ignore the many links between suffering and a positive outcome.

Magda Bozic was plunged into suffering in a shocking way. She lost most of her family in the wartime bombing of Budapest and her young husband was killed on the Russian front. She decided to migrate to Australia, but the pain of leaving Hungary was acute. Her touching description speaks to anyone who has had to say goodbye to their home:

The full impact hits you when you are on the station with your luggage. You look at the people around you with whom your whole life was a network, with whom you went through all that life meant to you, love affairs, happy moments, terrible times, awful grief — but it was all shared life. This small crowd of people stand around you with their awkward little presents. They hardly dare to look at you and you at them. You are thinking 'let's just have the strength to get through that five more minutes', but you break down and you weep. You get on that wretched train and it slowly, slowly moves away. They are standing and waving to you and you can't touch them any more ... From being one person with language, with home, with friends, you step ashore in another place and you're a migrant; you don't speak the language, you don't have friends, and you nod and smile and feel awkward.'[7]

I was very much moved by Magda's description of this painful leavetaking. Is that because she has created a metaphor for the exile of the human condition and the relentless demands that life makes on us to be ready to say farewell again and again? To take her words literally is poignant enough, but then there is so much loss underneath them. For what is left when one has been stripped of family, friends, home, hemisphere, culture and language? This is the suffering of the scourge. It could be a passport to madness. Yet Magda responded to it with all the strength of her character.

Instead of seeking haven in the Hungarian community of Sydney, she set off for Darwin. She learned the new language. She made a new marriage. She brought up her son and she built a productive and contributing life in Australia. Chaos had threatened her life, yet she held to the sustaining humanist philosophy that people are basically good, that we have responsibility for each other, and that every individual gesture towards the common good is worthwhile. Her story tells us what is possible for the human person. It does not promise that it will be easy but it suggests that we may choose how to look at difficult circumstances and how to respond to them. And it tells us that there is always hope. Magda could have chosen differently. She could have succumbed to despair.

And so could Brian Keenan, the Irish university lecturer kidnapped in Beirut by terrorists who imprisoned him for four and a half years in filthy, cramped conditions. Yet his confinement turned out to be a time of profound personal and spiritual encounter which he has documented in his book, *An Evil Cradling*.[8] I had to read the book in preparation for an interview with him but week after week I kept putting it off, because it was such a terrifying story. Somehow I could not avoid projecting myself into his fearful situation, and I knew that it would be beyond me. By the time I had finished *An Evil Cradling*, my fear was unabated yet I had recognised profound meaning in Brian Keenan's brave interpretation of what had happened to him. It is the sort of book I could take up for courage when I need it. This impression was reinforced when I met him and encountered his hard-won, deeply reflective maturity — and the charming Irish humour which, miraculously, he had retained.

Each of these powerful personal stories sheds more light on the tough subject of suffering and enriches our way of thinking about it.

They offer us the option of contemplating suffering as a rite of passage rather than as a brick wall.

When I talked with the distinguished biologist, Professor Charles Birch, he suggested that suffering is the experience that brings us closest to each other. He went on to say that God is with us in our suffering. These two ideas are encouraging in that they lend a depth of meaning to suffering that we may not have considered. He expressed them like this:

> Every experience I have, every experience that every creature has, is registered in the heart of God. In Christianity, the Cross is probably the greatest symbol of that because this is the symbol of God's participation in creatural suffering. You can't participate more in another life than to participate in the suffering of that life. God not only participates in the world so that it couldn't exist without him, but God participates in the feelings of the world.[9]

Charles Birch's claim that suffering brings us closest to each other was powerfully demonstrated in the outpouring of public grief when Diana, Princess of Wales, died at the end of August 1997. In the days after her death, members of the public gathered in unprecedented numbers to share their sadness for the loss of someone they felt had been part of their lives. Taken aback by their own depth of feeling, perhaps, people tried to identify the qualities they now felt bereft of. Forced into proximity by hours of gathering and the queueing to sign official condolence books, strangers came close to each other in an unusual way. Struggling to find terms to express what Diana had meant to them, they claimed that 'she cared', and that 'she understood the concerns of ordinary people'. These surprising statements came from people who did not know her personally, but yet felt close to her and were gathered to participate in mourning her untimely death.

It seems quite clear that it was mainly her personal unhappiness, disclosed in the controversial BBC television interview of November 1995, that allowed people to feel that they knew Diana. That was something they could readily identify with in their own lives: her suffering, her need to love and be loved, and her desire to do something worthwhile with her life. And it was her suffering that enabled her to give solace to the disabled, the homeless and the rejected of society. In hospices for the dying she met people for whom no pretence remained. They encountered her stripped of any artifice by their suffering. And when she found that a hug or the touch of her hand could bring them comfort and reassurance, this privately wounded young woman recovered some sense of her own worth and began to discern an authentic purpose for herself in public life. In her television interview, she said: 'So I went out and supported and loved people. People supported and loved me. The healing they gave me carried me through.'

This was an extraordinarily revealing statement. It provided a deep motivation for Diana's humanitarian advocacy in some of the least appealing and most vulnerable areas of need. She had given us indelible images of the face of compassion looking into the face of suffering, but she was not only giving — she was receiving solace there. She had discovered meaning in that spiritual connection with others which heals the isolated anguish of existential loneliness endemic in the West today. This had been revealed to her through her own suffering and it seems that she took her discovery into herself, so that it became part of her and nourished her and enabled her to reach out to others in need. She came to know that compassion means warm human presence to one another, that it requires being there, hand-to-hand, eye-to-eye, listening to each other's stories, sharing the vulnerability that is common to all humanity. This is why people said with heartfelt conviction that 'she cared'.

It was her own suffering that gave her the understanding and compassion to hold hands with a patient dying of AIDS-related illness even before it was quite established that there was no danger in doing so. The widely publicised image of this single action trans-formed the fearful public attitude towards HIV/AIDS. With genuine warmth and grace, she taught us how to do something we had thought impossible. Perhaps that was her most significant gift.

Mourners also claimed that Diana had understood the concerns of ordinary people. At first hearing, this seemed like sentimental wishful thinking. How could she really do that — a wealthy, privileged daughter of the aristocracy, a princess who lived in castles? Well, she exposed the emotional poverty within the castle walls and how it had undermined her self-esteem, and this is a suffering to which we can all relate. She was even prepared to risk embarrassment and public censure by describing her longing for love, for the comfort of 'a pair of arms around you'. This, too, is something we all understand. In articulating her own painful rite of passage through the unhappy years of her marriage, she provided others with a vocabulary for their experience. She gave a voice to many who had suffered in silence from postnatal depression, bulimia, unhappy partnerships and family life, from lack of love and the shame of failure.

Diana went on to disclose the benefit won from her ordeal. Not only had suffering brought her close to others, and allowed her to participate in their lives, it had also made her stronger. 'I am a very strong person,' she said in the BBC interview. 'I am a free spirit.'

In saying this, she gave a sign that suffering is not insuperable, that courage, companionship and new purpose may be won from even the darkest hour. It was the loving, vulnerable spirit of the woman that people were mourning, for it answered their own yearning. Diana spoke of people's needs, their feelings, hearts and hopes — terms easily ridiculed by cynical commentators. Yet these were words which many people were hungry to hear, after years of leadership characterised by pragmatism and economic rationalism in which humanity seemed to be disregarded. Diana may have been frivolous, imprudent and manipulative at times, but this fallible, modern young woman symbolised the dilemmas of her age and pointed a way through their messy complexity. For all her ingenuousness, she was a woman of loving spirit. And such spirit does not fade like headlines on newspapers. Spirit calls to spirit universally. Spirit belongs to soul and to the eternal.

Diana also enlarged the vocabulary in which love might be understood. She was failed more than once by the myth of romantic love, but she received love, and gave it, in other powerful public ways — through her endurance in an unhappy marriage, by devotion to her children and in her outreach to the marginalised and the suffering. This is a paradox worthy of further contemplation. If we will only remain open to the possibility of enlightenment, it comes in the most unlikely guises. Could Diana herself, the one-time fairy-tale princess, ever have foreseen that fulfilment and healing would come to her in an AIDS ward, or among cancer and leprosy patients, maimed children and the homeless? Or that her own natural affection and kindness would unlock an unprecedented flood of public donation to charity?

Charles Birch's other contention, that God is with us in our suffering, is not an easy one to grasp. While he claims that this is his experience, others feel that their suffering is evidence of the desertion of God, or the carelessness or even cruelty of God, asking: 'How could God let this happen?' For others again, it is the final evidence that God does not exist for, if he did, he would prevent suffering.

Those, like Professor Birch, who feel the companionship of God in their suffering are graced indeed. I have been told by some who have experienced it that this participation of God shows itself not in any dramatic supernatural revelation but through the compassion of caring people — doctors, nurses, other health practitioners, loving friends, family and neighbours. Perhaps that insight provides access to a challenging idea. It is reinforced by Rabbi Harold Kushner, in his best-selling book, *When Bad Things Happen to Good People*, where he quotes a 19th-century Hasidic rabbi saying that 'human beings are God's language'.[10] In the depth of our suffering, God, hope, meaning and purpose might seem absent to us, but we may experience them in what people do to help us at that time.

Emma Pierce has borne the suffering of years of severe mental illness, yet she too has garnered wisdom and purpose from her trial. She told me:

> The way I look at it, going mad is the best thing that ever happened to me. And I know that sounds a crazy thing to be saying but there were so many things I would never have learned any other way. Going mad is like being taken apart, right down to the foundation. And then you re-create. And then you begin to realise that who you are is not a discovery but a decision ... the first turning point was a

belief that total recovery from mental breakdown was possible. I've watched hundreds of people, over the nine years that I attended a group called Grow, develop this belief.

The other tremendous stepping stone for me was losing my youngest son one day. At that moment I discovered that I could love with total selflessness. And the reward from the knowledge that you can love like that is unbelievable. It's greater than a feeling of being loved by anybody — just that you can love. It nobody ever loves me again, as long as I live, I could live on that knowledge.

The central meaning for me is that the infinite Being, who created the universe, created me with love and still loves me. And that is an intrinsic value nobody can take away from me. That's the foundation that I'm now standing on. Please God I'll stand on it till the day I die . . . I suppose if God had another way of bringing us to him other than suffering, he'd use it. I don't think there's any other way us human beings will ever learn anything. We seem to have to suffer in order to grow.[11]

This is a tough statement and each time I hear it I want to reject it, but some imperative requires me to consider it. I have been told, far too often to dismiss it, that suffering can constitute a turning point which may reveal some of the deepest meaning in life. It is as though, when customary defences are ruptured, some new elements of understanding break through. It is then possible to see what was previously concealed. Something we have avoided or rejected knowing comes into focus. As a result, life becomes more meaningful; there is a new priority at the centre of our attention.

Although we cannot transfer such insight to each other like a magic formula, it seems that the telling of experience can strike a chord in the understanding of a receptive listener . . . a listener for whom the time is right to hear it. At a public gathering, a woman approached me with tears in her eyes to thank me for the interview I had broadcast with Dr Ron Farmer several years earlier. Ron Farmer is a celebrated psychologist who suffered a catastrophic nervous breakdown and embarked on a search through the spiritual traditions to find a new framework of meaning. Hearing Ron's story on the radio, when she was in mental anguish, had saved her from despair and given her a hopeful new direction. She said that it had saved her life.

Ron Farmer's talk was most notable for its intense candour. He held nothing back as he took us with him into the abyss of meaninglessness, and then retraced the steps by which he climbed out again to recover a sense of clarity and direction. He explained what he had to do to maintain the new peace of mind he had won from his terrible odyssey, describing the meditation he practised daily and the human values he now honoured in his everyday life. He told his story simply and with a sense of wonder at his own deliverance.[12]

In many cases, an episode of suffering redirects attention from self-absorption outwards to a wider communal concern: so that Fr Con Keogh established the Grow movement; Emma Pierce became active in that Grow movement and writes books on mental illness and the way to recovery; Yami Lester became an activist for Aboriginal justice and welfare; Paul Stevens turned his energy to helping others who'd also suffered loss of employment; Dr Ron Farmer made a series of self-help tapes which travel far and wide.

In each case, having faced and endured the challenge of their suffering, they found fresh purpose and, with it, the energy to act in that purpose to great effect. This lessened their feeling of being alone and isolated. Each one took on a new role in the world; they seemed changed, both to themselves and to people around them. Their activity carried the authority of authenticity because they were working, in their various causes, not out of a textbook but out of the successfully met challenge of their own lived experience. Most of us find the testimony of personal experience more convincing than 'expert' theory. And we feel a greater confidence speaking out of our own experience than out of theoretical information, until that information has been legitimated by experience. Certainly, this has been true for me.

The next story rewards reflection because it describes a specific instance of suffering, how it was endured and the eventual outcome. I was told it by one of Australia's most prominent church leaders, Reverend Dr Dorothy McRae-McMahon of the Uniting Church.

The big crisis moment for me was when I felt, or my husband and I felt we should end our marriage, which was a few years into my ministry, and that was the toughest thing that I've ever done in my life. For me, it was a total shattering of the person who I thought I was. I was faced with recognising that I had made vows that I could no longer keep and that I would have to shift my image, which was important to me, of being a respectable married woman and one who could sustain a marriage. I knew I was about to enter into hurting somebody else and, well, after many years of agonising, I came to a point where I just stood before God, and I felt as though I was going to step off a cliff, really, it felt like a moment of total danger and jeopardy. In the end all I could do was to say, on my knees, 'God, I can do no other', and to take that step and tell the Elders Council that I was about to end my marriage; which I did, and I was enormously fortunate in the people of Pitt Street Uniting Church. But first of all, I found the gracious arms of God underneath me in a way that I have never experienced before.

I just said, 'God, I am totally dependent on your grace; I have nothing else to depend upon' and there was the grace of God for me in a way that I have lived out of ever after. My life is full of thanksgiving for that experience of grace when I had nothing. I simply felt surrounded by a cloud of understanding and love and forgiveness. From people and from God, both. It was really a powerful experience of the God who is other than myself, and I had that experience of nearness. I've often experienced God most close at the point of death . . . when I'm in the most deathly experience of my life God has become so close to me . . . I think God hovers round death very, very closely. And that for me was a death experience — the death of a relationship. I experienced that with God very profoundly.[13]

It's easy to imagine Dorothy's trepidation in raising the question of divorce with the Council of Elders. As one of the most renowned of Australia's rare women ministers, would her admission of failure undermine the prospects of other women ministers in the eyes of the already sceptical? To her surprise, Dorothy's ministry was not diminished. On the contrary, more people trusted her with their lives because they said: 'Well, you're human too. You know what failure is

like and you can stand with us and accompany us towards forgiveness and new life and you will not judge us, because you yourself
have given evidence of your need of grace.'

There is much hope in regarding suffering as a gateway to deeper
meaning. Through the suffering of her divorce, Dorothy McRae-
McMahon won new insight, increased capacity for ministry and an
experience of personal grace. This is not to suggest that therefore her
divorce was a good thing. It is to say that suffering happens; this is the
way one person dealt with it; these were the outcomes. Once again,
Dorothy needed to live out of that 'experience of God's grace' when,
in 1997, she identified herself as a lesbian and had to face a painful
and very public division of opinion in her church on this subject. It
seems as though each episode of suffering, however unwelcome, has
the potential to refine and prepare us for the next.

One of the most widespread forms of suffering in western culture
is loneliness. I always feel a particular empathy for loneliness because,
for many years I suffered from it myself. I wanted desperately to
belong somewhere but could not see where or how that might be
possible. At times I did not feel real. It began in adolescence when,
for the first time, I realised that I was essentially alone.

The first terrifying intimation of loneliness came to me on the
day I was left at boarding school at the age of twelve. There were
sound reasons for sending an only child from a small country town
to boarding school. I know my parents made sacrifices to afford it.
They thought it would provide me with a good education. Yet I can
still feel the desolation of the day they left me there. Against our
intuition, the three of us were acting out a painful charade with a
pretence of normality. My mother breached her lifelong custom of
thrift to buy me a large expensive peach. I stood holding this treach-
erous gift in a brown paper bag with both hands as I watched my
parents in their small car disappear slowly down the long driveway of
the school.

I can still retrieve the taste of abandonment, the disbelief of it, the
constriction in my chest and throat, the exhausting responsibility of
having to survive this strange environment in a state of grief that

must be concealed. I did conceal it, but at what cost? With my mind, I accepted the reason for boarding school but the dull ache of separation from my home and my parents persisted, ready to break through at the slightest provocation.

As intended, I did make friends and have fun and meet the challenge of the academic work. But an institution does not love and care for individual children as most parents would and I was acutely aware of what I did not have. It was an Anglican boarding school, and I am sure they did their best for us, but why did morning and evening prayers provide no comfort to a homesick child? On Sundays we wended our way in a crocodile of damp serge cloaks across the sodden fields to church. The minister's sermons provoked only mass stifled giggling, and the hymns evoked in me a relentless melancholy which I tried to shake off afterwards like a dog freeing its coat of water.

Then there was the additional responsibility, in writing letters home, of shielding my parents from the knowledge of how much I missed them. It would have been ungracious to give them the burden of that knowledge.

The whole experience left me with a shocking impression that I was on my own, and that life was going to be a struggle against inexplicable odds and unpredictable blows that I was ill-equipped to deal with. Two years later, a move to another school was even more damaging to my precarious hold on self-esteem. Lacking an inner conviction of wellbeing, all I could do in those years was to develop some survival tactics. I learned to cultivate popularity by challenging authority in mild ways; I tried to be amusing and quick-witted, to achieve at sport and schoolwork; and to learn the idiom and culture of a new environment rapidly, for camouflage and acceptance. I continued to use these ploys into adulthood. They were all useful, both in journalism and in getting on with people.

But my tactics left me embattled and isolated. They were like tricks played in desperation, in which I had only limited confidence. And at a deeper level, in the spirit or the psyche, I retreated in adolescence into an anaesthetised state. It was my mother's death, while I was still a young woman, which convinced me that life was fundamentally chaotic, that there was no moral justice, that destruction could strike at random, without provocation, and that I was all but helpless in the face of it. This produced a person who was perpetually in survival mode, not lacking courage, but with no real conviction that there was much meaning to be found. As far as I could see, survival and security could be attained only by gaining a foothold and perhaps a fragile fortress through performance and achievement. This had some positive results but it was a dangerous way to live because my undue dependence on approval distorted personal relationships, while I remained insecure about my own intrinsic value as a person.

Relief would not come until middle age with an experience which reassured me of my own inner legitimacy and unique dignity. And that experience contained an image which, for the first time, gave me a satisfying way to think about suffering. To my astonishment, it was the image of Christ on the cross.

Christ on the cross. I had seen it a thousand times — the cruel death of that compassionate, radical young Jew whose message of love and justice was so threatening to the religious and political establishment of the day that they had to get rid of him. When I had noticed it at all, it had seemed an intensely moving but ultimately grim icon — a warning of the inevitable crucifixion of goodness by flawed human nature. Then suddenly, one day, it was flooded with fuller meaning when someone explained to me that defeat is only half its message — that, in fact, it offers the promise of not only death, but also new life. Death is hanging on the cross, but the story does not end there. Christ was crucified and then He rose to new life. That life has inspired and animated people for two millennia.

In the cross, the negative image of terrible suffering is enriched with the positive image of a gateway to new life. The two intertwine. The positive does not cancel the negative but accompanies it, and in this reconciliation of two conflicting images I was offered, for the first time, a way, albeit a very challenging way, to make some meaning of suffering and to invest it with a sense of hope. It was a revelation to me, an answer for which I had been waiting all my life.

However, as a modern woman, with my rational, scientifically conditioned ears, the whole extraordinary story of Christ was not easy for me to hear. When, to my amazement as a sceptic, I found myself somehow intuitively at home in it, then I found a gift indeed. As I reviewed my life in the light of the Christian insight, I saw that through no skill of my own I had been carried through innumerable crises, large and small — and that many painful events had in fact germinated new beginnings.

When a Moslem, a Buddhist, an American Indian, a Taoist, a Jew or an Aborigine tell you *their* guiding story, the language and symbols will be different, but it too will contain an explanation of how to live a full life, of what life's purpose is, and of the meaning of suffering and death. That is what the spiritual traditions have offered people over the centuries. For me, it happened to be the Christian cross that first turned the key to the wisdom of the ages.

Since the beginning of teenage I had found life a struggle and a mystery. Much as I wished that things were different, life seemed to present too many experiences of challenge and personal failure. This rewarding new-found concept of 'not only death but also new life' gave me a template of meaning to place upon all my instances of suffering, from the greatest to the least. I saw death hanging on the cross and I did not want to look at it. For that is the toughest question of our existence. Why do we have to suffer? Why do we have to die? Does death cancel out life? Is it the end? If so, what is the point of life? In order to live with hope we need to find satisfying answers to these daunting questions.

Over time, in my contemplation of the cross, the horizontal beam has come to represent death. This was the beam under whose crushing weight the young Christ staggered on his way to Calvary and to which he was cruelly nailed through the hands, while the vertical beam points upwards like the shoot of a plant, a vigorous sign of life. It is the body of Christ crucified, where the two intersect, which transcends the paradox. His suffering becomes the key to reconciling the opposites of life and death.

Church doctrine explains the crucifixion in much more elegant language yet, for some reason, I struggle to find my own plain words to interpret this unexpectedly convincing paradox to myself. In my own suffering, I may indeed cry out, as did Jesus himself, 'My God, my God, why have you forsaken me?' but the Cross also tells me I am not left to bear my suffering alone. I am invited to know Jesus Christ as one who suffered for all and as companion in my suffering. And if Jesus Christ is the son of God, and one with God, then somehow God suffers with us, rather than inflicting suffering upon us. Further, I may look within and beyond my suffering, both slight and serious, for the seeds of hope. It is mine for the asking. Do you know the story of the two thieves who were crucified on either side of Jesus, told in Luke's Gospel, Chapter 23, 39–43?

> One of the criminals hanging there abused him. 'Are you not the Christ?' he said. 'Save yourself and us as well.'
>
> But the other spoke up and rebuked him. 'Have you no fear of God at all?' he said. 'You got the same sentence as He did, but in our case we deserved it: we are paying for what we did. But this man has done nothing wrong.
>
> 'Jesus,' he said, 'remember me when you come into your kingdom.'
>
> 'Indeed, I promise you,' He replied. 'Today you will be with me in paradise.'

It is a story of exquisite comfort and promise even for those of us who feel the least deserving of mercy or reward. The image of home and homecoming is a powerful one in all literature and legend and it has always been one of the most compelling in my consciousness. The term 'home' gathers to it a powerful constellation of ideas including happiness, wholeness and origin. The yearning for home is most beautifully expressed by St Augustine when he writes 'Thou has created me for thyself and my heart is restless until it rests in thee'.

I was excited when I first read that, because it provided words for what I felt — that somehow, in the experience of human life, I had become separated from the mysterious source of my origin, my wholeness and my home which might be called God. Yet I recognise joyful fleeting glimpses of this origin/wholeness/home/God, and I long to know it again. For that is where I came from and where

I hope to return. This perception is vividly evoked for me by Wordsworth in a verse from *Intimations of Immortality from Recollections of Early Childhood*:

Our birth is but a sleep and a forgetting:
The Soul that rises with us, our life's Star,
Hath had elsewhere its setting,
And cometh from afar:
Not in entire forgetfulness,
And not in utter nakedness,
But trailing clouds of glory do we come
From God, who is our Home.

This seems just right to me. It captures the poignancy of my feeling that life, for all its richness, is a temporary exile. But how am I to find my way home? Various spiritual traditions offer various pathways. One convincing answer is to be found in the Christian understanding which tells me that the way back home is to be found in walking the challenging pathway trodden by Jesus Christ — that is, by living this extraordinary experience of life to the full — and apparently that means living by love *and* engaging with the crucifixion of suffering along the way. The last of the sufferings is death — which becomes the gateway through to new life, to wholeness, to 'God, who is our Home'.

This understanding almost defies expression in the language of today. It can be lived as a personal experience but it does not submit to scientific measurement. On the other hand, it is a way of life that works. People who live by loving those around them add enormously to the wellbeing of the world, and their own fulfilment is evident. Those who endure their suffering with courage show others a purposeful way to deal with the inevitable pain of life. And people who approach death with hope exemplify a positive way to live that offers a sense of direction and some peace of mind. One of Leunig's prayers goes:

That which is Christ-like within us shall be crucified. It shall suffer, and be broken. And that which is Christ-like within us shall rise up. It shall love and create.[14]

So it is the dramatic and moving story that makes the Christian insight most real for me. And the story is reenacted and kept alive in the sacraments. The sacramental ritual at the heart of Christian life is the Eucharist, and at the heart of the Eucharist is suffering. It is a ritual of new life emerging from brokenness, celebrated in the familiar domestic elements of wine and bread, fruit of the vine and the work of human hands. And the bread and wine speak of the inevitable suffering and transformation of all life, for the wine that becomes the blood of Christ was once grapes, now crushed and fermented into another form; and the bread that is consecrated into the body of Christ was once a golden field of wheat, now ground and kneaded and baked in the fierce heat of the oven into bread. The Eucharist is a beautiful and sustaining sacrament performed in memory of Christ at the Last Supper and on the cross. For Christians, that cross provides a signpost in the mystery, a way to think about the suffering and the brevity of the human condition, a recurring personal experience that after each 'death' there is the hope of new life. The year 2000 is not only the date of the Sydney Olympic Games. It is the anniversary of 2000 years since the birth and death of Christ changed the course of history.

However well I may accept the insights of my faith intellectually, emotionally and spiritually, at this early stage of my spiritual development I am still uncomfortable with the idea that suffering is to be welcomed. That is for the saints. Personally, I wish that the design of human life were otherwise, and devoid of suffering. But it is not, and I can do no more than encourage you to find an approach to it that satisfies you; to share with you my glimmerings of understanding so far; and tell you the stories of what others have discovered.

Many people have found satisfying explanations of the meaning of suffering in the spiritual tradition in which they were raised. Others look to the scholarship of Joseph Campbell and his study of the power of myth, a study that has much to reveal about the place of suffering in human life. Some seek a spiritual teacher. Other pathways include the Hindu and Buddhist traditions which offer a rich understanding of life, suffering and death without reference to an essentially personal God.

For those who prefer to think in non-religious terms, a sustaining image may be found in the metamorphosis of the butterfly — after the cocoon, wings — or in the rhythm of the seasons — after winter, spring. The humanist may be inspired by a glorious act of heroism achieved through human goodness. The Jungian may be satisfied by the testing of the psyche on its way to individuation. Some western-educated people, dissatisfied with their own society's organised religion or with the secular orthodoxy of science and rationalism, turn to the East in quest of meaning. The Lebanese poet, philosopher and artist Kahlil Gibran opened a window of understanding to many western readers, especially in the last 20 years of his life when he moved to America and began writing in English. In *The Prophet*, Kahlil Gibran writes:

Your pain is the breaking of the shell that encloses your understanding.

And elsewhere:

The deeper that sorrow carves into your being, the more joy you can contain.
 Is not the cup that holds your wine the very cup that was burned in the potter's oven?
 And is not the lute that soothes your spirit the very wood that was hollowed with knives?[15]

Such beautiful and truthful reconciliation of opposites gives welcome relief to the western mind conditioned to the painful *either/or* habit of thinking. Much of our suffering arises from this compulsion to choose, in which westerners are trained from childhood: black or white; pain or pleasure; your way or mine; religion or science; life or death. I have written earlier of the writer Barbara Blackman's pleasure in discovering, in eastern philosophies, the insight of *'not either/or, but both'*. This idea can bring resolution to many a confrontation, showing, as it does, the way out of an impasse.

Some of the worst suffering of the 20th century is epitomised by the Holocaust, in which millions of Jews, gypsies, homosexuals and incapacitated people were murdered, yet this catastrophic crime against humanity has yielded many stories of inspiration. Viktor Frankl, author of the classic *Man's Search for Meaning*, describes the response of a young girl to whom he spoke in the Nazi death camp of Auschwitz:

> 'I am grateful that fate has hit me so hard,' she told me. 'In my former life I was spoiled and did not take spiritual accomplishments seriously.' Pointing through the window of the hut, she said, 'This tree here is the only friend I have in my loneliness.' Through that window she could see just one branch of a chestnut tree, and on the branch were two blossoms. 'I often talk to this tree,' she said to me. I was startled and didn't know how to take her words. Was she delirious? Did she have occasional hallucinations? Anxiously, I asked her if the tree replied. 'Yes.' What did it say to her? She answered, 'It said to me, "I am here — I am here — I am life, eternal life".'[16]

Viktor Frankl is pointing out that the only real freedom we have is the freedom to choose a response towards our circumstances. He observed this, even in the extreme suffering of Auschwitz. He wrote, 'For what matters above all is the attitude we take towards suffering, the attitude in which we take suffering upon ourselves.' This is a very rewarding insight and it leaves the reader with the responsibility of finding and cultivating a personal attitude to life that sustains rather than defeats. At its most basic, this attitude could start with choosing to describe a glass of water as half-full rather than half-empty.

Suffering is one of the most crucial questions we encounter in the search for meaning. It comes in many guises and it comes again and again. There is much evidence for a bleak universe, indifferent to human life, devoid of meaning and characterised by random cataclysmic events. There is evidence for a universe in which evil seems, too often, to overcome good. Yet, in the face of this, many people find reason to hope that there is indeed a benevolent impersonal source of life; or even a personal God, in whose image they are made, who suffers with them and who is, in some mysterious way, their destination.

The choice is ours. If we want to live life to the full, we must find some context for suffering and a constructive way to deal with it. We need a reservoir of reason and courage to accompany us in our trials. Whichever religion or philosophy of life we choose to be our guiding light needs to have the integrity to carry us through suffering with a sense of hope. The alternative is to waste essential energy in panic and defeat. I write this with a real sense of struggle for, in the face of suffering, I have to rediscover my reason and courage and even my faith, over and over again. Finding a way to live with suffering — my own and that of others — has been the great challenge of my life.

I still dread suffering myself and I am enraged or heartbroken to see the suffering of others endlessly repeated in so many ways that defy understanding. Yet, for the sake of reality, I must acknowledge that all life is characterised by episodes of suffering. And, like everyone else, I must find the most hopeful way to bear it personally and to alleviate it for others. The wisdom of the ages and our own life experience demonstrates that we cannot choose contentment and reject pain any more than we can select day over night, or waking over sleeping. These apparent opposites are, in fact, complementary; they are integral to a whole reality, interdependent, each informing the other, indivisible. To banish one or the other is to refuse life.

interdependence

For your Journal

* What strategy do you have to face suffering?

* Think about a time of suffering in your life. What did you tell yourself about it? Did you blame someone else for it? Did that help?

* What sustained you and gave you comfort at this time?

* And what was unhelpful?

* What action did you take?

* Did the guiding principle in your life give you support and meaning to help you?

* Do you need a more satisfying approach? If so, what will you do about finding it?

* In hindsight, was there any positive outcome of that suffering? What was it?

* Explore ways in which a purely humanist perspective may give meaning to suffering.

* Is it your habit to see the glass of water as half-empty or half-full?

* Do you inflate one setback into an all-encompassing tragic view of life? ('This is the sort of thing that always happens to me.' 'I am generally unlucky.')

* Could you change this to say instead: 'This is an unfortunate event. I've been unlucky this time.'?[17]

Endnotes

1 Kahlil Gibran, *The Prophet*, Heinemann, 1926.

2 M. Scott Peck, *The Road Less Travelled: A New Psychology of Love, Traditional Values and Spiritual Growth*, Arrow Books, 1983.

3 Francis Crick won the Nobel Prize for Medicine in 1962, with James D. Watson, for the discovery of the molecular structure of DNA. This quotation is from his book *The Astonishing Hypothesis*, Simon & Schuster, 1994.

4 Yami Lester, Tape 191 in *The Search for Meaning Catalogue*, ABC Radio Tapes.

5 Fr Con Keogh, Tape 1 in *The Search for Meaning Catalogue*, ABC Radio Tapes.

6 Paul Stevens, Tape 19 in *The Search for Meaning Catalogue*, ABC Radio Tapes. Paul Stevens heads The Centre for Worklife Counselling: tel: (02) 9968 1588; fax: (02) 9968 1655.

7 Magda Bozic in *The Search for Meaning Collection*, Caroline Jones, ABC/Harper Collins, 1995. Also Tape 81 in *The Search for Meaning Catalogue*, ABC Radio Tapes.

8 Brian Keenan, *An Evil Cradling*, Vintage, 1993. Also Tape 199 in *The Search for Meaning Catalogue*, ABC Radio Tapes.

9 Professor Charles Birch in *The Search for Meaning*, Caroline Jones, ABC/Collins Dove, 1989. Also Tapes 27 and 109 in *The Search for Meaning Catalogue*, ABC Radio Tapes.

10 Harold S. Kushner, *When Bad Things Happen to Good People*, Shocken Books, 1981.

11 Emma Pierce in *The Search for Meaning Collection*, Caroline Jones, ABC/Harper Collins, 1995. Also an Audiotape, *Making Sense of Life Vol. 2*, ABC Shops.

12 Dr Ron Farmer in *The Search for Meaning Book Two*, Caroline Jones, ABC/Collins Dove, 1990. Also Tape 79 in *The Search for Meaning Catalogue*, ABC Radio Tapes. Address for Ron Farmer tapes: Self-Help Therapy Tapes, P.O. Box 118, Rozelle, NSW 2039.

13 Rev. Dr Dorothy McRae-McMahon in *The Search for Meaning Collection*, Caroline Jones, ABC/Harper Collins, 1995. Also Tape 189 in *The Search for Meaning Catalogue*, ABC Radio Tapes.

14 Michael Leunig, *A Common Prayer Collection*, Collins Dove, 1993.

15 Kahlil Gibran, *The Prophet*, Heinemann, 1926.

16 Viktor Frankl, *Man's Search for Meaning*, Hodder & Stoughton, 1974.

17 Martin E. P. Seligman, *Learned Optimism*, Random House, 1992.

11 LIVING WITH CHANGE

Try to love the questions themselves, like locked rooms ...
Live the questions now. Perhaps you will then,
gradually, live along some distant day, into the answer.

Rainer Maria Rilke[1]

God help us to change.
To change ourselves and to change the world.
To know the need for it. To deal with the pain of it.
To feel the joy of it. To undertake the
journey without understanding the destination.
The art of gentle revolution.
Amen.

Michael Leunig[2]

RAVAGED MEN WITH RUDDY, leathered skin and matted hair were slumped on the benches outside Pitt Street Uniting Church, wearing someone else's clothes and nursing bottles in brown paper bags. Like many others in the inner city of Sydney, they knew this to be a haven where everyone is accepted. The city plane trees funnelled a spirited nor'easter down to street level, fluttering our shirts against damp skin. We climbed the stone stairs out of the hot asphalt turmoil of midday traffic and shopping crowds into the cool cavern of the church. Huge brass vases of white and purple agapanthus and Christmas bush decorated the altar. We were met by Rev. Dr Dorothy McRae-McMahon.

She led us to the Peace Chapel. On a table covered with a white cotton cloth, a branch of bleached driftwood lay as a sculptured symbol of hard times. There was a candle for hope and a pitcher of water to symbolise the quenching of thirst. This is a church where the congregation, supported by imaginative ministers, create their own rituals to bring them through the bewildering changes of contemporary life. They have a healing rite for a divorced person in which the whole congregation witnesses the grief of the broken relationship and accepts it as a painful reality. As a community they support the divorcing person to enable them to express grief, guilt and sadness and to move on to the next stage of life, embraced in the community of the church rather than rejected for breaking the rules. This church stands as a beacon of Christianity, outspoken in asserting the dignity of all human beings and travelling with them for the whole journey, in times of both celebration and despair.

And we are here today for just such a ritual, a group of workmates perplexed and grieved by the termination of *The Search for Meaning* radio program on which we've worked together for eight years until this Christmas 1994. We are full of questions for which we have no satisfying answers. We are badly in need of a chance to acknowledge the pain of what has happened, and somehow to come to terms with it.

In her generosity of spirit, Dorothy has designed for us a liturgy entitled 'Water of our Tears, Water of our Life'. I am feeling overcome with gratitude to Dorothy for her sensitivity and her typically generous gesture of solidarity, but I have no idea what to expect from the liturgy. It's a new experience for me.

We've brought our own symbols to put on the chapel table: a small bundle of listeners' letters; the dried petals of a bunch of flowers sent from a listener's garden; a postcard recalling poignant and hilarious moments in the production process from Louisa Ring, the researcher who did much to shape the program. As well, to symbolise all the life stories told by guests on the program, I've brought a delicate seashell. Hold it to your ear and you can hear the ocean.

First, 'we recall the place of safety and joy which has been left, and the betrayals, fears and losses along the way'. Dorothy then invites each person in turn to speak, as they hold a small glass bowl of salt water to symbolise tears. In turn, hesitantly, we say our thoughts aloud, trying to express what we have been suppressing until now. We are sad because we will miss each other — a team of broadcasters who have become ardent collaborators in the cause of unfolding the stories of a great cross-section of men and women, revealing the truth of their lives. We mourn the loss for the listeners, who have written in their many thousands from remote mining towns, and along the outback dingo fence, from pensioners' high-rise flats and the loneliness of affluent suburbs to say that *The Search for Meaning* has given them something of value. We grieve, as well, that we have failed the listeners because we were not able to persuade the ABC manager of the value of the program, so that it might be allowed to continue. For two of us, this change means we have lost our jobs and, at a time of high unemployment, we are apprehensive on that count.

We pass the bowl of 'tears' and we shed some of our own and perhaps, in this naming of sorrow in a sacred place, the healing slowly begins. The scripture readings have been chosen to transmute the image of water from 'tears' to 'lifegiving river'. As I listen to Dorothy guiding us through this change and look at the swathe of blue silk she has cast on the floor to symbolise river, I can visualise eight years of life stories being poured out across the continent as a stream of living water. What richer gift could we have offered each other than our stories, the record of who we are, the scourge of the tough times, how we kept up our courage and what we've found to sustain us on the journey? What more could we want than to tell our story and to know that it is heard?

My sense of loss begins to transform into an idea of celebration: that, for one hour a week, for eight lifegiving years, we've been broadcasting across Australia an expression of the striving, the suffering, the strength, the doubts and the faith of a multitude of our countrymen and women; generous revelations of the spirit, beautiful in their transparency. Now the program has been declared redundant, but nothing can alter what it has meant to people and the nourishment it has provided.

Out in the street again, only an hour has passed, yet the daylight is a shock. We have been through a rite of passage. We do not have any new answers to what has happened, but now it seems easier to live with the questions. We have celebrated the endeavour on which we worked together. We have acknowledged that we put up a good fight to save it, and that we failed. We have mourned its ending. Now we know that we must try to move on, for change, however inexplicable, is the nature of life.

Somehow it should be night-time. I have the weary tranquillity remembered from childhood after crying. But with it, a mature sense that a dangerous crossing has been made in safe company, and that the sail is set fair for some new destination not yet quite discernible through the glare on the water.

Crises of change come to everyone. Living with the constant change of life's circumstances is more of a challenge today than it has ever been before because change is occurring so rapidly and is often incomprehensible. The enormous decrease in the availability of paid work poses a challenge that our society has not even begun to meet. It is already affecting millions of Australians and will dismay many more in the immediate future. Whatever type of change comes our way, it is necessary to find a way to deal with it because, like suffering, change is inevitable. As with suffering, we would like to avoid it. And, like suffering, if it is approached in a positive way it can yield rewards. In the absence of an effective strategy, copious energy is expended in stubborn resistance to change, energy that could be better spent.

A good place to start is in the construction of a realistic view of change. After all, we are in a constant state of change throughout life, and much of it is positive, even essential. Every moment we are shedding cells and growing fresh ones without thinking about it, to keep our bodies renewed and healthy. Our thoughts too are in a constant state of evolution as new information becomes available. By opening ourselves to experience, we grow in awareness and understanding every day. The inevitable ageing of the body may be accompanied by the getting of wisdom.

Similarly, you delight in the growing of your children; it is accomplished through change. You are pleased when exercise improves your feeling of wellbeing; that is accomplished by change — by walking, swimming or cycling, not by sitting still. After a disagreement and a reconciliation, a relationship may be deepened. It is changed and you are heartened by the change. The weather is in a constant state of change and you enjoy the variety of it. The garden is changing every day and that is a source of fascination and pleasure. Night follows day and you welcome the contrast. Change is the pattern of all life. While we live, we grow, and we grow by changing. Remembering all these things gives change a positive connotation, and that is a good foundation from which to consider change of a challenging nature.

This does not mean that every change is to be accepted without question, that we should be ready, slavishly, to follow each new fashion. Change is not always for the better and some of it should be resisted. But when change is forced upon us, how are we to cope well with it?

The most effective response to change lies in redoubling attention to your own sense of self, becoming clear about your values and maintaining your confidence in them, cultivating a positive mental attitude and keeping your body as healthy as possible. It is also vital to attend to the care of your soul by nourishing your spiritual life.

Imagine a ship sailing round the world on a voyage of exploration. It is subjected to dramatically varying weather conditions, to powerful currents and uncharted waters and it may even be attacked by pirates. Imagine, too, that it is well defended, splendidly equipped for navigation, constantly trimmed and painted and maintained; and that it is in the charge of an accomplished crew under a resolute captain sure of the mission of this voyage. Although the circumstances of the craft will change from minute to minute, the integrity of its preparedness gives it a fine chance of survival and success.

If you have a reasonably clear and growing idea of who you are and where you are going and why, then, like the ship, you have reliable resources with which to chart your course through the changeable ocean. Much of this book deals with ways to nourish your integrity, to sustain yourself spiritually and be clear about your unique purpose.

This remains the best way I have discovered to be ready for all the changes that life brings. With a confident sense of values, we can more readily make decisions on personal questions and on the difficult public issues for which we have responsibility as citizens in a society. We can form an opinion and take action based on our own values rather than be captivated by fashionable theories or economically expedient thinking. The only factor over which we have some control is ourselves. We could choose to see this as reassuring for it means there is something powerful that we can do ourselves to face change, something other than denial, playing the victim or being seduced.

Ritual too is helpful in facilitating the changes in our lives because it provides a setting in which mundane matters are put aside while a significant event is acknowledged with appropriate ceremony. How carefully every detail of a wedding ceremony is chosen, to make the wedding real and memorable. Funerals, too, are carefully planned, so that the grief of loss can be honoured and hope renewed. In a symbolic way, ritual gathers up the past into the present and looks towards the future. It is a setting aside of time to give emphasis to an important change.

Another feature of ritual is that it provides opportunity for a gathering of people to witness the change, to demonstrate that this is not something of merely individual concern, but of meaning for the community. The need for this in private lives is well demonstrated by what happens in cases of significant public change. The Governor-General Sir William Deane convened ecumenical services after the Port Arthur massacre of 1996 and the Thredbo disaster of 1997. And remember the celebration in Newcastle when the city took fresh heart from winning the 1997 Rugby League Grand Final, only months after the devastating news that BHP would close down the city's steelworks. The parties and street parade were a ritualising of new life being won out of defeat. It was a big public occasion which united the people of a city. The industrial change will still be tough but Novocastrians will negotiate it with renewed spirit and hope.

Similarly, the death of Diana, Princess of Wales, in August 1997 showed in a very dramatic, internationally public way the importance of communal gathering and ritual at a time of change. There is no meaning to be won and no solace to be found in the premature death of any young woman, mother of young children. And because people had projected so many of their own hopes and desires onto Diana, as a public figure, her death threatened their sense of equilibrium and accentuated their vulnerability. The event was a shock, a change of the worst kind and a reminder of the haphazardness of all human life. People's private losses were evoked from their hiding places by this public loss.

Whatever opinion we may hold of royalty, celebrity and the media's taste for sensation, it was a fact that, for whatever reasons, millions of people experienced Diana's death as a personal tragedy. They needed a way to express their feelings of loss and what it was about her they had valued, and they needed to put their sentiments into action. So they wrote messages on cards they had made themselves. They brought affectionate gifts. They made pilgrimages to Buckingham Palace and Kensington Palace. They did not want to stay at home but to gather at those significant places with other people, strangers united in their loss. Over and over, on television, we heard people say that they had come 'to pay their respects'. This is a very formal term, belonging to ritual not everyday life. Ritual and symbols mattered very much to people at that time. They helped to show intensity of feeling when words were hard to find. People were upset when, at first, the flag was not flown at half-mast on Buckingham Palace. They wanted the sovereign, Queen Elizabeth, to state her sorrow along with theirs, to invest it with royal formality. And the predominant symbols were the millions of flowers placed in swelling banks in front of the royal palaces, and later cast in front of the hearse as Diana was driven home to Althorp.

The sudden death of such a young woman was a potent reminder of everyone's mortality, so the challenge of the funeral was to put that death into some meaningful context for people, especially for those many whose grief was unmitigated by any belief in eternal life. There was discussion about the most appropriate form of funeral service. Should it be a state funeral or something less formal, to reflect the

Princess's style? They came up with a compromise. It had to be a public occasion that would cater for everyone who wanted to be there. As well as grieving her loss, it needed to celebrate Diana's life and the ongoing effect of her contribution. Her favourite charities must be represented to reinforce this important sign of hope and love. And any ceremony had to satisfy a populace no longer agreed on a common religious practice.

Writing in the Catholic journal, *The Tablet*, of 13 September 1997, Clifford Longley offered an interesting analysis of the outcome, suggesting that the people themselves had created an appropriate ritual:

> What happened transcended ordinary definitions of what is religious and what is not. The amazing scenes as the funeral procession wound its way through north London had nothing to do with conventional piety — people clapped, threw flowers, took pictures, even followed the hearse on roller-skates. They reinvented the protocol of public mourning for themselves, picking up their behaviour from the previous day's television. The amplification created by this daily resonance between media reporting and reality was extraordinary. The result was the most religious of any expression of shared feeling we have seen in Britain this century, with the possible exception of the Burial of the Unknown Warrior after the First World War.

The suggestion is that, even when a society sets religion aside, the religious imperative to create meaning from dramatic life events remains, and seeks satisfaction.

However we may wish to interpret it, both the religious and the secular ceremonial surrounding Diana's death provided a powerful illustration of the need for appropriate ritual to mark the losses of everyman and woman, although, for most of us, this will be done in private. The change that bereavement brings to our lives is very powerful and we need help to make our way through it. Fortunately, it is common knowledge today that grieving may go through stages of numbness, denial and anger as well as sadness, that the process will take time and that it will need the support of ritual and gentle, personal care.

In the past few years, a program called Seasons for Growth has been widely introduced into Australian primary and secondary schools, to support the many children experiencing the grief of loss through separation, divorce or death.[3] Based on research by the psychologist J. William Worden, it recognises the importance of social support in dealing with grief. Worden suggests that grief requires some active participation by the grieving person, and divides this into what he calls the four tasks: first, the task of accepting the reality of the loss; then, experiencing the pain of grief; next, adjusting to an environment in which the significant person is no longer present; and, finally, reinvesting emotional energy. The Seasons for Growth program has associated these tasks with the four seasons of the year, using typically Australian symbols to illustrate them, and training companions to accompany children through the process.

Participating students are first supported in coming to terms with the reality of their loss. This is the acceptance task of 'Autumn'. Next, they are given the chance to learn about the range of emotions that accompany grief and how each has felt these in their own loss. This is the experience of 'Winter'. Then they are provided with skills to help process their grief, in the adjustment task of 'Spring'. Finally, they are given the time to explore ways of letting go and moving on, in the reinvesting task of 'Summer'. The beautiful snow gum is the prevailing symbol of the Seasons for Growth program — a tree that survives through changing and difficult seasons, and is still able to flower profusely in late spring and summer. This practical and sustaining program has been applauded by academic evaluation and there are many moving expressions of gratitude from children who have taken part in it.

There is loss and grief in many of the ordinary events of life. When someone leaves work, her farewell party may be painful but it is necessary, to make a punctuation mark, acknowledge her contribution, regret her going and offer good wishes for the future. Again the ritual provides a time and a space for the contrasts of the situation to be accommodated, both by the departing worker and by the remaining group who will be altered by her going.

Even private life changes that are not easily shared can be marked by ritual. If the pain of a broken relationship cannot be discussed, perhaps it can be written down in order to express all that it meant, including celebration of the happiness it contained and the anger and sadness of its ending. The letter could be read aloud and then, when the time is right, it could be burned to make a dramatised represen-tation of what has been, and what has now passed, to make the change real. This provides a little ceremony, something to do, to give expression to emotional pain in a physical or material way, so that one can see flame, smell burning and touch ash. The letter that carried the story has now been transformed, symbolising the reality of the change and making manifest both the old and the new realities. People have told me that this has helped them to move on.

Although some will prefer private, individual grieving, there is value in expressing loss and, indeed, most feelings to someone else, so that your pain is heard and acknowledged as being both yours uniquely and an experience of the human condition. It is perilous to remain isolated at a time of significant change when there is solace to be found in the shared acknowledgement of individual loss.

The Pitt Street Uniting Church divorce ritual was a beautiful example of this. It was a tangible expression of an occasion when a group of people gathered to acknowledge their common fallibility and to express their solidarity for one of their number, in sadness for what had broken down and in hope for what new life can bring. The common cup, from which communion had been shared, was given to the person involved to take home. This common cup then became a receptacle of spirituality, resource and hope for the next challenge of change in that person's life, a reminder that there is a way through and that he is not alone.

There are many such rituals to be found in a book by Dr Dorothy McRae-McMahon entitled *The Glory of Blood, Sweat and Tears: Liturgies for Living and Dying.*[4] Other churches too are developing appropriate rituals to mark the separations of life. Often such rituals are designed by the people rather than the leadership of the church. Sometimes people request that their ashes be scattered in a place of great meaning for them. This can be both deeply affecting and at the same time satisfying, in that a dead person's wishes have been fulfilled — they have been united symbolically with some place of spiritual significance to them.

The ritualising of significant life changes facilitates our passage through them. This has been well recognised in traditional societies where there was a ceremony for every important stage from birth to death. Western society is weakened by the abandoning of such customs which are usually intertwined with religious practice. We are left with only a few of them — christenings, weddings and funerals. And so we modern people are often deprived of help at those times of change when we most need it. Our society is staggering with loss of many kinds — loss of employment, forced retirement, divorce, termination of a pregnancy, miscarriage of a baby or loss of a baby at birth can all be the cause of great pain, intensified by lack of public recognition. Such events need to be acknowledged with an appropriate ceremony, even if it is private, so that grief may be honoured and hope renewed.

I have always found change difficult. In my childhood, wartime bred a climate of uncertainty in which ordinary people had scant control over events and planning for the future was in suspension. It was like a disturbing folk tale in which we could only hope that 'Once upon a time' might one day turn into 'and they all lived happily ever after'. Yet there was a sense of unreality about it, reinforced by the knowledge that we could have no effect upon its timing. Perhaps this unstated communal impotence in the face of cataclysmic change communicated itself even to a small child.

I experienced change from an early age and should perhaps have become accustomed to it, but instead I saw it as upheaval, involving loss and insecurity. My father would come home on leave from the army, but would soon go away again. We went a long way on the train to visit him in camp, but soon we would be leaving again. My mother would take a job as housemistress in a boarding school, the only employment she could get with a small child in tow. Reluctantly, she would lift the suitcase down from the top of the wardrobe and we were again in a state of flux. To this day, I dislike moving out of the familiar schedule that gives me security. I sigh when I have to pack a case and waste energy in the process.

The times when I was happiest were the days of routine and a fair degree of predictability, even in wartime, at Granny Pountney's and at primary school in Murrurundi. After the war there was a move to another town, and then another, then to boarding school, then to a state high school. There were good practical reasons for the moves but, for me, each geographical change was accompanied by dislocation, by saying goodbye to people I was attached to, and by the strenuous effort of making a new home in a strange environment. I did not feel that my lot was improved by these changes and I succumbed to a good deal of unexpressed misery in making them. Then I generalised these experiences into an idea that change was undesirable and I carried this negative connotation into adult life to hang around the neck of any pending alteration in my circumstances.

However, if I survey those years of change through a different lens, and from the vantage point of maturity, I can see that each move opened up another potentiality for me. As a result of change in my circumstances, I encountered new people; my educational opportunities were enhanced; and my knowledge of the world was increased. At the time I did not realise that I had the freedom to choose my attitude to every event, and that is what makes all the difference.

My own most recent major change came in 1994 when *The Search for Meaning* program was taken off ABC Radio National.[5] It was not a life-threatening change but it was a significant incident for me. To hear how I handled it may teach you what not to do when you are confronted with change. My conclusion is that I did not manage it very well but that I learned a good deal from it.

I learned three important and very unexpected things. The first was that this change, which appeared to threaten my lifework, simply brought it into clearer focus. The second was that chaos can be creative. The third was that unemployment brings not only insecurity but also opportunity. Yet, when first the change was forced upon me, I had none of this clarity and optimism and it took a long time to come.

When I lost my job I lost a good deal of my sense of order.

Unemployment was no longer only a social injustice about which I had theories. It became a fact of my life. Suddenly I knew its demoralising effects personally. I discovered that to lose your job is to mislay part of your identity and much of your confidence. Contrary to expectations, enforced leisure is not agreeable. I missed the familiar structure of the working week. Monday mornings were the worst time. I missed the discipline of getting up at a certain time. I missed catching the ferry and drifting across the harbour, collecting my thoughts for the day ahead, while uniformed schoolboys, huddled into a scrum nearby, frowned and consulted over last-minute homework. I missed Circular Quay, the old busker quavering *Edelweiss* on the Jew's harp, women dressed for the city in suits and joggers, juggling cappucino in styrofoam cups, and everyone moving, maybe with stress but also with purpose, towards a destination.

I missed the bus ride, the men in suits studying folded newspapers or whipping out their mobile phones to have loud, one-sided conversations, urgent to them, comical to the onlooker. I missed the pigeons on Queen Victoria and the plane trees around St Andrews with leaves the size of dinner plates, and I missed joining the slowly-moving wave of students at Railway Square that would wash me up eventually on the steps of the ABC in Harris Street, Ultimo.

Ultimo, ultimas, ultimatum.

I missed greeting my workmates and hearing their overnight news, planning the day we would spend together. I missed communal morning tea, the in-jokes and shared anxieties of the workplace. Of course, at my farewell, they had said to call in any time and have a cup of tea, and they had meant it. But you can't call in on busy people and, besides, it is not a cup of tea you want but a resumption of your work, sitting concentrated on your own chair at your own desk.

I missed the sense that I was making a creative contribution to the society in which I live. I missed the purpose and the satisfaction of it. We were fortunate enough to have good evidence, from ratings, letters and tape sales, higher than any other program, that we were making something useful that people wanted. I missed the continual stimulation of thinking about ideas for the program. I missed the deep encounters of interviewing. I missed the listening that is my vocation. I missed the nourishment of it all. True, I had the faith and reason of my religion to turn to: and sometimes it sustained me but sometimes I forgot.

Over the past few years I had seen many colleagues 'made redundant'. That is a euphemistic term for an appalling practice that we have been conditioned to think is normal. I had seen their shock; the rejection of it seemed to shrink them. The men especially were bewildered. The unjust practice of economic rationalism which caused their sacking was harder to accept than a charge of incompetence or misconduct. There was no appeal against its inhuman criteria. And this was happening right across society, while a small elite in certain sectors enjoyed ever-increasing benefits.

I followed the progress of enterprise bargaining in industrial relations with growing bemusement. How do you bargain in an employers' market? We who are unemployed may be enterprising but we have no chips to bargain with. There are too many of us looking for too few jobs, while those still in work are pressured to do longer hours; and those who work at home unpaid are not even acknowledged.

Regardless of its purpose, quality or outcome, paid work is valued far above the vital productive unpaid labour of the parent, the home-maker, the honorary secretary of a body corporate, the emergency services, Meals on Wheels and community volunteers: their work does not register anywhere in the national accounts. The way we have come to describe and reward work in this society is confused and distorted. Some months after losing my job I saw in a newspaper that the manager who had terminated our program had left the ABC for a much bigger salary at a commercial network. His face laughed from the page in a photograph above the caption 'Smart career move'. For a few, the world of paid work is an amusing game, while for the bulk of the population the prospect of regular, full-time paid work is receding at a dramatic rate.

I found, as one of the many unemployed, that much of my grief was expressing itself as anger.

There were several layers to my anger. As a taxpayer and citizen, I was aggrieved by yet another ABC management decision based on mere personal whim in the face of hard evidence to the contrary. The ABC is a public utility for which I help to pay and I have firm ideas about how it should be administered — by best management practice, not whimsy. But then there was a deeper anger for a much more personal deprivation. It seemed unjust that I should be put out of the work to which I had given 30 years of my life. I had lost the opportunity to use my long and valuable experience as a public broadcaster. And, even deeper than this, I felt that for no intelligent reason listeners had been robbed of a rare reflective interlude in the media, an expression of spirituality in a society starving for it.

It was in this deepest anger that I learned something important for it revealed to me the depth of my desire to be part of enabling people to live life to the full, with meaning and purpose. After eight years dedicated to this endeavour, I had lost the most obvious means of achieving it. Now it was up to me to find other ways.

But how? I had not given any effort to imagining other ways. For a person who thrives on routine, organisation, structure and professional teamwork, how could anything be achieved in the absence of all these elements? I could not envisage it as a solitary endeavour. I lacked the support of the team on whom I had depended for creative partnership and practical help. Because I had been part of a team, I had relied on others for computer skills and, although I am a fast typist, I was badly out of date with contemporary technology.

And there was another problem — *The Search for Meaning* unit had become a resource centre over the years and, although unemployed, I was still receiving a large correspondence, redirected to my home; and wilting under the weight of trying to answer it alone.

I felt adrift in the chaos of my situation. Without structured days, I had to find my own way to organise time and, suddenly, there was never enough of it yet I was achieving nothing. Without program deadlines, there was no way of measuring achievement. I seemed to be working hard trying to create freelance opportunities yet made little discernible progress. And with no way to assess success, I had no incentive to allow myself any time off as a reward. I felt I must be constantly on duty, trying to make things happen. With only the sporadic earnings of the freelance writer, for which you often wait a very long time, there was no sense of income security, and I experienced a constant unease that drew me back to my desk to make another phone call, to follow up another possibility.

To lose your job is to lose your livelihood. In my case, as a contractor, there was no golden handshake of accrued sick leave, holiday leave and redundancy payment, nor even a note from the Chairman or the ABC Board. I did receive a pleasant, rather detached letter from David Hill who was also on his way out of the organisation and no doubt preoccupied. After 30 years I walked out of the door with my final week's pay packet and that was it. I was shocked at how casually and cheaply the organisation had shed me after an adult lifetime of service. As, increasingly, the corporate world insists on employing people as work units on contract, thousands of Australian workers know this dilemma. Sudden unemployment necessitates a significant rearrangement of priorities: how to pay the mortgage, pay off the car, support the family, how to keep living at the accustomed standard. It can't be done. I was luckier than many. I was fortunate to have some savings, even on my public servant's pay, but it goes against every instinct to live off savings for too long.

It was a humbling experience but, as the months multiplied into years, I found myself eventually submitting to my new situation, first in defeat and later with a slowly dawning realisation that there is actually some freedom in unemployment, even some opportunity, if only I chose to see it that way. I thought back over the wisdom I had heard in eight years of radio talks with my countrymen and women; how they had found new structures of meaning when old ones crumbled. I realised that I had to stiffen my backbone and find strength and resilience in my character. I remembered what Viktor Frankl wrote in his classic *Man's Search for Meaning*,[6] that whatever is taken from us, we retain the intrinsic capacity to choose our attitude towards our circumstances. That is our ultimate freedom. I rang others who had lost their jobs expecting commiseration, but I did not get it. Instead I got inspiration. They had all moved on creatively, making their own opportunities.

When I complained to one former colleague, 'But don't you feel they've taken your life away from you?' she replied, 'Oh, no, they've given it back to me!'

The funniest comment was: 'Snap out of it, Caroline. There's life after the ABC. That turkey has done you a favour.'

The idea of that self-confident executive as a turkey broke me up. I remembered turkeys from childhood farmyards, strutting self-consciously among the hens with their red dewlaps wobbling and their comical gobbling mating call, oblivious of their destiny which was the chopping block and the Christmas dinner table. The laughter was helpful, as it always is, if someone is brave enough to challenge the drama in which you are indulging yourself.

And out came my colleagues' stories, moving from initial grief and resentment to new, expanded achievements and a humorous backward glance at Aunty ABC's genius for losing so many of her best people. They taught me that I had clung on to my anger for too long and that, until I prised my fingers one by one from the resentful belief that someone else had decided my fate, I would be nailed to the past and unable to move forward. They had identified the truth of my situation, as friends so often do. It was good advice and, when at last I managed to follow it, it was liberating.

In addition, I was forced to reassess the meaning of unemployment in terms of the well-lived life. This is a culture that expects us to do things, to achieve and get tangible results. There are few rewards for living a modest life of integrity, based simply on 'kindness in another's trouble, courage in your own'. I began to appreciate having more time to visit a sick friend, to do voluntary work, to spend time with family or with a stranger who crossed my path, to make a long-over-due investment in personal relationships, to read and think. One day I sat in the sun for half an hour and watched the rainbow pattern of a prism reflected on the wall. It was a most unusual experience and, once I gave myself permission to do it, a rewarding interlude of rest and care for the soul.

I had to contemplate, too, the possibility that it was time I retired from a full-time job, to make way for younger broadcasters with new ideas. One angry Generation X journalist had put that to me when he said, 'Will your age group never get out of our way? You've had your turn, now move aside and give us our chance.'

I understood the point he was making. The trouble is that I've relished every moment of my fortunate working life. It's painful to let it go without a fight. At least I have the consolation of sharing that pain with thousands of my countrymen and women. Unemployment remains a national tragedy. I know that today with a more informed understanding. We are in need of urgent solutions. If I, with all my experience, maturity and good fortune, can find unemployment so shattering, what is it doing to the morale of our nation? My generation accepted work as a birthright but, apparently, there will never be full employment again, so we must find creative ways to redefine employment in order to give young people, especially, a sense of worth and purpose.

As my circumstances required me to move out into a wider world, looking for new work, my horizons were extended. I did two presentation jobs with the Lend Lease Corporation where I was fascinated to gain insight, for the first time, into an enlightened management style. It was a revelation to see how executives collaborated with their teams, how employees were cared for in many ways as whole human beings with family responsibilities, and how productively they responded to this consideration. I was also interested to see how specific projects were carried out by setting up *ad hoc* management committees that disbanded on completion of the project. This was chaos theory at work in the most effective way and it stimulated my imagination for my own situation.

Slowly I began to receive invitations to use *The Search for Meaning* experience in fresh ways: to spend a day with a group of people trying to discern a new corporate direction; or to facilitate the personal story-telling of a group, helping them to listen to each other and to share their experience in order to establish more common ground for their project. As well, I began to write pieces for the opinion pages of major newspapers. I had more contributions rejected than accepted but I persevered with this new discipline.

Friends and colleagues suggested a variety of ways in which *The Search for Meaning* experience could be adapted for workshops, but I did not put this into practice; and then came the idea of writing a book on the subject — not a collection of interviews like the previous four books but one addressed directly to the reader. And so I began to write this book. I could never have managed it while working full-time. It had taken a long while for this fact to dawn on me but, at last, after much resistance and heartache, I saw the relative freedom of my situation and I was grateful for it.

As I persevered with my several strands of endeavour, I began to feel that I was on track again, so far as my life purpose was concerned. And that was relieving and reasssuring. But it was still very different from having one central, full-time project. The disorganisation of it continued to torment me. I had been reading about the creativity of chaos with increasing irritation and disparagement. Finally I just gave in. When it became too much for me, I stopped worrying about the piles of mail pouring into the letterbox and mounting up on my desk. I stopped worrying about all the phone calls I had to answer. Occasionally, I would have a one-day blitz on them and catch up to some extent. I tried to follow the dictum to distinguish what was urgent from what was important. And I allowed myself to concentrate on the major priority of the book, ranking other demands by measuring them against my deepest value and purpose — that of furthering the search for meaning and spirituality in our community.

To live with disorganisation goes against my every instinct yet, when I accepted the chaos of my situation, I found that interruptions sometimes provided fresh insight for my writing. I began to trust that, as long as I had the spiritual compass pointed in the right direction, what happened along the way would only serve the cause. Sometimes it worked; at other times it did not and I reverted to a sense of being overwhelmed and underpaid.

One year after my unemployment began, I was invited to contribute interviews in *The Search for Meaning* style to a commercial radio Sunday night program *In Focus*. I was glad to take up the opportunity. Two years after I became unemployed, Deborah Fleming invited me to become an occasional contributor to her new *Australian Story* program on ABC television. I felt ambivalent about working with the ABC again but I said yes, since the show would share much common ground with *The Search for Meaning*. Deborah Fleming's aim was to enrich current affairs television by moving away from confrontation into the exploration of issues through the telling of people's stories, especially those at a turning point. It turned out to be a professionally redeeming experience because Deborah is an excellent manager and an exceptional communicator who knows how to build and maintain a creative, loyal team and get the best out of them, on a shoestring, and in spite of various other quintessentially ABC impediments.

With my finger in so many small pies, my working life became even more chaotic and I simply had to trust that, because my various jobs were aligned with my values and life purpose, somehow I would be able to do them. Assuming this attitude like a cloak, even when at times I couldn't quite believe in it, has been helpful. One of my part-time employers insisted that I get an answering machine. Stubbornly, I had always rejected the idea. When I accepted it, it made a helpful difference to my time management. Another employer allowed me to use one of their office computers to write this book. Until then, I had resisted learning how to use a computer. Now I am a complete convert.

It was very moving for me that some of my sustenance in this difficult time came from the testimony of guests who had spoken on *The Search for Meaning* programs. Reading through the books, listening to old interviews on tape, I came again upon stories that strengthened my resolve and illuminated my understanding of how to deal with change. I realised that the program was still alive. It had just gone underground to nourish people like me in our continuing quest.

Having given all my copies away, I bought *The Search for Meaning* video at an ABC shop and was greatly encouraged to see again the story of natural therapist Dorothy Hall.[7] She is one of that generation of strong figures who stood firm for their belief in alternative health care against critics and opponents in orthodox medicine and the powerful drug companies. Her books (such as *What's Wrong with You? The Natural Health Book*) brought practical information about wholesome food and better health to a huge audience in simple language. Dorothy explained to me how her lifework had been fuelled by a tremendous, driving anger. She thought that anger turned into zeal provides the energy to change things. Even as a child, she felt angry that so many people spent their lives diminished by illness, fatigue and difficulties. She felt this was not what life should be about. Very early she determined to study medicine, but the money was not available for her to go to university. Instead she turned to the study of natural therapies, especially herbs, and how they might be used to help sick people back into harmony. It became the vocation to which she gave the first half of her life.

In mid-life, Dorothy found the perfect partner and spent eight marvellous years with him. I spoke with her two years after his sudden, premature death. It had shocked her and yet, she said, it left her feeling not half, but whole, because of the love they had shared. She was 59 at the time of our conversation. This is how she set about dealing with the change in her life:

> I've reached an age which perhaps a lot of women dread and which I found, when I came to it, was a very welcome experience. It is a time of great change, where I've reassessed the relative values of what I have done and what I want to do from now on. It's terribly important to know what are the real needs and values you've learned in the earlier part of your life, and which of those areas you choose to go on with from here.[8]

Dorothy said that she had reached a state of contentment which was distinguished from happiness in that it was not a rising spiral of exhilaration, but rather a deep-seated feeling somewhere around the solar plexus that says:

> This is your spot, this is where you're comfortable. I feel, at this stage of my life that, for the first time, I'm not only Dorothy Hall, but what I was born: Dorothy Hamilton — a Scottish lass who has found another little bit of Scotland in Australia, with lovely old pine trees and stone walls and beautiful red soil and a rich open area to work in, to create something beautiful. And this stage of my life, I feel, is the time to be

creative. For a younger person, creativity is a fairly desperate thing, something that you have to strugggle with, something that you have to quickly launch and get on and make your mark and climb your mountain. For a person in the second or even the third stage of their life, I think creativity is something they can do with hindsight. And I found that what I want to create is paradise on earth: gardens.[9]

As I watched Dorothy's story again, I was fascinated to see that plants were the source of two strands of her vocation. Her grandfather had been Government Botanist and, before she could say ordinary words, she was calling plants by their Latin names. This inherited delight in plants led to her work as a herbalist, therapist and teacher. Now, in later life, that same wellspring of deep interest was to bloom in the creation of a magnificent, intricately designed garden, that would display both extravagant beauty and her lifelong scholarship.

There is a reassuring continuity in the way Dorothy interprets her past and her present. Some of her experience has been tough but there is no regret. It's all been useful; it can all be reappraised and sifted to provide a foundation for how she will live her life in future. Dorothy's story is a sustaining one to contemplate at a time of change in your own life.

Another day, browsing through *The Search for Meaning Collection*, I came upon my talk with the painter Judy Cassab. She and her husband John Kampfner lost almost everything during the war, their homes and almost every member of both their families. John was taken to a forced-labour camp while Judy worked under false papers in a factory in Budapest, stealing medicines and using her artistic skill to forge passports for the Resistance. Unable to communicate with each other for three years, John and Judy 'met' in spirit each night at a certain star they had appointed in the northern sky. John says those spiritual meetings are what kept him alive. In 1951 they came to Australia with their two small boys and, in delayed shock, Judy had a nervous breakdown. She remembers it like this:

It was all too much on top of what we lived through, to arrive and have the studio window on the south instead of north. What it is that made one feel strange about that, I can't explain; but everything was different. I remember looking out over Bondi Beach and thinking, 'Will I ever ever get on the other side of that ocean again?' I didn't think I would. If I want to touch any of my friends back in Hungary I imagined a very long knitting needle that one could push through the Earth and then one could only scratch their soles, their feet. It was a very alienating time.

There was no home to be sick for, because I had such awful memories. I really didn't want to ever go back, so it wasn't home-sickness. Maybe it was Europe as a larger home that I was homesick for. But I must say that no country in the world could have been kinder and more helpful than people were in '51 (in Australia) — absolutely fantastic.

We had very little money. I wanted to go into a factory and work for a while, to be a help, and my husband wouldn't hear of it. He said, 'You are a painter. I don't want a frustrated wife: you stay and paint.' [10]

Early in the 1950s, Winston Churchill's book, *Painting as a Pastime*, inspired many people to take up amateur painting, so Judy earned something from teaching. With fellow artist, Ukrainian-born Michael Kmit, she made weekly excursions to comb the junkshops for old framed photographs, paying as little as sixpence for them. They carted their bargains home, took out the rusty nails and cleaned and painted the frames. As the photographic paper was of good quality, they made use of it as well, by overpainting it. By 1953, Judy was able to give her first one-woman show, and the rest is written into Australian art history. She has won many prizes and become one of our most celebrated artists. Judy says that her marriage has been just as much a gift as being born a painter. When they married, John promised that she should paint every day of her life, and so she has.

When I asked Judy what brought her hope, comfort and strength through all the deprivation and change in her life, this is what she told me:

My belief, which I was born with and I think which is a gift (like being a painter), because I had nothing in my upbringing to make me a believer. On the contrary, my father was an atheist, and the whole family was not really religious. And I remember I prayed every night of my life, and it's a part of my life. I feel that I have this higher power within me, and I believe we all have the power within us, if we recognise it.

And I don't think anything ever happened that shook this faith in me — even the terrible things which happened. It was very difficult to bear but I'm not questioning it, because that would make it impossible to live, I think.

About belief, I'd quote the motto in Franz Werfel's book of Bernadette: 'For those who don't believe, every explanation is in vain. And for those who believe, every explanation is unnecessary.' So, I'm not trying to explain it.[11]

On Friday nights, John and Judy light candles in remembrance of those they've lost and in gratitude for a life which epitomises much of the sacrifice and upheaval of the 20th century.

Over the years, I have gathered many such life stories and each one has increased my store of resourcefulness and hope to call upon in times of challenge. The common thread of the storytellers is that they were true to themselves. This involved exploring themselves and their deepest values and then being faithful to those values. The testimony of human experience is more powerful than any theory about how to deal with change. For this reason, it is strengthening to read quality biography and good literature that explores human character and potential.

As I grow older, in this world of increasingly rapid change, it seems important to be discriminating in choosing the media images on which I will dwell. Occasionally, I waste a bit of relaxing time on shallow magazine gossip but I know it does nothing to stimulate the mind or care for my soul. Thoughtful works of art, films, books, theatre, well-researched documentaries and journalism have the capacity to nourish individual development of character and create a whole-some, compassionate community life. When change comes, as it does in greater and lesser degrees, to every life, we will deal best with it if we have given patient and faithful attention to building up our inner resources of integrity, hope and purpose, both individual and communal.

For a person who dislikes change and is most comfortable with stable routine, these past several years have been a time of enormous challenge for me. Sometimes I have made it more difficult for myself, by fighting for too long against something that I had to accept. Another mistake was blaming someone else and hanging on to anger about the change for too long before transforming it into energy to pursue my purpose in a fresh direction. At times, my faith sustained me with its promise of hope out of brokenness. At other times, I forgot to look towards it; I forgot to nourish my spirit and care for my soul; I forgot to pray and to ask others for help and their ideas, falling instead into that anxiety of independence in which the weight of the world seemed to be on my shoulders alone.

I can acknowledge now that this change has been a painful but very educational time and that it is not over. Somehow I have come to accept that life is characterised by change and that if only I will go with it, keeping my compass pointed due north, then change may be creative and I will strive to adapt to it and work constructively to use it.

I am almost disbelieving of this alteration in my attitude to life. I recall my mother telling me that I would be surprised when I found what made me happy. And so I am. In my youth, and even a few years ago, I would have repudiated out of hand the life I live today. After all, I've lost the job to which I gave my life. My voluntary commitments outnumber those that pay. I find tremendous sustenance in friendship and sharing ideas with colleagues, yet I live much of my life in solitude. I lend a hand where I see a need, in a way that would have exhausted me previously. Now it tires me, but I am satisfied that the effort is worthwhile — that it connects me in some small but meaningful way into universal life. None of this was part of the dream that I was sold in my youth. I was never going to be one of those middle-aged women with grey in my hair driving a little white car, happily going to functions alone, or curled up at home with a good book. And yet I am all those things now. Like everyone else, I still have to grapple with life's problems but, at a deep level, I enjoy a peace of mind and a sense of purpose and joy that I have never known before. Materially, it is a modest and simple life.

Spiritually, it is rich. The difference between then and now is that gradually my sense of values has altered and deepened and been reoriented from the purely personal to the communal, the universal and the ultimate, and I have a growing sense of my own authenticity as a person. Change, then, has been good for me. I can hardly believe that I am writing this, but it is true and I need constantly to remind myself of the fact.

For your Journal

* If you are experiencing change now, what are you feeling?

* What do you fear?

* Think of a time of difficult change in your life. Reflect on how you dealt with it.

* Can you see with hindsight any benefits of that change?

* What did you learn from it?

* In what way are you now more resourceful as a result of that change?

* Think of a time of positive change in your life. What benefits did it bring? Store them up to invest in the next change that faces you.

* Is there an image from this chapter that you would like to conserve, to return to at a difficult time of change?

* Return to the statement of purpose you wrote at the beginning of your journal. Are you achieving your purpose or does it need restating?

Endnotes

1 Rainer Maria Rilke, *Letters to a Young Poet*, trans by M. D. Herter, Norton, 1993.

2 Michael Leunig, *Common Prayer Collection*, Collins Dove, 1993.

3 Seasons for Growth National office, 9 Mount Street, North Sydney 2060; tel: (02) 9929 7001.

4 Dorothy McRae-McMahon, *The Glory of Blood, Sweat and Tears: Liturgies for Living and Dying*, JBCE, 1996.

5 For a full account of this matter, see the Introduction to *The Search for Meaning Collection*, Caroline Jones, ABC/Harper Collins, 1995.

6 Viktor Frankl, *Man's Search for Meaning*, Hodder & Stoughton, 1974.

7 Dorothy Hall in *The Search for Meaning Book Two,* Caroline Jones, ABC/Collins Dove, 1990. Also in *The Search for Meaning* video, ABC Video catalogue number 12574.

8 Dorothy Hall in *The Search for Meaning Book Two*.

9 Dorothy Hall in *The Search for Meaning Book Two*.

10 Judy Cassab in *The Search for Meaning: Conversations with Caroline Jones*, ABC/Harper Collins, 1992.

11 Judy Cassab in *The Search for Meaning: Conversations with Caroline Jones*.

12 SPIRIT OF THE GREAT SOUTH LAND

*In our tribe, Wandjina made the whole world, birds,
trees, rocks, animals, people, you and me. He gave us the land
divided equal and gave us totems to look after.
He punished us when we made mistakes. He is said to be
our grandfather's God before we were born and
those with and before him.*

Maurice Umbagai, Mowanjum, Western Australia[1]

IT WAS IN 1988, the year of Australia's bicentennial celebration of
white settlement, that I was invited to Alice Springs to work alongside colleagues in the Central Australian Aboriginal Media Association
as they established new television programs on the Imparje network.
It was the first time I had been to Central Australia to stay. I was
unprepared for the shock of both place and people.

Belatedly, I began to listen to the profound creation myths that tell
how the Aboriginal world began: how everything was summoned
into existence by sound, as the legendary Ancestors sang the land into
being. The origin of the Ancestors is told in various ways: for some
groups, the Ancestors emerged from eternal sleep beneath the surface
of the land; for others, they came from the Milky Way. They roamed
across the continent. They called life out of the matrix of the land.
They sang out the name of everything that crossed their path — birds,
animals, vegetation, rocks, waterholes and people — and established
an intricate network of relationships and responsibilities among all
living things. This act of creation left the imprint of songlines or

dreaming tracks, invisible trails of words and musical notes. As Bruce Chatwin puts it in *The Songlines*, 'a spaghetti of Iliads and Odysseys, writhing this way and that'.[2]

And there is much more: those songlines, which tell the story of how things were created, require maintenance. The creation was not a finite act. It did not happen once and for all. It is a spiritual process continuing in a sort of eternal 'now' but dependent on the cooperation of human beings. The song must continue to be sung along the song-lines in order for the creation to continue to flourish. Those who belong to a certain area must sing the songs and tell the stories that criss-cross their area, to keep them alive. This is how everything in the stories is kept going, including the people. And this is the meaning and purpose of a life in which everything and everyone has a place; and in which group responsibility devolves into an intricacy of individual totem responsibilities. The interconnection and interdependence of all that exists is exquisitely meaningful.

Once you open your mind to it, this stirring account of creation makes lucid the Aboriginal claim of belonging to the land, which falls so strangely on western ears, conditioned to the idea that land belongs to them.

I have sketched only the outline of a complex system of thought and belief that gives Aborigines a sophisticated and completely satisfying psychological and spiritual framework for life. In possession of even this simple sketch, it is easy to see why Aboriginal people need to be in their own place. They have crucial sacred work to do there. Suddenly it is easy to grasp the anguish of separation from land and all that it means. To be taken from your land is to be taken from your meaning, from your whole purpose in being. Once this understanding took a foothold in my imagination, it never left.

In the western view, imagination has been devalued as a means of knowing, inferior to reason. Recent research into the separate functions of the linear-thinking left brain and the more intuitive right brain are changing this supremacy of reason over imagination. It is considered now that our logical, rational capacity is only one part of a greater capacity that gives insight into a fuller reality. This in turn throws new light on the meaning of the myths and values of old religions like that of the Aborigines.

Bede Griffiths makes a helpful commentary on this in the introduction to his book, *Universal Wisdom*[3], when he contrasts the way of thinking employed by the people of ancient times with the modern way of thinking.

> The people of ancient times did not think with a small part of their brain, as we have learned to do. They experienced the world in its totality with the totality of their being. A myth is not a fanciful story about the beginning of the world or some supposed divine event. It is the concrete presentation of the reality of the world as manifested in the imagination and engaging all the faculties of the human being. To understand the myth one had to be initiated into a total way of life and through it discover the meaning of human existence. Today we are searching for a myth which will give meaning to our lives, now that the myth of Western science has betrayed us. Western science created the myth of a universe of solid bodies moving in space and time, obeying mathematical laws, but this myth has collapsed. As science itself has discovered, we know now that matter is energy . . . The universe appears as a vast ocean of energy organised by an intelligence, of which our human intelligence is a reflection . . . the universe is a living organism, undergoing continuous evolution . . . This takes us back to the understanding of ancient, tribal people, as Christopher Dawson[4] has noted, 'Primitive man does not look upon the external world in the modern way as a passive, mechanical system, a background for human energies, mere matter for the human mind to mould. He sees it as a living world of mysterious forces greater than his own . . . which manifest themselves both in external nature and his inner consciousness.'

This explains the cross-purposes that sometimes bedevil negotiations between Aboriginal and white Australians over questions of land ownership. Somehow two very different systems of thought must engage with each other. Common understanding is made possible only by great efforts of intellectual generosity, to be applauded and facilitated when they occur.

My own understanding was deepened in conversations I have had with many Aboriginal people including the poet Kevin Gilbert, who explained to me that he knows himself to be 'a part of the continuous spirituality and personality of this created universe'.

> Right from our early beginnings we were taught of the sanctity of the total life around us. There's a difference in the white appreciation of creation. Their belief is that man was created from clay, and out of this substance he took an ascendancy, or a superior position, over all other things. The Aboriginal way is that everything created is equal and sacred: that the soil, the clay, the rocks are all sacred; and that all have a personality ... I had the strength of knowing that my creator is not above me somewhere, but is always with me; that, whatever the substance around me, that creation flows to me, through me, within me; that the universe is part of me, as I am a part of it. And I think that, once you know that, there is no fear ... there is complete belonging, and life and death is just a constant flowing ... a continual renewing.
>
> So, this presence is an ever-flowing thing with me. There's no need to meditate distinctly; there's no need to go to any church; there's no need to think spiritual or religious thoughts. There's a constant flowing of life and we are very much part of that life ... [5]

It is a captivating and sustaining view of life and I was in awe of Kevin Gilbert's fluency in articulating his faith in it. His calm conviction was utterly persuasive. It explained everything for him, even loneliness:

> There is an incredible amount of isolation in the white community ... because people haven't learnt to belong. Nobody should be homeless in this land, and yet there is an incredible amount of homeless people. You cannot build a nation until there is a national spirit. [6]

I am constantly taken aback by the compassion that Aboriginal people have for white Australians. White settlement has very nearly destroyed them yet they continue to exercise their patience and imagination on reconciliation. It is as though their responsibility for land must perforce be extended to anyone on that land, no matter how peculiar the manner of their arrival. One can only revere a spirituality that creates and sustains such people. In Central Australia I had an extraordinary encounter with another elder, whose name in English is Kevin Buzzacott. He told me he had been thinking long and deeply about the relationship between white and black in Australia.

Although I did my best as we spoke to avoid the direct gaze, natural to the westerner but so offensive in Aboriginal custom, in the course of two long conversations I did see his eyes. They were of a different order to the eyes of any European. They were opaque windows to some ancient dimension, way beyond my ken. They seemed akin to the darkness of rocks with lighter tracings like serpentine riverbeds snaking through saltpan. They seemed to hold the memory of aeons, not centuries. They were looking both inwards and beyond, rather than being focused on me or even particularly in the present. Because he knew I was a broadcaster, Kevin spoke to me in order to communicate something important to the outside world.

He was troubled by the discrepancy he saw between whites and Aborigines. Even though many Aborigines have been dispossessed, many know their identity because they know their place and their name and their kinships and their responsibilities in cultural law — whereas white people did not emerge from this land and have never been 'named' in the Aboriginal way, so they are not yet at home. From the security of his own rich psychic sense of belonging, he thought this to be an untenable position for whites and a serious obstacle to communication and reconciliation. He was devoted to the idea that if somehow whites could be 'named', then they could truly belong here and the gap in understanding between black and white could be bridged more readily.

His tact in expressing his ideas was immaculate. He never mentioned invasion; and it was not until later I came to realise that colonisation has no place in the Aboriginal perspective. It is quite unthinkable that anyone would choose to abandon their place of origin, their land, the sacred place in which their identity, duty and meaning are vested. Yet the unthinkable had happened, and with generous vision he was searching his imagination for a solution to this unprecedented problem.

His earnest concern with naming reminded me again of my own delight in finding the hymn by Christopher Willcock SJ, which includes the line 'I have called you by your name, you are mine' — how much this had meant to me in my own search for identity. And even in contemporary secular Australia, where many religious rituals have been discarded, most parents still seek out some form of naming ceremony for their newborn children. There is a recognition of the need for naming as an important rite, although people may not be able to explain the powerful instinct that causes them to do it. The naming ceremony, whether conducted in a church, temple, mosque or synagogue, or by a civil celebrant, is not a private matter, but one to which the parents invite witnesses and for which they still nominate godparents. This is a fascinating anomaly in what is said to be a predominantly secular society — the unconscious desire to honour a ritual which the workaday reason would probably deny. Such is the power of naming, in the psyche.

One of the first imperatives when white settlers came to this country was to name everything. Like animals marking out their territory, they labelled places for various political and sentimental reasons, ignorant of the fact that these places already had names. On the one hand, noble patrons and statesmen back in the old country had to be appeased or flattered. As well, the yearning gripe of exile could be assuaged slightly by calling a strange new place by a nostalgic name from home, 10 000 miles away. In the same way, the earliest white artists could not help but superimpose the familiar images of home onto a savage landscape which intimidated them. Memories of home were their only defence against its strange, indifferent terror; their only means to keep it at bay, to pretend that its vastness was not so, nor the gnarled, nightmarish contortions of its vegetation and topography.

Naming was a crucial adjunct of taking possession. The imperious straight lines of state boundaries announced a complete disregard of the existing culture by cutting through the geographical features that delineated Aboriginal Australia. I remember the shock when I first saw a map of Australia marked out in terms of Aboriginal understanding of the land — the contrast with European maps was so dramatic. Although only one-dimensional and perforce over-simplified from an Aboriginal perspective, it was a honeycomb of curves and crevices determined by river valleys and mountain ranges, marking the areas to which various groups belonged. It was a concrete representation, related to the logic of geography, rather than an abstract grab for real estate across a continent which the newcomers had neither fully explored nor yet understood.

My own forbears were among the early white settlers. They included a master mariner, timber-getters, pub-keepers, providores to the gold rush, farmers and builders. They encountered Aboriginal people in both tension and friendship. They pioneered with courage and initiative in the understanding of their time. I honour their achievement and what they created, and I benefit from it, but I cannot divorce myself from the ravaging aspect of colonisation in which they were participants, however unwittingly. Deep, terrible and sacriligious hurt was inflicted on Aboriginal people. Its ramifications continue to this day. Now that we understand with greater insight the terrible effects of white settlement on the cultural values and spiritual foundation of Aboriginal people, the way is open to recognise the steps we must take to right a historical wrong.

The law leads the way, but the facts of our history need to find a home in every person's heart and spirit so that desire for reconciliation may be heartfelt, voluntary and overwhelming. This would be a giant step forward in the clarification of meaning for all Australians. At a meeting of the Women's Reconciliation Network, to which I belong, I heard it suggested that the loneliness, the restlessness and rootless-ness of many white Australians grows out of the half-unconscious race memory that they are living on stolen land, and therefore have no real sense of belonging even though they want to belong.

My talk with Kevin Buzzacott was broadcast on *The Search for Meaning* program on ABC Radio National,[7] so at least I was able to carry out my undertaking to tell people across the country of his proposal. Wise elders of the white community, people like Dr H. C. 'Nugget' Coombs and others, had argued publicly decades before for a treaty with Aboriginal peoples. They had the sensitivity to know that we can achieve neither national identity nor integrity without a transparent acknowledgement of our history. It is something which, in a spiritual sense, newcomers need more than Aboriginals.

People who have settled land in Australia for several generations have developed a love of their country but it is still a huge leap for many urban westerners to make, from a concept of land as real estate for exploitation to land as the mother of sacred place and meaning. The day on which that insight dawns may hasten the arrival of a national identity that has so long eluded us. Real progress is being made in recent years, with goodwill on both sides. But until we achieve reconciliation, with justice, must we remain, in the branding words of our own great novelist, Xavier Herbert, 'a community of thieves' and at some level suffer the unhappiness of it? Today, a 'community of thieves' seems an inappropriate term to apply to the exiled men and women transported here against their will by English governments. And it hardly describes the refugees from the Irish potato famine who were more sinned against than sinning. Yet it contains the germ of an uncomfortable truth when applied to the policies of the governments which administered white settlement.

Somehow, Australia has to become home both for her original inhabitants and for all successive generations of immigrants. Their stories too need to be heard, as part of a dialogue in which all may learn from each other.

Reconciliation is a crucial goal for Australia in the context of the search for meaning, and I am convinced that it could be achieved more readily if white people had Aboriginal friends in the towns and cities, met some Aboriginal people steeped in their law, and travelled to the more remote areas to see and feel the spirit of the land. So long as we cling round the edges of the continent, our understanding of Australia and our capacity to belong here will be incomplete.

My first experience of the desert was in the late seventies when I spent some time driving and camping out on the Nullarbor plain, awed by the vast, singing silence of its space; and fascinated by the resilience of the plants and creatures which have adapted themselves to win a tough living from it. I took dozens of photographs of those enduring life forms and I can look at them in my journal today when I need to find personal courage or adaptability.

Ten years later, my first flight across central Australia in clear weather was one of the most alarming days of my life. For there below, hour after hour, the vast emptiness of the landscape offered me no reference point. It seemed a vacuum into which I could vanish without sound or trace. Ochre melted into magenta, claypans swirled and dazzled in grey whorls. I was mesmerised by the repetition of dry rivers writhing across endless desert. I could not press my face sufficiently close to the porthole to see it all. This was my country yet it was unintelligible to me and my imagination ached with the infinity of it — the grand emptiness which only gradually I comprehended was humming and droning with 'the Iliads and Odysseys' of the Ancestors, a story beyond any measure of time I knew. I reeled back from its immensity into the enclave of my modern mind and found only a house of cards.

And then, although reason rejected the fact, I remembered that an extraordinary people have clung here for aeons against savage westerlies brandishing a scourge of sand, threatening eviction. And that they have laid a template of meaning on this appalling landscape. They call her 'mother' but how demanding she is of their obedience. They were created out of her in the wilderness and, with sublime imagination, they answered her eternal command to maintain her fantastic creation: they hollowed out the didgeridoo to groan her labours back to her. They chattered to her in clapsticks and echoed her eerie sighs with the bullroarer. They danced for her in the guise of all that was made in her image; they sang her birds on their migration paths; they painted her in all her myriad manifestations, divining a symbolism of immense complexity to do so. They chanted her stories back to her in infinite cycles. They frequented her sacred chasms to receive the spirits of their children. They kept her taboos; they propitiated her with ritual and ceremonies that pulsated the retold legends rhythmically, hour after hour, out into the dense, black, star-encrusted nights pressing on the desert. Towards morning, as the campfires died, the children fell asleep and the stories they had been told crept into their dreams, to sustain them with law and meaning for a lifetime.

The communal discipline of all this effort was beyond anything that contemporary life demands or has to offer. It is of an all-engrossing spiritual order in which inner landscape is in communion with outer, and both are answering to their Source. Is it too great a leap to suggest that this intense communication of creator and created breathing each other in and out, in and out, became the holy spirit of the Great South Land, a spirit that many of us sense but find difficult to describe or touch?

After my long, illuminating flight across the heart of my country, I arrived in Alice Springs, astonished to see Albert Namatjira's paintings come to literal life. Yes, the colours really are cobalt, scarlet and viridian. What I had thought must be the naive palette of a primitive was his vivid daily reality, and the shapes of his rocks and trees not fanciful after all.

Then I came into the presence of the people themselves, people who have succoured their families and kept their laws and carried their faith and honoured their creator through more ages of time than any other human group. I was touched by the dignified stillness of many Aboriginal people, their way of listening before speaking. When I went bush with one group, I wondered at their intimacy with the land, their skill in conjuring grubs from tree roots, gathering wild plums and honey, digging yams from the red earth and finding water hidden behind the bark of trees. I felt wistful for my own youth and longed to join the gleaming children revelling in billabongs beside their mothers pulling edible roots from beneath the lily pads.

Perhaps you will go there yourself: to match wits, if you can, with the Aboriginal sons and daughters educated in western culture — the lawyers, philosophers, historians, politicians, broadcasters, poets, bush-men, designers, tour guides and artists who can give you a comparison between European and Aboriginal perspectives with challenging erudition.

Perhaps you will be exasperated, as I was, by lack of punctuality until you appreciate that family business, sorry, men's and women's business is sometimes more important than getting to work on time. You may be shocked, as I was, by the ravages of alcohol and sugar and the injuries of domestic violence — scenes that white society can hide but which become public for black people dispossessed of their home. You may decry the schisms in black politics until you recall that white politics is based on the adversarial model and rife with factions. If you join in the common complaint of 'Where has all the money gone?', remember too that Aboriginal money management was learned in government departments from white bureaucrats and politicians, and from sometimes unethical shopkeepers. When you deplore the slowness with which change comes, someone will explain to you the wise, leisurely process of consensus decision-making. To Aboriginal people, democracy often seems like entrenched conflict, and Darwinian theory is a white myth used to legitimise colonisation — to be tolerated, politely, but never taken seriously.

Criticise the unruly custom of sharing all possessions if you will, but ponder the selfishness of its opposite in other societies. Decry a demonstration in Redfern, New South Wales, but reflect on its motivation as a cry for justice and participation. When you have encountered the gentle courtesy, the dignity and wisdom of bush people in their own place, you will appreciate more deeply the lost heritage that some angry urban Aborigines are mourning. When you have seen the resourcefulness of people on their own land, you will understand the anguish of the dispossessed. When you have slept in a swag in the desert, watched over by great clusters of immanent stars, you will know why Aborigines give up the ghost in prison cells. When you have actually contacted the spirit of the people of the land, when you have made friends, asked questions, listened to stories; when you have spent time in that other world, you may be changed by the experience in a way that is valuable for the fulfilment of your humanity.

I do not claim that all Aboriginal people everywhere are spiritually aware and sensitive, just as I'm not saying all westerners are ignorant and materialistic, but I do contend that Aboriginal culture teaches a spiritual relationship to the land, and to each other, from which all Australians may benefit.

You may come to believe, as I do, that spirituality is not just an optional extra for us Australians, a matter of choice or philosophical fashion. It was here long before we came. It is as real as the air we breathe, as real as the Southern Cross that hangs like a benediction in our night sky. It is here now, palpable, potent. It is awaiting our engagement and our surrender. Once I began to open myself to the Aboriginal understanding of life, it became part of my history, intertwining with all the other stories I have inherited and which form my identity. I see it as the great gift of the Aboriginal people. They offer it freely to welcome newcomers to this ancient continent and to give them the passport to belonging here. It is the genius residing at the root of Australian culture and illuminating Australian spirituality.

Aboriginal spirituality has been generous in its engagement with Christianity. Some indigenous people were gracious enough to enter into dialogue with the god of their colonisers. It is moving to see how Christian and Aboriginal spirituality have encountered each other in some communities, each enlivening the other. Perhaps it is not so surprising, since a reading of the Book of Genesis strikes many echoes in the creation legends of the Aboriginal Ancestors. Other Aboriginal people deplore the imposition of Christianity upon their own deeply felt spirituality and will have none of it.

My encounter with Aboriginal people refreshed my sense of spirituality and informed my faith more deeply. The living landscape entered my imagination; my sense of individualism was diminished and my consciousness of community enhanced. I was confronted with my own lack of freedom in relation to timetables, privacy and possessions. I was humbled to hear the fluid ancient languages of my country spoken and not to understand a word of them — Arrente, Walbiri, Pitjatjantjarra, Luritj. I was shamed to see some of my countrymen and women living in poverty. I was warmed, during my later visits, to be addressed as 'Sis' by some of the women. As friendships grew sufficiently to allow candour, I was told, 'if only white people would at least say that they are sorry for what has happened, it would help a lot . . .'. Such a simple, obvious sentiment that many would feel, yet hesitate to express. Former Prime Minister Paul Keating's expression of sorrow in his Redfern speech meant a great deal to Aboriginal people. In Central Australia, I recognised reconciliation between black and white to be a crucial undertaking; and I understood the truth of Kevin Gilbert's assertion that you cannot build a nation until there is a national spirit.

The Aboriginal broadcasters I worked with gave me beautiful gifts — a carved wooden goanna decorated in pokerwork; a watercolour landscape by Jillian Namatjira; and a silk square, batik-dyed in the pattern of honey-ant dreaming, made at Soakage Bore by the oldest artist of the Alywarra people. The Aboriginal artists of Utopia at Yuendumu produce this ethereal silken beauty out of plastic buckets of dye in a remote sandy riverbed and hang it out to dry on the trees.

I wore my glorious scarf as a blessing the day I went out with a Catholic priest and nun on their regular circuit to celebrate Mass in the desolate camps on the outskirts of the Alice. For me, it was to be the occasion of another powerful instance of forgiveness and, when I was invited to write something for the bicentennial year, for the *Age* newspaper on 31 December 1988, I wrote about that day:

In the late afternoon I am sitting on the red earth in a wretched fringe camp, part of a huddle of men, women, tow-haired children and snappish dogs. There is no running water here, no shelter. The people look as if they have been tired for many years. Their eyes are sore, their legs thin and wounded.

The children eagerly set up a little stool on the dry ground for communion as they have done so many times before. In the middle of Mass, as the priest invites us to offer each other the sign of peace, I turn my face hesitantly towards the face of the woman beside me in the dust, terrified of what I might read there.

'Peace be with you,' she says, not in her own language but, generously, in mine. She forgives me even before I have asked forgiveness. But that is not quite absolution.

In this public place, in this 200th year of white settlement of Australia, I, Caroline, ask my Aboriginal countrymen and women for your pardon. I am deeply sorry for all the pain and dislocation which Europeans coming here has brought you. I respectfully offer you my grief for all that you have lost which is justly yours. I acknowledge you as the enduring, beating heart of this country. I honour your religion, your songlines, your ancestors, your law, your Dreaming. I respect your sense of the sacred in all that is created. Could you guide us out of our anxious chattering thoughts into the revelation of our dreams; away from the edges where we cling, into the heart where we need to go, to let go, to find ourselves; will you lead us from clamour into deep listening; out of our restless, acquisitive activity into our nature, our being; out of our certainty into faith?

Perhaps I ask too much, and too late. But still I ask for this gift of your forgiveness, your invitation to stay and your guidance on the way forward.

Of course, we must take responsibility for finding our own spiri-tuality, not dump another demanding load onto Aboriginal people. But their spiritual example is one of the great gifts of Australia to anyone else who comes here. It is neither just nor wise to build a society for the 21st century on anything but truth and equality. In our hearts, all decent Australians know that. In 1967, 92 per cent of Australians voted to give citizenship to Aboriginal people. It was an important spiritual and political milestone. In 1992 came the Mabo decision of the High Court, and with it the healing of the lie of Terra Nullius — that the land was vacant when whites came. More progress. Yet the social conditions of too many Aborigines today remain a shame, and a symbol of national poverty of spirit for all the world to see.

Differences over land claims continue to create new division between Aboriginal and white Australians. Painful as this conflict may be, we have no option but to wrestle with it and follow it faithfully through to resolution. It matters for the sake of the integrity of the nation, and for all of us. Paradoxically, it will turn out to be a gift. Through creative compromise, our modern form of thought, char-acterised by acquisitiveness and individualism, can be renewed by the larger spiritual vision of Aboriginal understanding, if we will allow it. That is what we need to listen for, behind the rhetoric of 'certainty' and 'rights' and 'leases'. These are but surface static on a grand and worthwhile bid for reconciliation that is essentially spiritual in nature. If we achieve this, we will achieve a measure of honour. We will have forged, out of conflict, and through generous intellectual and imaginative labour, a new creation. It will have the ingenuity of the best of modern Australian thinking, underpinned by a strength of spiritual wisdom that is the very stomach and soul of this land.

For your Journal

* What aspects of Aboriginal spirituality speak to you?

* If you are feeling resistant to what I have written, try to express the basis of that resistance.

* How have you felt the influence of Aboriginal spirituality?

* What are your feelings about the relationship of reconciliation to national identity?

* Do you have a sacred place in the landscape?

* Do you feel a spiritual relationship with places outside Australia?

* What are some of the ways in which naming is significant in your life?

Endnotes

1 Extract taken from *The Aboriginal Children's History of Australia* published by Rigby (nd).
2 Bruce Chatwin, *The Songlines*, Elisabeth Sifton Books, Viking, 1987.
3 Bede Griffiths, *Universal Wisdom*, Fount, 1994.
4 Christopher Dawson, *Progress and Religion*, Greenwood Press, 1983.
5 Kevin Gilbert in *The Search for Meaning Collection*, Caroline Jones, ABC/Harper Collins, 1995. Also Tape 25 in *The Search for Meaning Catalogue*, ABC Radio Tapes.
6 Kevin Gilbert in *The Search for Meaning Collection*.
7 Kevin Buzzacott, Tape 17 in *The Search for Meaning Catalogue*, ABC Radio Tapes.

13 LIVING WITH SPIRIT

It's in the memory, that's where home is.

Elie Weisel[1]

*The stuff of the world is there to be
made into images that become for us tabernacles
of spirituality and containers of mystery.*

Thomas Moore[2]

IN THIS CONCLUDING CHAPTER, there's an expansion of the concept of living life to the full and with greater spiritual richness. There is also an invitation to identify your most treasured possessions to see what they have to tell you; some reflection on the need to detach from possessiveness; encouragement to persevere with your journal; an idea about the value of adding a fresh element into a difficult situation; and some more thoughts on breaking out of individualism into the spirit of community.

One spiritual resource that most of us have in abundance is a store of memories. Memory is the rich repository of our experience, the home of our story and a resource from which to create the future. Using imagination, memory can be drawn upon to quicken a sense of meaning and strengthen a conviction of identity and purpose.

My imagination contains a collection of treasured images that I have gathered over a lifetime. In one powerful sense they are my home. They form the vivid furniture of my inner world. I can savour them at will, or sometimes they appear unbidden behind my eyes. In periods of uncertainty I revisit them as touchstones of an eternal reality to which I claim allegiance. They have a wistful quality about them, a scent of home and, perhaps, of destination. They provoke excitement, a holding of the breath as though to listen for a distant half-remembered sound. A number of them appear earlier in this book and here are three or four more of them.

§

THE RAIN HAS stopped for a while. My father is feeding five magpies on the wet lawn. They take scraps of yesterday's sandwiches from his fingers. They're standing on long, cautious legs in a half-moon around him, throats extended, carrolling, taking it in turns to stalk forward for a morsel. He is in his morning dress of sandshoes, shorts held up with an old necktie around the waist and a cotton shirt. The veins stand in cords on his outstretched hand. His thin skin is mottled with the dark spreading bruises of age. He bends his knees to reach down to the birds' level and waits patiently for them to approach.

'They know me by now,' he explains, with a modest smile, just in case I may think that, in his 92nd year, he is proud to have won the trust of wild creatures.

Later, when I am leaving, he packs a little bag for me from his pocket-handkerchief garden. It contains the first two tomatoes to ripen on his vines, mignonette lettuce leaves, and a bunch of mint and parsley with a wad of damp paper pressed around the stalks to keep it fresh. The gesture is unbearably moving, too profound for me to feel at that moment. I save my tears for the journey home in the car. I have started my grieving early, so as to expend some of it before he goes, as though to avert a flood. The car is perfumed with mint and tomatoes. Their aroma stirs even deeper filaments of memory, like fronds of seaweed swaying lazily in the current on the ocean floor: when I was a child, my mother soothed my sunburnt back with the cool flesh of a tomato cut in half.

§

AFTER DARK, a slight breeze disturbs the lace curtains. A page turns in my memory and I see behind my eyes the night time garden in *Howard's End*, the film based on E. M. Forster's novel. Is it a crab-apple tree, dense with blossom, past which Margaret (portrayed by Vanessa Redgrave) glides through her beloved garden, looking in at her family through the lighted windows? I am looking in too. I resonate with her deep spiritual love of the garden, a love that is different in kind from her detached affection for her family. Time has dissolved. This sequence exists in eternity and cannot be imprisoned in minutes or hours, just like the memory of my father with the magpies, and the little bag of tomatoes and mint from his garden, passing from his hands into mine. These potent images are both past and present. They replay over and over again into infinity.

§

THERE IS A VERY early memory of lying in my pram, looking up through white mosquito netting into a jacaranda tree. It is an alluring memory. The feeling is one of ecstasy. I am safe and warm because enclosed in the pram, and presumably not yet separated from my mother's identity. And I am absorbed into the mauve haze of the jacaranda blossoms, some of which have fallen onto the netting and are close to my face. It is a complete experience, lacking nothing for contentment. This image has accompanied me through life. If I am asked for my earliest memory, this is what I tell.

Jacaranda is a cornerstone of my story; it could be my totem. Each year I wait with heightened awareness for the first suggestion of a pale halo of colour on the October trees. There are many of them in the prospect from my window. As the colour deepens and then saturates whole trees, I know an expansion of spirit which allows me access to the quality of that early memory and helps to answer the perennial question, 'who am I?' It's not a rational answer, more like an intimation that, if I long for and recognise the essence of jacaranda, then I am somehow related to that jacaranda and, through it, connected into the seasonal nature of things.

I was alarmed when I heard an authority on Australian native trees complain that jacaranda is an import, no better than a weed, and should be eradicated. Although this may be factually correct, it was jarring to me because of my psychic connection to jacaranda which has the same reassuring effect as the knowledge that I can love, or that I can be moved to tears. Even when they are painful or almost unbearably poignant, these experiences are all evidence of what it is to be human and I am grateful for them.

Many of my recurring images are sensual. I feel the wet grass on the soles of my feet. The full-throated carrolling of the magpies fills my ears. I smell the tomatoes and the mint sharply and the drenched fragrance of the tree in bloom. My eyes move around the image, exploring it as one does a painting or a person. The eyes are drawn from one point to another to another, making a criss-crossing pattern, making it real. It is a refraction of the half-asleep experience of childhood, in which my eyes travelled the familiar furniture of the bedroom, to establish the reality of my environment, and to locate myself in it.

I find great freedom and security in the imagination. It is a rich world I can visit at will, a deep well of sustenance. It is my refuge, the place where I can retreat from futile conversation or tedium. It is the place where no one can follow, the place where I can rest, where I can feel what I am feeling, where nothing needs rational justification. It is the private place of the psyche which I share only by choice.

The peace researcher Dr Elise Boulding places critical value on the power of imagination. She told me we are unlikely to achieve a peaceful world if we do not put some effort into imagining it. She encourages people to think in concrete detail about a world without armaments. How would the economic system change, the society, our approach to science, trade and international relationships? Dr Boulding says that many people have never considered these possibilities, and this constitutes a barrier to their being realised. The same could be said of our own lives. If you never imagine it being different, fuller, more satisfying, then you may be blocking those possibilities. John Lennon had the same idea with his song, *Imagine*:

Imagine all the people living life in peace
You may say that I'm a dreamer
But I'm not the only one.
I hope one day you'll join us
And the world will live as one.

There is an interesting film called *Enchanted April* which was made in 1992, directed by Mike Newell.[3] It concerns Lottie, a young woman in Edwardian England, who longs to escape a stifling, conventional marriage in cold, dreary, rain-soaked London. Seeing a newspaper advertisement for a villa to rent in Italy, she is seized with an inspiration to take it up. She finds three other women to share the expense with her and so initiates an adventure that will bring important changes to each of their lives. The unaccustomed leisure of the holiday and the warmth and beauty of the setting prompts each one to a personal stocktaking. We watch their increasing openness to the present moment, and the transformation of their relationships.

What most captured my attention was Lottie's imagining of a place where things could be different. She was frustrated, longing for something more, and she conjured it into being. Then, instead of turning her back on the old life, she carried it with her into the enchantment. She invited her husband to join her and coaxed the pompous, materialistic fellow into a more generous frame of mind in which he became aware of the needs of other people, including his wife. As the film ended, with the holidaymakers returning to England, you knew that they were taking the experience home with them, that each had gained in self-knowledge and authenticity and that the potential of their lives was greatly enhanced from that time onward.

The opportunity of fulfilment was not tied to a particular place. It was a state of mind that could be carried from sunny Italy back to rainy England and into their future. They did not have to choose *either* Italy *or* England. They could have the benefits of both. There would be little change in circumstances for any of the characters, but a revolution in their enjoyment of life because, not without pain, they had chosen a new attitude towards it and rearranged their priorities accordingly. The last scene includes the classical image of a discarded wooden walking cane, stuck into the ground and sprouting into leaf on the fertile Mediterranean hillside.

The art of *Enchanted April* is a reminder that the literal happenings of every day can be transformed if only we give them some imaginative attention. Glimpses of eternity are available in countless ordinary events of life and, when they are acknowledged, they enrich experience and enlarge a sense of meaning.

Some situations in life seem intransigent. You may feel trapped and fret that you cannot change things. The first instinct is to get rid of an awkward tension, at home or at work, to escape it. That cannot always be achieved, but imagination may lead you to an inspired solution. It may enable you to add a fresh element to a difficult circumstance in order to improve it.

For instance, an elderly couple without transport may be getting on each other's nerves. One is constantly agitating to go out. The other is longing for some peace at home. They are at loggerheads. There is too much pressure on their relationship. But the introduction of a third party to provide a regular outing for one satisfies the needs of both. It is for only a few hours a week yet it breaks the cycle of aggravation, providing respite from what seemed an inescapable stress. The two people who were locked in an unhappy conflict gain some relief through the interest of an outsider. They see that they are not isolated in a small world of which they are the only inhabitants. Someone else has become aware of their needs. The third party also brings news from his own world which provides a fresh talking point in a flagging two-way conversation, even if that derives only from discussion of the visitor. This small solution came into being because someone imagined the situation differently.

As Thomas Moore suggests in his book, *Care for the Soul*,[4] one reason for feelings of emptiness is that too little of a person's experience has been registered or integrated to become part of them. The squirrel gathers nuts not only to eat today but to store in its nest for winter. We understand this concept well in relation to our material needs, but neglect it in an emotional and spiritual sense.

§

ONE DAY WHEN I arrived at my father's house he was engaged in what I soon came to think of as a spiritual exercise, although he may not use that term himself. He was in the laundry cutting the stems of soaking hydrangeas at an angle, with secateurs. Next he carried the drenched heads to his workbench and crushed their cut ends with a hammer. Then he laid the hydrangeas on an old towel and carried them upstairs where he began to arrange them in two vases. He is a very masculine type and it enriches the image of manliness to see his creativity with flowers. The heavy pink and deep blue heads were wayward. He was patient and completely concentrated, placing a bloom then stepping back to get the effect, and forward again to make another adjustment. It was his last job for the morning and he was tired but the task had significance for him.

My father has grown these hydrangeas in a compost heap in his tiny back garden. He has watched them, pruned them, watered them, and waited all year for their blooming. This day was the climax of a long process and he was honouring its evolution. Nothing was wasted. He had cultivated beauty and now it was rewarding his soul. He was in a reverie, no more to be interrupted than a priest at his devotions. The atmosphere in the room deepened and shimmered as he created his work of art. He had broken out of time and was playing in the eternal — and all in the modest domestic art of arranging cut flowers.

§

THE PACE OF contemporary life encourages us to squander experience as though it were infinite, to move on from one event to the next, in search of novelty and in the illusion of progress. Moving on is seen as being desirable in itself but it may come at a high price. What is the point of all our doing, however exciting, however novel, if nothing is harvested from it and integrated into increased under-standing and insight?

The custom of keeping a journal, as this book has encouraged you to do, may help to provide some reflection time as you mull over and record what happened on a certain day. The onrush of time is slowed as you search for words or pictures, a symbol or an object to describe some incident, how you felt about it, and how it may have touched your heart and soul. To choose even one instance a week for attention is worthwhile.

The mere listing of events is less valuable than a record of your response to them. In this work of conservation, experience is distilled and clarified. You make it part of you, to enliven your spiritual life and give a heightened sense of significance to your days. Another advantage is that, in documenting your own unfolding story, you give it authenticity. You affirm that you have a story, that it is a continuing story, unique and worth recording; and that you are surrounded by other people whom you influence and by whom you are touched. This may seem like stating the obvious but many people underestimate the validity of their own story and consider it unremarkable, especially when compared with others, such as celebrities in popular magazines. Some people find it difficult to imagine they have a story. Life seems to them like being tumbled about in a washing machine, lacking any semblance of control, purpose or direction. And without a firm sense of continuing story, our sense of inner legitimacy is less well established, leaving us more susceptible to feelings of emptiness.

Remember that a journal can be as simple as a scrapbook. A large project book of bound butcher's paper from the newsagent can provide a home for evocative pictures cut from magazines; for a motto, verse, prayer or quotation that provides a signpost or inspiration; for a feather or leaf found in a special place; for sketches, photographs, the map of a journey, a card sent in friendship at a tough time — anything you want to recall and treasure; anything that sets another piece into the jigsaw puzzle of the story you are building up, your own story. Such a book grows gradually into a spiritual resource. It gives you a window onto your inner landscape. You can open it any time to gain access to your unique sensibility, to what attracts you most deeply. It becomes a conservatory of your desires and concerns and will reflect back to you what matters most to you, where you find beauty, what nurtures you, what wounds you, what engages your compassion — who you are.

Patterns will emerge as you scan the images you have gathered, giving an insight into your enduring priorities. As time goes on, you may be moved and enlightened by this record of your true self and your spiritual journey. At the very least, it will give you a sense of continuity and satisfaction that you have kept important clues discovered along the way, and that you can revisit them. Choosing what goes into the scrapbook might best be done instinctively, just as you pick up certain shells on the beach and leave others. If it catches your interest, if it is intriguing, gather it. It will reveal its significance for you later.

The new enthusiasm for researching and documenting the family tree provides an important opportunity for believing in your own story. You start to wonder about those antecedents of yours whose engagement with all their struggles gave rise to your own life. What were they like? What was the source of their courage and their determination to overcome the odds that beset them? Have some of their characteristics emerged in you, several generations later? Is it some experience of theirs, which you are carrying, that gives you those eerie moments of *déjà vu* in a place you have never visited before? You find in yourself a new sense of gratitude for all their striving, for all that they suffered and endured — because their perseverance has given you life. In reviving their story, you are laying the foundation of your own, making it real.

And then you come to understand that you, too, are laying a foundation for all those other lives that are touched by the way you live. Not only your biological children, if you have any, but everyone who comes into your orbit feels your influence, for better or worse. They are all enlivened by your generosity or diminished by your lack of care. They all take example from your character, from your communal spirit, your personal encouragement, your faith, hope, joy, love and sense of justice. Your life furnishes the imagination of your peers and of the next generation. How you choose to live is a matter of significance, for this alone. Pope John Paul II expressed this in an encouraging and inspiring way when he said, 'Remember, your life may be the only Gospel some people will ever read.'

And how you choose to live depends on the steadiness of your sense of inner self; the vitality of your values and your conviction of meaning and purpose. When you review your life, it is unlikely to be by your possessions that you estimate your success, but by your personal integrity and by the quality of your relationships. And whatever else may be uncertain in life, these are matters over which you have a great degree of control.

You may argue that some are given much more promising circumstances than others, that it all depends upon the hand you are dealt. But is that entirely true? The keeping of a record of your life, however fragmentary, can lay a template of coherence on your experience and win meaning from even the most appalling circumstances, in time, if not immediately.

When Stan Arneil, in his early twenties, was suffering with his fellow prisoners of war, forced into cruel labour on the Thailand–Burma Railway, he kept a minimal record of the ordeal on scrounged scraps of paper. That record was published 40 years later as the classic *One Man's War.*[5] The book is a testament to the existence and endurance of the human spirit and it has seen many readers through tough times of their own. It tells how starving men, stripped of everything, found not only the will to survive but compassion for each other. They died in their thousands, but 'no man died alone'. In brief vignettes, Stan Arneil recounts how men kept their faith in life and in each other for three-and-a-half wretched years of deprivation.

Not every prisoner of war would remember those years as Stan Arneil does. For some there were no redeeming features in their ravaging experience, but for that young Australian platoon sergeant it was the getting of wisdom. After the war, he never lost a sense of gratitude for a glass of clean water from the tap, and a roof over his head. In his wartime diary, without knowing it, he was writing the blueprint for the life he would live from that time on and nourishing his spirit for the job ahead.

During his ordeal, Stan treasured his memories of life at home and, even in the depth of deprivation, he could imagine how things might be made better. After the war, he redeemed his suffering into a creative life of service. When he got home, he campaigned to found credit unions in Australia, a movement that would secure the future of countless disadvantaged families. With his wife Dorothy, an ex-servicewoman, he made a life of dedication to his church, to the survivors of his battalion and to his community; and raised a large family.

He could as easily have succumbed to bitterness or depression. But instead he kept the belief that the journey was worth travelling, that there was a destination, and that he would be answerable at the end for the state of his soul. This had sharp reality for him and gave him a spur and a clear sense of purpose. Although he lost his parents while he was still very young, they had bequeathed to him a religious faith and a sense of values by which he set his course throughout life. When he had setbacks, and there were plenty, he felt them badly but he did not suffer lack of meaning. Why? Because he had a story to live by. He was a Christian and he held the belief that a life of love and self-sacrifice was a gateway to the prize of eternal life.

All the stuff of Stan's life was transformed into soul — hard work, anger, battles, outspokenness, humour, worship, kindness, love. Along with countless others, I was myself a recipient of his generous encouragement in difficult times. He was so clear about his purpose that it was the most luminous aspect of him and you could not help but be touched by it in his presence. He was the quintessential dry, craggy Australian and he shone with spirit. While there was sadness at his Requiem Mass, there was also celebration of a lifetime's devotion, and a reminder that human life is a matter of free will, that it is the sum of the decisions you make. It was Stan Arneil's choice to live as though life is a sacred journey of the soul in the world, with love of God and his fellow man and woman the defining purpose. And this chosen way made him one of the happiest people I've ever met.

When something goes wrong in my life, I reach for his book and it always helps. The record of his prisoner-of-war days puts my problems into perspective and gives me a way to approach them. I think of how he used to throw back his head and laugh; how he always made time for you; how he loved people and saw their needs and worked to fulfil them. And I draw from the memory real inspiration about how to live a good life. Who knows what inspiration *your* life provides to the people around you? It is the greatest gift you have to offer.

Not everyone will be suited by keeping a written journal to conserve memories and furnish the imagination. Some find writing a tedious exercise that only distances them from their imagination and spirituality. Collecting pictures and images will suit them better. There are those who appreciate best the look of things and the feel of things. They prefer to make something with their hands, or to collect objects that become symbols of a day that lifted the spirit. Such objects can become tangible containers of mystery. The sight of them or their touch can snap the bonds of time and allow entry into that wider dimension without boundaries where the spirit can run free. For this reason people carve wood and make gardens and collect shells, seedpods, leaves, rocks, semi-precious stones, souvenirs of potent places, books, kaleidoscopes, candles, ornamental boxes and many other symbolic objects.

It is customary for the followers of some religious traditions to make a little shrine in the home or the workplace. You may see such homely reminders of spirituality in your local Chinese or Thai restaurant. War veterans tell moving stories of Vietnamese refugees suddenly forced to abandon their homes with nothing in their hands but their shrines, gathered up instinctively in the frantic moment of departure. *In extremis*, driven from their hearth, they saved the objects that were receptacles of their spiritual life.

You may like to reflect on which objects in your own home carry that sort of significance, and perhaps create your own shrine. What is it that you would rush to save in case of fire? If you consider the reason for your choice, you will soon see its place in your spiritual life. It is important to conserve tangible objects that hold spiritual significance for you and to pay them attention. I have a number of treasured possessions. They are things a burglar would not even notice for they are not of material value. There is a pottery jug and several bowls that my mother made. They are the bearers of her imagination, for she fashioned their shape with her hands from pliable clay. She chose the glazes in which she would fire them. They are practical pieces, for daily use. They were part of her domestic life and now they have become a treasured part of mine. There is the wooden inlaid tray that my father made, permanent home of the teapot and cups standing ever ready for afternoon tea. Concern with honouring ancestors has traditionally been an aspect of the spiritual life.

I have cushions and framed works embroidered by my god-daughter. Apart from their creative beauty, they bring her person to life in my home and remind me of our love for each other. And then there are the gifts of other people who have great significance in my life: two exquisite small sculptures by Barbara Mimovic given to me by friends at the time of my confirmation; paintings by my aunt; lovely embroidered linen from my stepmother's family; a French carriage clock from Granny on my father's side; and two dinner plates which she must have used every day and from which I draw the strength of familiarity.

There are two astonishing plaster casts, one bronze, one silver, of my own head. They are like death masks but they recall the lifegiving companionship of the best friend who made them, and the hilarious time we had, years ago, devising a way for me to keep breathing through a straw while she encased my face in wet plaster to make the cast. Other pictures, objects and photographs hold sustenance for my soul, evidence of my identity and confirmation of my story. There is a photograph of me with Sir Yehudi Menuhin whom I revere for the sensitivity of his music-making and the generosity of his teaching and encouragement of young people. He is presenting me with a citation for the Media Peace Prize at Sydney Town Hall. We are in profile and, since we both have prominent noses, it is quite a comical picture, but still it is a dream-come-true to be depicted with one of my spiritual heroes. Then there are shelves of books which hold the ideas that inspire me and nurture my philosophy of life and provide it with intellectual framework.

Another sacred object is the bleached, brittle shell of a sea urchin. It was posted to me years ago as an expression of affection. I remember so clearly unpacking layer upon layer of cotton wool, and my wonder at discovering it intact. I rejoiced at the delicate masculine sensibility that would despatch a symbol of fragility and endurance on a perilous journey through the post with its touching tribute. On a day when life seems difficult, just a glimpse of that sea urchin shell restores my spirit. Contemplating it, I am filled with gratitude.

It is difficult to overestimate the value of affirming people, in their being and in what they do. We can afford to be spendthrift with appreciation. It is seldom wasted. I have two beloved aunts who always encourage me. That is simply their habit, no matter what the circumstance. They never fail to remember my birthday and they are always ready with praise for me. In doing this, they have restored my failing confidence many times, and revived my spirit. Such encouragement is often neglected in the routine of family life, to be replaced by a frank and all too frequent criticism reserved especially for family members. But familiarity should not be allowed to breed contempt. My father and stepmother are always ready with their thanks for anything I do around their home. They remind me that this is something we could all choose to do for the people near us. If the habit turns out to be infectious, then that is a bonus.

It's not always practical to bring home things that enchant you. You may catch sight of a beautifully designed garment or piece of jewellery, way beyond your means, in a shop window. Rather than mourn its unattainability, you can spend a little time with it, wonder at its beauty and absorb it into your imagination, to keep forever. My mother studied fashion in the magazines and then made our clothes herself, to get the effect without the expense. A home with a harbour view may not be within your price range but you can ride the ferry at little cost and drink in the vista of the coves and waterways.

The addiction to possess is a distracting preoccupation when you can readily enjoy things without owning them. The imagination is a store on which there are no limits except the ones imposed by you. Paradoxically, a craving to own things is not always satisfied by winning the lottery and buying them. Physical possession brings worries and responsibility and sometimes feeds an addiction to want more rather than satiating the desire, as expected.

A millionaire told me that money buys comfort but not peace of mind nor happiness, and his melancholy expression accentuated his disappointment in the discovery. I asked him if he envied anyone and he replied that a garbage collector probably lived more happily than he did. Why couldn't he adopt a simpler lifestyle himself? Because, he assured me, once you've had a Rolls Royce, you want it and need it; you feel you can't do without it. However, he had found one thing that his money could buy to nourish the spirit, and that was art. His collection was his deepest solace, his only window onto serenity. Being a shrewd businessman, he was pleased that his source of spiritual sustenance also had value as an investment commodity. He asked me if I realised that the value of a crucifix was calculated by the degree of serenity it conveyed. I had to admit ignorance of this claim. The less affluent of us need not feel deprived. We can go to the art gallery, or browse through library books of great art, and escape the huge cost of insuring the Rolls Royce.

We are conditioned to an ideal of personal ownership and it takes some eluding. I am not altogether free of it, but a degree of liberation from the need of personal possession has been one of my most important discoveries. It came to me first through a stretch of the imagination, at a stage of my life when I regretted having no children of my own. The sadness of this was not easily ignored but the idea came to me to volunteer for regular visits to a home for disadvan-taged children and that gave me a new view of my problem. I came to understand that I could love and care for children in various fulfilling ways without having given birth to them, or claiming possession of them. I have always been grateful to the children, to the matron who allowed my visits and the nursing staff who tolerated my inexperience.

And there were other opportunities too, like the support of charities that care for children and those that allow you to sponsor needy children in deprived communities. Some of the most satisfying work I've ever done was that of a trainer with Elizabeth Campbell's inspired Peer Support Program, a communication and leadership scheme that benefits school children of all ages Australia-wide. For two years I had unbounded energy for this work because it was fuelled by one of my deep spiritual and emotional desires of that time. In helping to make the experience of many children safer and more confident, I was cured of the self-absorbed yearning for one child of my own. This would not assuage everyone's need, but it helped me.

To gather up the contents of this book I want to tell just two more stories. One is about a woman who is not in the public eye and the other is of a man well known to you. Their common thread is a commitment to live life to the full.

I met Michele Fehlberg at the end of a six-year period in which she had suffered seven stroke-like episodes and been diagnosed with multiple sclerosis. It is not difficult to imagine the utter dislocation of this capable woman's life at the age of thirty-eight. At first, she had been partly paralysed and confined to a wheelchair. At that time she found it difficult to speak at all.

By the time we met, she had made considerable recovery but was having difficulty with her hand movements and could not walk far. Multiple sclerosis interferes with the messages coming from the brain. Although Michele's mind was clear, she was frustrated by faltering speech, which was dispiriting for someone with a love of language. Before her illness she spoke Greek, Spanish and German but cannot retrieve them from her memory now. A woman with two tertiary qualifications, she was disappointed to be no longer working. She felt that her retirement on medical grounds was not entirely justified and she was sensing the partial loss of identity that comes with a retirement not freely chosen.

Michele felt that she had lost a great deal and was apprehensive about the future, yet she was striving to make the most of all that was meaningful and possible for her. In spite of physical disabilities she prepared her own nutritious meals and walked four blocks to the local pool, swimming laps and doing aquaerobics — for exercise and also to give vent, in physical activity, to the frustrations of a limiting illness. She worked as a volunteer for two half-days each week for Amnesty International. She planned to visit the Fauves Exhibition then current at the New South Wales Art Gallery, very enthusiastic to see Matisse, Derain and Dufy in their glorious original colour. She sang once a week with a choir.

Music has always been a spiritual solace and inspiration and she treasures it now more than ever: Bach, Brahms, Vaughan Williams, the Fauré Requiem. The great Catalan master of the cello, Pablo Casals, is a kindred spirit to whom she can relate especially now in her time of struggle. She had visited his home in Spain and drew great sustenance from his sublime music-making and from his philosophy of life. She was thrilled that her father had found recently, in a second-hand shop, a book on Casals that she had longed to own for many years.[6]

When I pressed her further on the question of spiritual life, she told me that she finds nourishment in an expansive sense of the tran-scendent, neither personal nor limited by definition, and made real in art, music, nature and the love of friends and family.

Seeing the great effort needed to manage every simple task, I could only imagine what it cost her each day to achieve the attractive, individual style of her dress; and I marvelled at the quiet beauty of her expression, humbled but not defeated. Her daily life was testing and tiring. She was frustrated by a feeling that, at times, her brain was not functioning as it should, although, in her company, I was aware of slowness but of no other impediment to a lively intelligence. The future of her health was uncertain. Yet her choice was to acknowl-edge the hardship, the hurt and the anger of her situation, and to make the most of every possibility. I felt greatly moved by her honesty and her struggle and encouraged in my own life by meeting her. So we learn from each other.

And then there's the story of the eye surgeon Professor Fred Hollows.[7] Although he attained hero status, any of us can relate to his approach to life for he was not rich or handsome or a man set apart from common humanity. In fact, nobody could have been more down to earth than he was. He was not always the easiest of company because he was not prepared to waste time on niceties. People some-times found his frank, outspoken manner confronting, but he was intent on achieving his objectives and if you didn't like it, that was too bad. He had no time to waste.

The first important thing to notice is that he had identified his life purpose very clearly and that everything was devoted to the achievement of that purpose — to eradicate needless blindness, especially among underprivileged people, in his own country and in developing nations. It was what he loved to do. It had become part of him. Few of us may be driven by such a large and public cause but Fred Hollows' example is a prompt to find our own unique purpose and be faithful to it, whether it is a grand humanitarian work or the more private intention of being a listener or a loving person in your family.

It's worth noting too that Fred Hollows knew his own story well and that it gave him strength and continuity. His father's family were coalminers, refugees from the Industrial Revolution in Lancashire. At the turn of the 19th century, the English working classes were beginning to realise what they had lost in order to gain the wage slavery of the factories. Fred's grandfather brought his daughter and nine sons to Australia and then to New Zealand. One of his father's uncles was a founder of the Workers Education Association in New Zealand, and of the first Factory Inspectorate.

Fred told me that, in his family, it was accepted that individual and even family survival were not as important as social institutions and community survival. This was made clear to him from childhood. He remembered vividly an incident when he was walking with his father through their home town of Dunedin in New Zealand. Mr Hollows senior was a railwayman and a keen chrysanthemum grower. As they walked past a flower bed in a public garden, young Fred picked a flower. In the same instant, his father gave him a cuff across the ears and told him that those flowers belonged to everyone and he must not steal public property.

That event became a significant lifelong metaphor. For Fred Hollows, meaning grew out of what was good for the group. The most important thing was the relationship between people and the structures that serve that relationship. He was able to achieve great things in eye health in the Aboriginal community and in Nepal, Eritrea and Vietnam because he poured his whole self — his conviction and his spirit — into that work. He could imagine solutions and he could fire others with the spirit of his vision. It was the very giving, the communality of his life, that lent him energy, excitement and fulfilment. He was a patient enabler of disadvantaged people, teaching local doctors his surgical skills and finding ways for them to develop technology in their own countries, so that they would own the means to secure their future eye health.

Fred Hollows' humanitarian work was not achieved solely as an exercise of the scientific mind. He was passionate about the people among whom he worked. He researched their needs by listening to them. He lived with them and ate with them and got to know them and he told detailed affectionate stories about them. His life was a total engagement which left less energetic people breathless in his wake. He made no pretence to being a saint and he was honest in acknowledging the unconventional chapters of his life and remaining loyal to them.

His sources of spiritual nourishment were varied. He knew what they were and he paid some attention to them, if not enough. Certainly, his work was one vital element of spiritual nourishment. His family was very important to him, and an open house where there were always guests coming and going. He loved the high-risk adventure of mountaineering and he read verse. Keats was a favourite. I will always remember him sitting opposite me reading *Ode to a Nightingale*, in his gravelly voice, with his glasses on the end of his nose. His cancer was already well advanced and he was moved by the words of this poem published in 1820 when some still believed that the nightingale lived forever:

Thou wast not born for death, immortal Bird!
No hungry generations tread thee down;
The voice I hear this passing night was heard
In ancient days by emperor and clown:
Perhaps the self-same song that found a path
Through the sad heart of Ruth, when, sick for home,
She stood in tears amid the alien corn . . .'

He repeated the last three lines and commented on their simplicity and poignancy. He also liked to quote from Shakespeare and he preferred the King James translation of the Bible, for the poetry of its language. Verse was precious to him because, as he put it, it lyricises human communication, 'explaining, developing and enlarging something by an economic use of words, in a way that no other form of literature can do'[8] He thought that poetry, in its piquant use of language, allows a heightened form of consciousness.

He also enjoyed chess and woodwork. To design and make an original piece of furniture could provide him with recurring delight and he hoped that one day he would be considered an adequate cabinet-maker. The concentration of turning wood on a lathe underneath the old sandstone house in which he lived gave him a rest from other concerns.

The entity greater than himself for which Fred Hollows had reverence was humanity itself. His sense of eternity was in the continuum of human life and the notion that his existence might contribute to supporting or developing another human being. He believed that the essential attribute of being human was care for each other — that we look after the weak, the young, the sick and the old, that we don't kill each other fighting our way to the trough. He was disparaging of those who believed the essence of existence was to be found in self-promotion or climbing the hierarchy and he liked to quote the Christian gospel: 'What profiteth it a man to gain the whole world and lose his soul?' He would follow this up with: 'And blokes who try it, they end up losing their souls, you know?'

In his humanitarian ideals he was strengthened by his own heroes, who included traditional spiritual leaders and some great figures, both male and female, from the Communist movement. Several of his children were named after them. He took his definition of God from Paulo Freire: 'that within man which causes him to socially strive for liberation'. His varied taste in spiritual resources was well demonstrated at his funeral, held in the most unlikely venue of St Mary's Catholic Cathedral in Sydney, with the eulogy given by one of his close friends, the Communist writer Frank Hardy.

Thousands of people lined the streets outside the cathedral to do Fred Hollows honour because there was a sense that, at his passing, Australia had lost a national hero who was first and foremost a man of and for the people. His dogmatic views on some controversial issues did not endear him to everyone but many were ready to honour a man who had lived by the courage of his convictions and lived life to the full. Perhaps we recognised in him a capacity for authentic life, lived with passion, that we wanted for ourselves.

In concluding with something of Fred Hollows' and Michele Fehlberg's stories, I want to leave you with the idea that living life to the full, with meaning and spirit, is not an unattainable goal for the few. It's open to everyone. There is a naturalness about it which, once caught, becomes a sort of second nature. It grows out of paying serious attention to the discovery of who you are and what your purpose is. It is not a withdrawal from the world but a commitment to waking up to all the possibilities of life, to engaging courageously with life, taking in its rich experiences so they become part of you; to giving all that you uniquely have to give.

It is the discovery and cultivation of a philosophy of life that has integrity. It is a dedication to follow your passion, to care for your soul and hearken to your heart and imagination and intuition, as well as to your head; to become a listener as well as a talker; to be forgiving of others and of yourself; and to develop a practical and hopeful way to navigate change and suffering. It requires you to have a coherent sense of your own story and to find a spiritual home for that story. It invites you to nurture reverence for a concept greater than yourself and to express that reverence in some regular observance, like religious ritual, prayer, meditation or, at the very least, in a habit of reflection. Living to the full requires you to laugh and enjoy, to be grateful for the astonishing gift of your life, to identify and take care of your sources of spiritual nourishment, and to find a community of faith in life that will challenge you and keep you in good company.

At the same time it is vital not to remain stuck in a self-absorbed adolescence of 'searching for yourself'. Reorientation from the purely personal to the communal is a significant progression on the spiritual journey, and it is that reorientation which has led so many people to their fulfilment in life. This has been demonstrated in almost every story in this book. Just as long as you're not like the bootmaker whose family went barefoot or the social worker whose children were delinquents. It is important that your work in the community is a larger expression of your personal life, not an avoidance of it.

At those times when meaning and purpose seem elusive, remember that you will always find companionship for your search in other people's stories, if they are told with generous depth and candour. Reading or hearing about the lives of others gives you clues to how they've transformed their everyday experience into food for the journey. No matter how alienated you may feel, the story of another human person is like calling to like. No one else's prescription is just right for you but, in recounting their hard-won wisdom, they can keep you company and refresh your imagination, lift your spirit and, above all, renew your courage and hope for the way ahead.

§

As I complete this writing, I am at home. I am in place. It is Sunday, early evening. A spatter of rain on the windows is drawing my attention. Magpies are crying their last melancholy carol of the day and the sound strikes a corresponding chord in my soul. A late sailing boat is making for home up the molten river. The liquid amber tree is bare against a pale grey sky. These images gather up hundreds of my Sunday evenings over the years, like so many stitches on a needle. But it is my unique life that I am knitting, and that life must incorporate even the dangerous time of Sunday evenings, conjuring homesickness, yearnings for what has passed, and apprehension of what is to come. It is my life and I rejoice that I am alive in that life. It is my responsibility to claim it and explore it, to negotiate the suffering of it with hope; to celebrate the gift of it with gratitude; and to remember that I have only to reach out a hand to find companions of the way.

For your Journal, some Reminders

* How are you conserving your story? Are you keeping a journal, diary, scrapbook or collection?

* If you are too busy with things that will not matter ultimately, how could you make some changes?

* How could you pause more often to absorb beauty?

* How could you allow more time for your spiritual nourishment?

* What are your most treasured possessions? Make sketches or cut out pictures for your journal.

* What sacred meaning or story do they contain for you?

* What are the sustaining images or memories that you carry in your imagination? Have you photographs or symbols of them for your journal?

* What else could you do to furnish your inner landscape, to provide you with sanctuary and meaning?

* How could you take more time to savour your experiences, reflect on them, harvest some wisdom from them, build up your sense of self and authenticity?

* Do you need to reflect on an awkward situation in your life, which may be relieved by the addition of a fresh element?

* Is your spiritual search purely personal, or are you now able to invest some time in the spiritual wellbeing of the community? How?

* Who are some inspiring people for you? Is there a picture of them in your journal? Is it time to reflect on their story again, to take it into yourself for nourishment.

* Review your statement of purpose at the start of your journal.

* Have you made a new friend to add to your list?

* Have you a new entry to make on the page listing things you are good at?

Endnotes

1   Interview with John Cleary on *Meridian*, ABC Radio National, 18 February 1996.

2   Thomas Moore, *Care of the Soul*, Harper Perennial, 1992.

3   *Enchanted April*, directed by Mike Newell 1992. A BBC Films Production in association with Greenpoint Films. Released by Warner Bros.

4   *Care of the Soul.*

5   Stan Arneil, *One Man's War*, Alternative Publishing Cooperative Ltd, 1981. Also *The Search for Meaning Collection*, Caroline Jones ABC/Harper Collins, 1995, and *The Search for Meaning* video, ABC Video catalogue number 12574.

6   Pablo Casals, *Joys and Sorrows*. His story as told to Albert E. Kahn, LEEL Pie Publishing Ltd, 1970.

7   Professor Fred Hollows, *The Search For Meaning: Conversations with Caroline Jones*, ABC/Collins Dove, 1992. Also Tape 133 in *The Search for Meaning Catalogue*, ABC Radio Tapes.

8   Professor Fred Hollows in *The Search for Meaning: Conversations with Caroline Jones.*

How to Use this Book
for
Group Discussion

THE BENEFIT OF using this book as a resource for group discussion is that you can support each other in the belief that the quest for meaning, values, inner legitimacy and spirituality is valid and worthwhile. Belonging to a group increases your sense of connection. It adds to the purposeful structure of your life. If the group works well, you will gain sustenance from being regularly in a situation where you are heard and respected. It is stimulating to have a venue in which discussion, rather than argument, prevails; in which all contributions are met with interest and contemplation, rather than criticism.

Membership of a group gives you an opportunity to tell something of your story and your experience of the search for meaning. You will clarify what you have discovered by expressing it. Sometimes you don't know quite what you think until you say it out loud. You will enlarge your perspective on the search for meaning by hearing from others. You will be dedicating regular time to your spirituality. Attending the group will prompt you to keep adding to your journal. And who knows what other doors it may open?

It is important to establish, at the start of the first meeting, what participants hope for from the group, to ensure that you have aims in common and that these include care for all members. I suggest making a list of the group's expectations. When you think it is complete, it needs to be agreed that everyone subscribes to it. It will be useful for future reference, to check whether original hopes are being fulfilled, and as an informal constitution if the group begins to run off the rails. Although this will go some way to defining the group's purpose, you need to do something more specific to enhance the possibility of its success.

The next task for the group is to make its own rules. All participants need to agree on the rules. You may like to incorporate some of the following:

1 What we discuss is confidential to this group. People need to feel safe in order to disclose things that matter to them.

2 For each meeting, we will ask one person to volunteer as facilitator.

3 The responsibility of the facilitator is to open the discussion with a brief summary of the day's subject; read out the questions for discussion at the meeting; perhaps suggest a short interval of silence for people to collect their thoughts; invite people into the discussion; thank them at the end of their contribution; when necessary, indicate tactfully that it is time to move on to the next member's contribution, (e.g. 'George, thank you for what you've shared. I look forward to hearing more from you in the general discussion time. And now I'm sure that, like me, you would enjoy hearing from Mary.')

4 Listening is a crucial factor of our group discussion process. It is quite as powerful as the telling of our stories. The success of this group will depend on the quality of our listening to each other.

5 We will listen to each other without judging or giving unsolicited advice. Each person's story is sacred ground, not an invitation to argument.

6 At the conclusion, the facilitator will announce the date and venue of the next meeting and ask for a volunteer to act as facilitator.

You may also like to consider these issues:

* Decide where and when meetings will be held. If questions of group comfort such as smoking or air-conditioning are important, agree upon them.

* Do you need to decide how many meetings there will be, or will you leave it open-ended?

* Decide the duration of each meeting, and keep to it.

* People's sense of time varies and one or two members may speak at greater length than others. So it can be desirable to have a volunteer act as time-keeper. One effective time-keeping strategy is to allocate each participant an equal period to make an initial contribution without interruption, with another period designated for open group discussion.

* Leave a few minutes at the end of each meeting for an evaluation, brief and to the point. This should be a frank disclosure of how each participant experienced the meeting, moving round the circle so that each person has a chance to speak uninterrupted. First, what did they most appreciate about the discussion? Did they feel listened to? What do they hope for from the next meeting?

Group discussion can be disrupted or derailed in various ways. Power struggles can surface, or clashes of personality. Although this is disappointing, it needs to be dealt with openly if the group is to be lifegiving and enjoyable. Someone may want to promote a particular religious view or argue fine points of dogma. This could prove tedious and unproductive. In *The Search for Meaning* interviews, I avoided this by encouraging the discussion of concrete experience rather than too many abstract ideas. Evaluation time is a good moment to expose any such difficulties as they arise and decide, as a group, on any new rules that may need to be made.

Before embarking on a group discussion, I suggest you work through this book on your own, although this may be unsatisfactory to extroverts who are ready to share the experience right from the start. If you decide not to keep a journal, then you need to come to a group with your responses, in note form, to the questions at the end of each chapter so that you have reflections to share, rather than reflex actions.

A group could be two in number. Six to eight is ideal. More than eight and the time available for individual contributions is too short and may cause frustration.

The most lengthy chapters to manage will be the early ones, in which people are exploring their story as a whole. I have two suggestions:

1 You may decide to stay with this section for several meetings, allocating plenty of time for each one to tell their story. The telling of their story is valuable for each member. For the first meeting, you could try giving three people 20 minutes each. If this turns out to be too short, then adjust accordingly for the next meeting. The telling of a full chronological story in every detail is beyond the scope of group discussion but responding to some of the questions at the end of each chapter should help participants to put some structure into their story, and some boundaries on it.

2 Alternatively, you could decide, as a group, to begin with Desire of the Heart, Grace, Care for the Soul, Sacred Time or Living with Change. This would make for a more manageable discussion. Working gradually through all the chapters will bring out the essence of the whole life story and may avoid the difficulty, for both teller and listeners, of tackling the whole saga at one sitting. This was a problem that had to be resolved with *The Search for Meaning* interviews on radio. Researcher Louisa Ring and I experimented with many questions to help guests to tell the crucial aspects of their experience without becoming exhausted or daunted by the enormity of the endeavour. The solutions we discovered are now chapter headings in this book. As you will see, experiences of suffering, desires of the heart, sources of spiritual nourishment, sacred time, finding one's identity, forgiveness and instances of grace each provides a way in to telling some vital aspects of a life story, and offers a way to make the telling of it manageable.

There is no reason why a whole chapter has to be the subject of a meeting. Sometimes that is far too much to attempt, and will result in a discussion that lacks focus and may be unsatisfactory. You could discuss just one aspect of a chapter, in relation to each member's experience. Or at times you could nominate just one point to be the subject of a whole meeting. For instance, in relation to the Living with Spirit chapter, participants could be invited to bring a treasured possession to the meeting, and tell the story of it. This could give rise to a rich and useful discussion.

You could deal in a similar way with the section in Desire of the Heart on the things you love to do. Identify just one of those things each and expand on its spiritual significance.

When you join a discussion group, you need to take some responsibility for its success. The experience does demand patience and generosity and you will learn something from it. However, you do not need to stay if it is not meeting your hopes.

Caroline Jones may be engaged to visit discussion groups or gatherings. Write to her c/- ABC Books, G.P.O. Box 9994, Sydney 2001.